"Genuinely extraordinary masterpiece with a global appeal. You will be trapped within the pages of 'Pillars of Parenting' – exploring its rich and versatile deposits. Its classical approach, well-researched facts and relatable recommendations, make this Book a magnifying glass for the noble task of parenting."

Roland Akenji Fongwa
Senior Pastor, Royal City Mission
African Regional Office

"Masterful and captivating 21st-century parenting guide. Comprehensive presentation of core values in an eclectic and stimulating way that every parent can relate with."

Eyong T. Enoh
Professional Footballer, Former Ajax and
Vice Captain Cameroon National Team.

"A balanced delivery of practical parenting principles. A timeless road map for navigating present day challenges. A must read for raising difference makers."

Edwin C. Awasom
Houston Police Department TX, U.S.A

"As a Millennial parent, I find this book an indispensable tool. It is a must have for parents seeking to achieve positive outcomes."

Dr. Brenda B. Suh-Lailam
Director of Clinical Chemistry and Point of Care Testing at Ann & Robert H. Lurie Children's Hospital of Chicago. IL, USA

"The author has carefully and skilfully crafted a parenting guide. It will help any millennial who cares about raising children in a responsible, informed and balanced manner."

Dr Arllen Ade
PhD in Professional Counselling.
Regional Pastor, Mclean Bible Church. VA, USA
President, ABC's Counselling.

"Excellent read. In a simple, yet effective way, the author communicates very profound truths backed with facts for the custodians of our future – the Millennials – as they build the most important and fundamental unit of society – the family."
Drs Ade & Anikphe Oyedeji
Consultant Psychiatrist and Geriatrician, Cheshire North West, U.K.

"The author's clarity of presentation demonstrates a deep knowledge of divine principles. He represents a generation of dynamic authors who have a strong impact on lives."
Richard Schwéry
Minister and Business Executive, Switzerland

PILLARS
OF
PARENTING

Timeless Secrets for Millennial Parents

JESSE Y. SONG

CORNERSTONE
PUBLISHING HOUSE

PILLARS OF PARENTING

Copyright © 2019 by Jesse Y. Song

British Library Cataloguing in Publication Data.

A CIP catalogue record for this book is available from the British Library

ISBN: 978-1-9162817-0-7

Printed in the U.K

First Printing 2019.

Cover Design by Don Judex @ JGArtz

Ordering Information:
Quantity Sales: Special discounts are available on quantity purchases by corporations, associations, schools, seminaries and others.
For details, contact the publisher.

www.cornerstonepublishinghouse.com

DEDICATION

 These are the inspired words my mother taught me. Listen, my dear son, son of my womb. You are the answer to my prayers, my son.
[PROVERBS 31:1-2 THE PASSION TRANSLATION]

I wholeheartedly dedicate this book to my dearest mother of blessed memory Marie Ngem Kimbu – unmatched and unparalleled parent of all times; I could never have had a better parent.

"At the end of your life, you will never regret not having passed one more test, not winning one more verdict or not closing one more deal. You will regret time not spent with a husband, a friend, a child, or a parent."
[Barbara Bush, Former United States First Lady]

TABLE OF CONTENTS

ACKNOWLEDGEMENTS

> *Feeling gratitude and not expressing it is like wrapping a present and not giving it.*
>
> [WILLIAM ARTHUR WARD, AUTHOR AND SPEAKER]

This book reflects many decades of teaching, training and research. During this time, I have been the fortunate beneficiary of the most encouragement, guidance and support from my many friends, students, colleagues and associates. I am grateful to my siblings Brenda A. Kimbu, Dr Shawn A. Chiambah and Lesi N. Nayuoh, for shaping and moulding me with their love and support. I am also indebted to a host of the manuscript, art, and production team of editors, who worked valiantly to bring this project to a successful conclusion. My sincere thanks to The Nutrition Source Team, Department of Nutrition, Harvard T.H Chan School of Public Health for the permission to use 'The Healthy Eating Plate'.

I humbly convey my gratitude to all those professionals who have influenced my concept of parenting, whose names I do not have the privilege of knowing, but whose input has made an invaluable contribution to my study of parenting. There are indeed others whose names I may have inadvertently omitted here but who I want to heartily thank as well. Extraordinary acknowledgement also goes to all the members and Leaders of Royal City Mission U.K., U.S.A, Cameroon and South Africa for their commitment and loyalty. To Dr Cynthia Ndeh, Laurencia Newi Kwanga, Emmanuel A. Siben, Daniel Tah, Madri Muchuo Iwoi and Casandra Dimala for their invaluable assistance in making this book a reality. I wish to express enthusiastic gratitude to the millions of parents, whose labour behind the scenes in most cases goes unappreciated.

This book is a tribute to their dedication, commitment, and sacrifice. Finally, with exceptional thanks and appreciation, I take this moment to offer a special acknowledgement to my wife Immaculate, for her dedication and support, and whose parenting skills have been a tremendous blessing to our four children.

PREFACE

> *Parenting is a unique life journey,*
> *not a sentimental destination*
>
> [JESSE SONG, AUTHOR PILLARS OF PARENTING]

The 21ˢᵗ-century Millennial parent is often at a considerable loss on how to translate statistical figures into a straightforward 'child-centred' blueprint. With hundreds of conflicting ideas and techniques, a 'one-stop' parenting guide containing evidenced-based information is indispensable

With more than 25 years of leadership and counselling experience, I have seen *'the good, the bad and the ugly'* of parenting and witnessed firsthand in counselling sessions, the detrimental effects of mediocre parenting. All round, there are countless examples of people with dysfunctional lives, not because their parents were evil, but merely because they were ignorant of the fundamental principles needed to navigate the journey of parenting. Positive parenting is not merely a social construction or a culture-bound phenomenon; it is the development of a committed relationship between parent and child within a nurturing environment. While most of us aspire to be exemplary parents, we may also find ourselves bewildered and frustrated by the endless challenges.

This book focuses on Millennials – individuals who reached adulthood around the turn of the 21st century – born between 1981 and 1996. This cohort was raised in an electronics-filled and socially-networked environment. They are the generation that is the most diverse and tolerant of differences. More than 25% of Millennials are now parents with the proclivity to challenge long-held traditions on marriage and family. This book is an essential companion to parents, students, counsellors, academic institutions, religious organisations, child policymakers and stakeholders. The various chapters provide valuable information, statistics and recommendations that promote healthy child development. A dominant feature of the book is its ability to provoke reflection in the readers, both on their own experiences and on the wider society. The various chapters present principles, recommendations and statistics that when consistently applied, will increase the likelihood that children are raised with the right experiences and desired outcomes. In the end, is that not the ultimate desire of all parents?

Statistics are presented in a concise way to inform, guide and revitalise the parenting energy of yet-to-be, expectant, new and exhausted parents. This book can also minimise parental shortcomings and prevent 'history from repeating itself'. Your personal experience with your parents will profoundly influence your perspective on the way you practice parenting. There will be repercussions if the parenting strategies applied in your upbringing produced detrimental outcomes in your life. Regardless of the stage in your parenting life, you can find fulfilment in reading and applying these principles to the best of your ability.

Pillars of Parenting does not offer a 'one size fits all' quick fix to parenting challenges. It presents a broad range of enthralling topics that foster sustained commitment and dedication in achieving realistic goals and objectives. So, if you are the type of parent who wants a massive positive change with minimal effort, then this book is not for you. Remember that reading a book does not automatically produce results; instead, results are a consequence of the amount of energy you expend on putting into practice what a book recommends. Maximising the benefits of this book entails reading it alongside other books that cover other relevant aspects of parenting.

The fifteen chapters of this book are not an academic treatise, nor claim to offer a panacea to all parenting challenges; nor a day to day prescriptive recommendation of parenting techniques and strategies. Instead, it provides valuable information which when assimilated and implemented, will produce a fruitful and satisfactory parent-child relationship. Raising children is not about going from one point to the next. The parenting life is about the journey, and the key to loving parenting is to enjoy the ultimate ride with *'Pillars of Parenting'* as an essential front seat passenger.

"We know the excitement of getting a present – we love to unwrap it to see what is inside. So it is with our children. They are gifts we unwrap for years as we discover the unique characters God has made them."

[Cornelius Plantinga, Former President,
Calvin Theological Seminary]

INTRODUCTION

> *I came to parenting the way most of us do – knowing nothing and trying to learn everything.*
>
> [MAYIM BIALIK, AMERICAN NEUROSCIENTIST]

Millennials are the first generation to come of age in the new millennium. According to Pew Research Centre, 82% of babies born in 2016 were the children of Millennial parents.[1]

An essential feature of Millennials is that they are generally better educated, ethnically diverse and make up the majority of the global workforce. While the view that Millennials are obsessed with technology at the expense of family is inaccurate; the global environment predisposes them to various paradigm shifts in parenting. One of the misconceptions of the 21st century is equating child-rearing with parenting - both interchangeable terms in certain contexts, since some aspects of parenting involve child-rearing (the process of bringing up a child). Parenthood is the natural state of being a parent, like motherhood or fatherhood, while parenting is the task that promotes and supports the physical, emotional, social, intellectual and holistic development of a child from infancy to adulthood. Parenting has a higher level of involvement and commitment than child-rearing. Parenting emphasises responsibility, exemplary behaviour and high demand on emotions. Parental responsibilities also include great communication skills, resources and energy, which all goes beyond just the physical wellbeing of a child. Becoming a Millennial parent is a once in a lifetime experience. Parents are children's first and lifelong educators. Conversely, children are parents' most pivotal educators on parenting matters. Because children are each unique in their individuality, there is no single "right" way to raise them. As they guide, listen and learn, parents become better with their children, and know them better than anyone else.

Chapter one introduces the Millennials (also known as Gen Y), who by their time in history, reflect a new mindset and outlook of the world – the reason for which their perceptions on parenting warrants a closer look. The focus of chapter two is voluntary childlessness or being childfree – the rising popular choice amongst many Millennials not to have children. This chapter looks at the various misconceptions and puts forward some reasons behind this popular trend. Whatever the circumstance, both men and women can still enjoy a fulfilling life without children, if they so decide. Even though attitudes about the roles of men and women in raising children often differ, the role played by one parent is not more important than that of the other. Both play complementary roles in promoting a positive emotional well-being of a child, including a positive sense of self and the ability to cope with stressful situations. Responsible parenting does not necessarily mean fulfilling a child's every desire, but meeting a child's primary need for care, stability, safety, respect, wellbeing and emotional support. Good parenting (the totality of the responsibilities of raising a child) is more important to the academic success of a child than a good school.

Some parenting roles and responsibilities can be accomplished in some instances by people without a claim to biological parenthood themselves. Most animals have the innate instincts to guide their young through a comparatively brief period from infancy before the new generation becomes independent. Humans have a distinguishing characteristic in the much longer length from infancy to youth, and the enormous magnitude of the reliance of their young. Therefore, humans need the appropriate knowledge, guidance and the necessary support mechanisms to enable them to carry out their parenting duties with dignity. Chapter three introduces parenting styles and offers recommendations for parents to understand their children's uniqueness and to adapt parenting styles accordingly. Parents can deal with conflicts before they escalate by determining the appropriate parenting style, which takes into account the personality of the child. Every child is different – even within the same family.

The University of Harvard Centre on the Developing Child, in an article 'Science of Early Childhood Development', comments:

"All aspects of adult human capital, from workforce skills to cooperative and lawful behaviour, build on capacities that are developed during childhood, beginning at birth. When we invest wisely in children and families, the next generation will pay that back through a lifetime of productivity and responsible citizenship." [2]

Research shows that the majority of books concerning infancy and upbringing are from the western world. As a result, the parenting practices of other cultures are being discarded in favour of western parenting philosophy. Chapter four reinforces the fact that parenting literature must be expanded to glean from the rich diversity of the parenting heritage of other cultures. Chapter five introduces the prevalence and adverse effects of absent fathers. Extensive research show that children from fatherless homes are more likely to be poor, become involved in drug and alcohol abuse, drop out of school, and suffer from health and emotional problems. No single factor can fully explain why parenting operates in a particular way. Positive factors, such as a child with an easy temperament, loving family history and a good standard of living, enhance parenting – whereas negative factors such as a child with a challenging personality, an abusive past and adverse economic condition present risks. Parenting practices around the world share major significant objectives – ensuring a child's wellbeing; preparing the child for life as a productive adult and as a transmitter of cultural values. Indeed, The National Academy of Sciences further outlines four primary responsibilities for parents: maintaining children's health and safety; promoting their emotional wellbeing; instilling social skills, and preparing children intellectually.[3]

The aforementioned parental responsibilities cannot be discharged without sensible, practical 'child-specific' principles, which are covered in chapter six. This chapter also envisages best outcomes for children through reasonable, practical and compassionate discipline – especially as it relates to professional parents, who may find it challenging to create time and energy for their children or who may struggle in maintaining a 'work-parenting' balance. Achieving such a balance is the Eldorado of any parenting journey. Chapter seven examines the strategic positioning of children and the interconnection with the sports of archery. When we let our children fly like arrows, we understand that we have been chosen to be the bow in their lives to 'shoot' them in the right direction. This chapter also examines the sacrifice it takes to be a good archer – likewise, a good parent.

Sexuality education, which encompasses sex education, has rapidly metamorphosed into Sex and Relationship Education (SRE). Contentious questions have been raised at several levels; at what age should children start receiving such education; what topics and how much information should be taught; what role should cultural sensitivity and awareness play in lesson delivery? Children in some cultures are not given any information on sexual matters since such discussions are considered taboo. In other cultures, pressure groups and radical sex education campaigners are pushing their agenda into the curriculum – without giving due diligence to appropriate age-related content – thereby destroying the innocence of children. Chapter eight examines these issues, and the various challenges encountered in the implementation of sexuality education policy, including recommendations on the options parents have to curtail the unhealthy excesses in the curriculum. Chapter nine explores the worldwide reality of single parenthood and the multifaceted challenges they encounter. This chapter proposes recommendations to help mitigate these challenges. Chapter ten addresses interparental conflicts, which are a normal part of intimate relationships, but if handled constructively pose few risks for children. The principle of 'best interest of a child' requires parents and the state to safeguard and promote the welfare of children at all times and in all circumstances. Children should never be used as pawns or weapons in divorce or custody battles. 'Best interests of a child' concept derives from Article 3(1) of the United Nations Convention on the Rights of the Child 1989 ('UNCRC'), which states that:

> *'In all actions concerning children, whether undertaken by public or private social welfare institutions, courts of law, administrative authorities or legislative bodies, the best interests of the child shall be a primary consideration.*

Why is parenting achieved with relative ease for some but full of challenges for others? Why are some parents sensitive, responsive, and emotionally engaged with their children, whereas others are unresponsive, detached or even abusive? The answers to these questions must consider the many different factors existing between parent and child and within the immediate socio-cultural framework, which embeds parent-child relationships. Under-parenting and over-parenting are becoming more and more popular concepts. Over-parenting aims for perfection in parenting which cripples children as they move into adulthood, rendering them unable to cope with the inevitable setbacks in life. Naturally, there is also such a thing as under-parenting too, and research demonstrates that lack of parental engagement usually results in poor behavioural outcomes in children, partly because it produces grounds for the young to be too dependent on peer pressure, social media and dysfunctional 'celebrity' role models as elucidated in chapters eleven and chapter twelve. Parenting guilt – the sentiment that you, as a parent, are not doing a good enough job in raising your child – is the natural fear that comes from within and lurks around in mind. Parenting without guilt is the main thrust of chapter thirteen, which draws inspiration from the ancient parable of the prodigal son – a parable of a good parent with a wayward child. Concisely, chapter fourteen provides practical guidance for parents dealing with issues of 'parent-child' abuse and 'child-parent' abuse, while chapter fifteen concludes the book with a journey into the basic rules of life from the perspective of renowned historical figures.

A diversity of sacred texts, translations and paraphrases are used throughout this book for ease of reading and simplicity of understanding. These texts are paramount as they provide a blueprint in the often lonely world of parenting. Professor Laurence Steinberg, specialist in child and adolescent psychological development at Temple University, in his book, '*The Ten Basic Principles of Good Parenting*', provides guidelines based on social science research – some 75 years of studies confirms that good parenting helps foster empathy, honesty, self-reliance, self control, kindness, cooperation, cheerfulness and motivation. This helps protect children from developing anxiety, depression, eating disorders, anti-social behaviour, and alcohol and drug abuse.[4]

While this book has been written within the socio-historical backdrop of the United Kingdom, its principles are universal and pragmatic in their application. Understanding parenting from a global perspective uncovers the problem of adapting Western research to non-western cultures. An attempt has been made by the author to introduce readers to the productive parenting practices of other cultures. However, translating theories of optimal child outcomes into measurable objectives has been a challenging pathway for developmental psychologists and child policymakers.

The author has been inspired by *"10 Famous Parenting Quotes,"* published by Education.com which provides parenting advice through ten relevant quotes from a diverse array of individuals. "But while the world evolves at a rapid rate, the best parenting advice stands the test of time," says education.com. Five of these quotes include:

"Children are educated by what the grown-up is and not by his talk."
[Carl Jung]

Swiss psychiatrist Carl Jung was best known for his theories about personalities, but raising five children may have been his proudest achievement. Jung knew you can't simply tell your kids what to do—you must lead by example.

"Parents can only give good advice or put them on the right paths, but the final forming of a person's character lies in their own hands."
[Anne Frank]

Perhaps her family's struggles taught her that no parent could guarantee a child's success or failure. Instead, she recognized the wisdom and morals parents could pass on to their offspring. While these tools will give children the best start, it's ultimately up to them how they're used.

"If you have never been hated by your child, you have never been a parent."
[Bette Davis]

There's nothing glamorous about those occasions when your children are cursing you out for laying down the law. Their behaviour can sting, but don't let that weaken your resolve. The best parents know they can't play the good cop all the time.

"It is easier to build strong children than to repair broken men."
[Frederick Douglass]

Children thrive when they're challenged, given responsibility and encouraged to assume leadership roles.

"Children are apt to live up to what you believe of them."
[Lady Bird Johnson]

Lady Bird Johnson was one of America's most loved First Ladies who believed that praise and support help children reach their potential.

Various studies suggest that the best adjusted children are reared by parents who find a way to combine warmth and sensitivity with clear behavioural expectations. Good parenting helps promote intellectual curiosity, motivation and the desire to achieve.

CHAPTER 1

MILLENNIAL PARENTING – THE QUEST FOR RELEVANCE

“ *Delight yourself also in the Lord, and He will give you the desires and secret petitions of your heart.*
[PSALM 37:4 AMPLIFIED BIBLE, CLASSIC EDITION] ”

THE MILLENNIAL GENERATION

For decades, the exact definition of 'Millennials' has differed from one source to another. Where the "Millennial" generation ends, and the "Post-Millennial" generation begins, has been in debate. However, Neil Howe and William Strauss, authors of the book '*Millennials Rising: The Next Generation*', are widely credited with naming the Millennials – a term used to define a cohort consisting of individuals born between 1982 and 2004.[5]

Their work was the extension of the book *'Generations: The History of America's Future'*, which presented the view that groups of people who grow up in a particular time of history share similar characteristics such as beliefs, values, attitudes, and behaviours.[6]

According to Iconoclast, a consumer research firm, the first Millennials were born in 1978. Newsweek magazine reported that the Millennial generation was born between 1977 and 1994. In separate articles, the New York Times pegged the Millennials at 1976-1990 and 1978-1998. A Time magazine article placed the Millennials at 1980-2000.[7]

At the turn of the century, other organisations, such as Pew Research Centre offered well-reasoned arguments for classifying generations by studying and measuring public attitudes on critical issues across demographic groups. President of Pew Research Centre, Michael Dimock says that generations are a lens through which we understand societal change, rather than a label with which to oversimplify differences between groups.[8]

Technology and how people communicate and interact is another generation-shaping consideration. Dimock points to Baby Boomers as a generation that saw TV become dominant – dramatically changing their lifestyles. Generation X experienced the computer revolution – dramatically changing their work life, and Millennials came of age during the internet boom – dramatically changing their communication. Dimock explains that the Millennial cut-off of 1996 is key because it points to a generation that is old enough to have experienced the 9/11 terrorist attacks, while also finding their way through the 2008 recession as young adults. This generational cut-off point is not an exact science, but a tool that enables the analysis of different shifts in how age groups experience the world – socially, politically, economically and technologically.

Pew Research Centre guidelines for categorisation:[9]

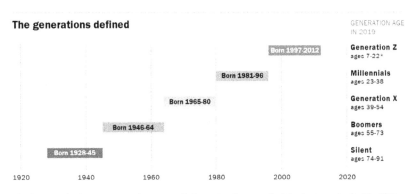

The generations defined

	GENERATION AGE IN 2019
Born 1997-2012	**Generation Z** ages 7-22*
Born 1981-96	**Millennials** ages 23-38
Born 1965-80	**Generation X** ages 39-54
Born 1946-64	**Boomers** ages 55-73
Born 1928-45	**Silent** ages 74-91

1920   1940   1960   1980   2000   2020

*No chronological endpoint has been set for this group. For this analysis, Generation Z is defined as those ages 7 to 22 in 2019.

PEW RESEARCH CENTER

- The Silent Generation: Born 1928 – 1945 (74 – 91 years old)
- Baby Boomers: Born 1946 – 1964 (55 – 73 years old)
- Generation X: Born 1965 – 1980 (39 – 54 years old)
- Millennials: Born 1981 – 1996 (23 – 38 years old)
- Post-Millennials: Born 1997 – Present (7 – 22 years old)

According to the Deloitte Millennial Survey, Millennials, who are already emerging as leaders in technology and other industries will comprise 75% of the global workforce by 2025 and will want to work for organizations that foster innovative thinking, develop their skills, and make a positive contribution to society.[10]

This cohort conspicuously stand out for their use of technology – 93% own smartphones; 86% use social media; 53% own tablets; 78% subscribe to home broadband; 84% report using Facebook, and nearly 100% say they use the internet.[11]

FAMILY AND PARENTING VALUES

Don't let anyone think little of you because you are young. Be their ideal; let them follow the way you teach and live; be a pattern for them in your love, your faith, and your clean thoughts."

[1 Timothy 4:12, The Living Bible]

Millennials are said to share a typical period of history, shaped by the historical events and experiences of that time. As a result, their upbringing, values, attitudes and behaviours have been significantly shaped by this period.[12]

They are responsible for the majority of purchases from groceries to automobiles, and some have started to settle down with homes and children of their own. Contrary to previous generations, they are more tolerant of a wide range of non-traditional behaviours concerning marriage, family, parenting and social order. According to Pew Research Centre, 82% of babies born in 2016 were of Millennial parents.[13]

According to some experts, they differ from previous generations in their perspective on parenting. For example, they get parenting advice online and are not committed to marrying before having children. They significantly have more single women with children, more people cohabiting without being married, more mothers of young children working outside the home, and more inter-racial marriages. They are more receptive than previous generations to these newer patterns of behaviour.[14]

Demographer David Foot refers to the Millennials as "*Baby Boom Echo*," since they are the offsprings of the Baby Boomers.[15]

Boomer parents played a crucial role in the upbringing, development and worldview of Millennials. However, the critical factor is to understand the circumstances that influenced the childhood of Boomers – brought up in the 1960s and 70s when the floodlights of the social revolution had been switched on, revealing a contrary, anti-authoritarian and colourful society. These socio-cultural changes fuelled by rock 'n' roll music and the quest for 'freedom' flooded the Baby Boomer generation with a new set of 'untested' values and lifestyles – rebellion against traditional values, individualistic culture and the obsession for material possession.

"Not all Millennials think alike. A demographic is not a psychographic."

[Andy Dunn, U.S. Businessman]

THE IMPACT OF THE GREAT DEPRESSION

The Latin maxim '*Nemo dat quod non habet*' which means that no one can give what he does not have, reflects a quote from Jesus in the gospel of Matthew '*Freely you have received, freely give.*'[16]

Notwithstanding some exceptions, this quotation may be generally true of the parenting received by the Silent Generation which invariably affected the quality of parenting given to their Boomer children. This, in turn had a ripple effect on the parenting received by the Millennials. The Great Depression and the Second World War had a huge impact on the upbringing of the Silent generation; which in turn significantly shaped their view of parenting; and consequently the parenting practice of the Boomers and ultimately the Millennials. Richard Pells and Christina Romer in Encyclopaedia Britannica describe the Great Depression as:

"A worldwide economic downturn that began in 1929 and lasted until about 1939. Its severity varied substantially across countries, from United States where it originated; followed by Europe; and mild in Japan and Latin America. Its social and cultural effects were no less staggering, especially in the United States."[17]

Writing on the impact of the great depression on home and family, Encyclopedia.com, comments:

"The Great Depression challenged American families in major ways, placing great economic, social, and psychological strains and demands upon families and their members. Both working-class and middle-class families were drastically affected by the Depression. Traditional conceptions of gender roles prevailed during the 1930s; accordingly, men were expected to

be the breadwinners of their families. Unemployed men felt like failures as a result of their inability to provide for their families. Unemployed men often found themselves hanging around their homes, irritating their wives; quarrels became more frequent between husbands and wives. At times, men withdrew emotionally and even physically from their families and friends. Children of impoverished families often remembered their fathers as emotionally distant and indifferent. Some unemployed men took up drinking. Some deserted their wives and families altogether. "[18]

The Baby Boomers, through no fault of their own, were faced with two significant challenges, viz:

1. They were raised by the Silent Generation, faced with the socio-economic and political problems of the 1930s.
2. They were brought up in a cocktail of socio-cultural changes of epic proportions, characterised by civil and women's rights movements, a countercultural tsunami of fashion, the Cold War and other events that combined to blur moral lines and challenge the status quo.

CONCLUSION

Next Avenue contributor and Boomer Parent, Richard Watts in his article *'A Boomer Parent's Apology to Millennials'*, says *"perhaps it is time for us as boomer parents to take a good hard look at what we did."* [19]

Watts offers an apology for the following reasons:

1. We decided to give our kids everything we did not have and rejected teaching them some of the hard lessons we had.

2. We insisted our kids succeed and make us proud according to our expectations, no matter how much tough-love parenting we overlooked to ensure that raising them was fun.

3. We gave them too much and anesthetised their drive.

4. We behaved like drone parents, seeking out and removing obstacles and adversity to their success. Like growing a palm tree indoors, we protected them from the wind, fertilised them and kept the storms away.

5. We thought we had their best interest at heart, but in reality, we were making them look good to make us look good.

6. We let our love for them hijack our parenting skills.

7. We were afraid to risk their affection when we should have equipped them with the life tools that only come from allowing them to struggle, persist and recover on their own.

Watts further makes some promises to Millennials as the way forward.

1. We Boomer parents will encourage you in whatever endeavour you attempt, whether it is a success or a failure.

2. We will only give advice when you ask.

3. We will share with you and your children the struggles and setbacks we experienced when we were kids because recognising and discussing our failures can teach more than boasting about our successes.

4. We will withdraw our financial support (perhaps over time), and allow you to feel the struggles, the independence and finally pride that results from victory over adversity.

5. We will begin to accept the reality that we Boomer parents are only going to be on this planet a short time, and our lasting legacy will be the tools and traditions we leave with you, our Millennial children.

6. Sorry, we got a late start at being your parents - but we have never stopped loving you. We were intentionally spoiling you, unintentionally.

"Millennials are the greatest assets in any organisation"

[Jesse Song, Author 'Pillars of Parenting']

CHAPTER 2

CHILDFREE LIVING – THE REALITY OF MILLENNIALS?

> *Children are God's love-gift;*
> *they are heaven's generous reward.*
>
> [PSALMS 127:3, THE PASSION TRANSLATION]

VOLUNTARY CHILDLESSNESS – CHILDFREE LIVING

Childless or Childfree – two terms often used interchangeably, yet with different meanings. Being "childless" refers to the condition of being without children. This implies that everyone who does not have children would like to have them but is unable to conceive or carry a pregnancy to term. However, being "childfree" means that one does not want to have children at all – the condition of being without children. Certain common taboos still surround women without children, whether childless or childfree. Nonetheless, around the globe, the trend of voluntary childlessness is rapidly increasing and much less stigmatised than it used to be – and even applauded in certain circles. Not every childless woman is happily childfree, and not every childfree woman regrets their decision not to have a child.

Skipping the parenting stage of life is a rising popular choice amongst Millennials. One common misconception is that childfree couples are either infertile or unable to have children physically and are in a perpetual state of grief. Another misconception is that childfree couples do not like children. Going childless has even been labelled as a trend by some experts, with some early writers portraying childlessness as *"a mode of ultimate feminism."*[20]

Some Millennials are childless by circumstance; others have tried fertility treatment with no success; whilst others have partners who do not want to have children, or are perhaps still searching for the right person to have children with. Whatever the circumstance, it is still possible for both men and women to appreciate and enjoy a fulfilling life without children. The advocacy of choosing not to have children has permeated public discourse in ways unseen in previous generations. Of those English and Welsh women born in 1946, a mere 9% did not have children by the age of 45. For women born in 1970, that percentage almost doubled to 17%.[21]

Amy Blackstone, a professor in Sociology at the University of Maine, writes:

"Today, about 15 per cent of women never have kids; there are not that many people who, early on, say, 'I don't want kids,' Even the childless are more likely to begin uncertainly or assuming they will have children. It's only with time that they decide against it."[22]

Childless and childfree families are generally overlooked by family scholars and in popular discourse. However, this is one of several family forms that have evolved in the western world since the 1970s. Studies of childless adults reveal that they create bonds to fulfil many of the same functions that families with children fulfil.[23]

Time Magazine cover story *'The Childfree Life: When having it all means not having children'*, author, Lauren Sandler underlines that people choose not to have children for diverse reasons, not just out of economic hardship. She includes interviews with women who are substantially happier with their family, friends, travel and work-life because they have made a choice not to become parents.

Unfortunately, one of the pivotal predicaments with the article is that most of the interviews were granted only to women. There are very few male voices, but the childfree opinions come mostly from the women. In many cases, some men do not want to have children too. Having children – and not having them – is not something unique to women. Sandler attempts to justify it by explaining that the pressure to procreate falls mainly on women or as Pamela Smock of the University of Michigan says "childlessness defaults to women."[24]

The reasons for childfree living are diverse and specific to various individuals. Amongst these are:

- **Awareness of environmental impact of overpopulation**
  Some Millennials frequently express concern about the state of the world and are reluctant to have children in an overpopulated and environmentally challenged future.

- **Freedom from responsibilities**
  According to Elaine Tyler May in her book '*Barren in Promised Land*', the freedom from child-care responsibilities is another reason for childfree living.[25]

- **Freedom of travel**
  A meta-analysis from 1987 found that the childfree mostly anchor their decision on the freedom to travel.[26]

- **Freedom and autonomy**
  Other studies on childfree women found that there was an overwhelming focus on the benefits of freedom and autonomy of not having children.

- **Economic cost**
  A study in the U.K. by the Centre for Economic and Business Research for the insurer Liverpool Victoria (LV) show that the projected cost of raising a child born in 2016 from birth to 21 years old increased to £230,000 – an increase of 65% since 2003.[27]

- **Conflict with Career and work**
  The ability of children to conflict with work is a challenging factor for many women, whereas having children for men may well mean working more than they would have otherwise

had to. According to a 2012 study, women who wanted fewer children had a significant allure in a rewarding career, fame, and in generating new ideas and discoveries.[28]

A study by the Federal Reserve Bank of St. Louis found that parenthood appeared to result in lower productivity when the children were 12 and younger, with mothers averaging a 17.4% loss.[29]

- ## Finding substitutes for children

  Dogs and other pets are gradually becoming the new "children" for many couples these days. A study in the Journal of Mental Health Counselling found that dog owners placed their dogs as close as or even closer than family members and in 38% of cases considered their dogs to be the closest of all.[30]

  Researchers in *Society & Animals* Journal reviewed multiple studies and found that the death of a companion animal can be as devastating as the loss of a relative.[31]

- ## Impact on relationship with a partner.

  Some hold the view that children will have a negative impact on the relationship with their partner. Paul Dolan, a professor of behavioural science at the London School of Economics, said evidence shows that the traditional markers used to measure success did not correlate with happiness – particularly marriage and raising children. Dolan's book, Happy Ever After, cites evidence from the American Time Use Survey (ATUS), which compared levels of pleasure and misery in unmarried, married, separated, divorced and widowed individuals.[32]

Some of these reasons require more robust scrutiny; nonetheless, they show that the choice for a childfree living is on the rise. However, people – both men and women – with or without children, in the long run, report being similarly content with their lives. The Office for National Statistics (ONS) released a report *'Childbearing for women born in different years, England and Wales: 2016'*. Emily Knipe, Population Statistics Division, Office of National Statistics, writes:

> *"Women born in 1971 who completed their childbearing in 2016 had an average 1.90 children per woman, fewer than their mothers' generation (born 1944) who had 2.21 children, and the lowest level on record. Childlessness was higher for the 1971 cohort (18%) than for the 1944 cohort (11%), which is one of the main drivers of falling completed family sizes by the end of childbearing."*[33]

Psychiatrist and Philosopher Neel Burton in his book *'For Better for Worse: Should I Get Married?'* attributes the decline in marriage as another reason for the rise of childless or childfree women. Many people associate marriages with children, and being celibate accounts for one of the strongest predictors of childlessness.[34]

Not everyone agrees with the childfree philosophy. In 2015, Pope Francis during the general audience in St. Peter's Square at the Vatican, said:

> *"A society with a greedy generation, that doesn't want to surround itself with children, that considers them above all worrisome, a weight, a risk, is a depressed society. The choice to not have children is selfish. Life rejuvenates and acquires energy when it multiplies: It is enriched, not impoverished."*

"The soul is healed by being with children."

[Fyodor Dostoyevsky, Russian Novelist and Philosopher]

ANTINATALISM

Antinatalism is the view that it is morally wrong to bring new life into existence (including humans), because doing so would exposes them to pain and suffering. Antinatalists draw inspiration from David Benatar's notion that coming into existence is serious harm, regardless of the feelings of the human being once it comes into life. As a consequence, it is always morally wrong to create more sentient beings.[35]

Since the life of a new human being can unavoidably contain pain and suffering; antinatalists, therefore conclude through philosophical reasoning, that it is better for human beings not to be born. So having a child means foisting life on another person without his or her consent. It goes further that a born individual experiences pain and suffering of life, which would have been prevented, if the parents not procreated and brought that person into existence. Diane Bandy, antinatalist from Pennsylvania, writes;

"The anti-natalist and childfree community is growing rapidly with younger folks, especially millennials. Our parents thrust us into the world, but they won't be living our lives for us. There's no way to predict your future or your child's – but there will be guaranteed loneliness, disappointments,

frustration, fears, illnesses, long work hours, and pain. Reproduction and
parenting have been falsely glamorized. I never saw any logic to the idea
that parenting is life-affirming.'[36]

"Children are renewers, ground breakers and world-shakers,
bearers of new seed, heralds of a new age. Instead of letting the problems
that surround us frighten us from having children,
we should recognise God's pattern of using new life to mend those problems,
to bring renewal and fresh hope."

[Mike Mason, Author 'The Mystery of Children']

TOKOPHOBIA

Tokophobia – occasionally also called severe Childbirth Anxiety
(CA) or Fear of Childbirth (FOC) – is a phenomenon describing
the fear of pregnancy and childbirth, rather than merely a rational
decision not to have children. Women who have this condition have
a pathological fear of giving birth, and will often avoid becoming
pregnant, even though they want to have children. Tokophobia may
occur in women who have never given birth to a child, but it may
also affect women who have had prior traumatic birth experiences.[37]

Given the number of years that women have had prenatal and
postnatal complications associated with delivery, Tokophobia was only
officially identified in 2000 by Dr Kristina Hofberg, Britain's leading
expert on the syndrome, in her article *'Tokophobia: An Unreasonable
Dread of Childbirth'*. Hofberg stated her surprise in finding out how

common and high the rate of suffering was, yet experts had largely overlooked the issue – so incredibly important to many women."[38]

A study in the Royal College of Obstetricians' and Gynaecologists' yearbook found that one in five women, when pregnant for the first time, reported extreme fear about childbirth, while 6 per cent described a fear that was 'disabling', and almost one in seven of the 370 childless or non-pregnant women interviewed by Hofberg reported a morbid dread of childbirth sufficient to postpone or avoid pregnancy altogether.[39]

Tokophobia can develop due to several causes, including a fear of the unknown; fear of pain; loss of control and privacy; fear of childbirth in your family; past sexual abuse; a concern for the life of the infant; anxiety disorders; frightening birth stories from other people; gynaecological issues (problems with reproductive organs), lack of trust in medical practitioners. Tokophobia can cause severe impairment to strength or the ability to function, but with an excellent supportive multidisciplinary care, the desired outcome is possible. Men can also experience tokophobia. Studies have found that men with tokophobia often have a severe fear regarding the health and safety of their partner and child.[40]

"The potential possibilities of any child are the most intriguing and stimulating in all creation."

[Ray L. Wilbur, Third President of Stanford University]

HAVING CHILDREN — OBLIGATORY OR OPTIONAL?

This question raises a profound ethical issue which is not just a matter of whether or not God "expects" us to have children, since He is sovereign and all-knowing, and is aware that not everyone may end up having children. The critical question is whether one can fulfil his duty to God successfully without children. In the Old Testament Scriptures, children were an external physical sign of God's blessing. Even so, infertility was not a reliable sign of God's displeasure. Many couples in the Scriptures, such as Elkanah and Hannah (parents of Samuel), Abraham and Sarah (parents of Isaac), and Zechariah and Elizabeth (parents of John the Baptist), were godly men and women who had been sterile or barren for years. Nowhere does the Bible state that every marriage should have children. Again, the absence of children is not an indication of God's displeasure. Families or couples without children are as important to the Kingdom of God as those with children. It is not uncommon for some to hold the view that couples without children (much like single people) may devote additional time and energy to focus on the work of the kingdom than those with children.[41]

Having children in itself is not a measure of success since childless people can end up just as satisfied with their lives as those with children. The value system in the New Testament places a high premium on spiritual fruitfulness and multiplication than on physical blessings. Married, single, with or without children, every individual child of God is an essential and integral member of God's family. For many, God's plan may involve having children, whether naturally, medically or through adoption, while for others, children do not constitute part of His program.

"Every child is a different kind of flower, and all together, they make this world a beautiful garden."

[Author Unknown]

CONCLUSION

There remains tremendous socio-cultural pressure on both women and men, but particularly women, to have children. This pressure may remain mostly unexpressed. However, even without any form of constraint, many people would still embrace the desire to have children. Children have the unique potential of adding meaning and purpose to our lives. The creation of another human being is almost transcendent, and their dependence on us, at least in the early years, can give us a strong sense of meaning and significance.

CHAPTER 3

PARENTING STYLES – TRAINING ACCORDING TO PATTERN

Train up a child in the way he should go [teaching him to seek God's wisdom and will for his abilities and talents], Even when he is old he will not depart from it.
[PROVERBS 22:6, AMPLIFIED BIBLE]

PARENTING STYLES

For many decades, developmental psychologists have studied the effects of parenting style on child development and behaviours. However, it is difficult to create a link between cause-and-effect in relation to specific actions of parents and later behaviour of their children. Despite these barriers, researchers have postulated the existence of connections between parenting styles and their effects on a child. These effects may well carry over into adult behaviour.

Parenting styles are the different ways parents interact with their children. In practice, many parents find themselves naturally using a blend of different styles, adjusting and changing strategies as children grow older. The use of a particular style will depend on the parent's preference as the family progresses. Nonetheless, a suitable method for one child may not be suitable or appropriate for another child. It is not unusual to find that children reared in substantially different environments can later grow up to have similar prominent personalities with one another. Contrarily, children who were brought up in the same household could grow up to have astonishingly different characters. Researcher Diane Baumrind in the 1960s produced some of the most well-known research on parenting styles. Baumrind and many subsequent researchers focused on two essential aspects of parenting: '*responsiveness*' and '*demandingness*'.[42]

According to their research, parents high in *responsiveness* are attuned and sensitive to their children's signals. Responsiveness also includes warmth, reciprocity, clear communication, and attachment. Parents high in *demandingness* monitor their children, set limits, enforce rules, make maturity demands and use consistent discipline. These two aspects of parenting create four general parenting styles. Even though different researchers give different names to them, the four Baumrind parenting styles have well-defined names and characteristics: Authoritarian, Authoritative, Permissive or Indulgent and Uninvolved.

- **Authoritarian (High Demandingness, Low Responsiveness)**

  The authoritarian parenting style substantially leads to children who are obedient and proficient but rank low in happiness, social competence, and self-esteem.

- **Authoritative (High Demandingness, High Responsiveness)**

  This parenting style significantly tends to result in children who are happy, capable, well-adjusted and have high self-esteem.

- **Permissive or indulgent (Low Demandingness, High Responsiveness)**

  The permissive parenting style often produces a child who ranks low in happiness and self-regulation. These children are highly likely to experience problems with authority and generally tend to perform poorly in school.

- **Uninvolved or Neglecting (Low Demandingness, Low Responsiveness)**

  Uninvolved parenting ranks the least across all aspects of life. Children of such parents tend to lack self-control, have low self-esteem, and are usually less competent than their peers.

Parenting style can have long-lasting effects on a child. Each method looks at a different perspective in raising a child and can be distinguished by many different characteristics. Nonetheless, it is not unusual for both parents to have different ideas on parenting as one might prefer a more permissive approach, whereas the other a more authoritative approach. What is essential is for both parents to agree to work together on a combined approach which takes into account the temperament, personality and best interest of the child.

"The greatest gifts you can give your children are the roots of responsibility and the wings of independence."

[Denis Waitley, Motivational Speaker]

AUTHORITARIAN PARENTING

In this parenting style, children are expected to follow strict rules and their behaviour is modulated to the highest standard. These parents set robust regulations and make sure that children understand the consequences of breaking the rules. Authoritarian parents do not explain the reason behind these rules. Instead, they enact the regulations and enforce them by applying consequences with little regard for the child's opinion or feelings. Parents who exhibit this style are often reported to be domineering and dictatorial. They do not allow the child to get involved in problem-solving challenges or obstacles. Their primary outlook on parenting is summarised as *"spare the rod, and spoil the child."* A child's feeling is not considered when consequences are applied, and obedience is demanded without question. While these parents have towering requests, they are not very approachable and expect their children not to make mistakes. Authoritarian parents may prefer the use of punishments instead of discipline (see chapter 6). Children of authoritarian parents have a higher risk of developing self-esteem problems because their opinions are generally not valued.

"Children need models rather than critics."

[Joseph Joubert, French Moralist]

AUTHORITATIVE PARENTING

Authoritative parenting also set rules and guidelines that children are requested to follow; however, they are more democratic in their parenting approach and monitor their children's behaviour. They are confidently assertive, but not intrusive and restrictive. Authoritative parents balance setting clear boundaries and encouraging their children to think independently. They are sensitive and understand their children's needs; however, they do not let their children get away with breaking the rule. A child's feeling is considered when consequences are applied, and obedience is demanded with consideration given to the child's viewpoint. They validate their children's self-esteem while also emphasising that adults are fundamentally incharge. They use positive discipline strategies to buttress good behaviours – like praise and reward systems.

Authoritative parents dedicate time and energy into preventing behavioural problems before they arise. When children fall short of expectations, these parents are more supportive, nurturing and forgiving rather than punitive. Authoritative parents are conscious of a child's needs; are willing to pay attention to questions asked and expect good behaviour from their children. It is this fusion of expectation and support system that helps children of authoritative parents develop skills such as independence, self-esteem, self-control, and self-regulation. Researchers have found that children with authoritative parents are most likely to feel comfortable in expressing their opinions. They are likely to be good at making decisions, evaluating safety risks on their own and have higher prospects of being independent and well-behaved.

"Seven things every child needs to hear: I love you,
I'm proud of you, I'm sorry, I forgive you, I'm listening,
This is your responsibility, You have what it takes."

[Josh Shipp, Teen Behaviour Expert and Motivational Speaker]

PERMISSIVE PARENTING

Permissive parents, also known as indulgent parents, are astonishingly over tolerant and rarely implement any rules or structure or a strong sense of self-discipline. They have very few demands to make of their children. They are inclined towards being very loving, yet provide few guidelines and rules. These parents are non-orthodox, lenient and avoid confrontation; do not require mature behaviour and allow considerable self-regulation. They usually do not put much effort into discouraging poor choices or bad behaviour and often step in only when there is a severe problem.

The permissive parenting style is often practised by parents who take more of a friend role than of a parent role.

According to Laura Markham, author of *'Peaceful Parent, Happy Kids'*, permissive parents have a hard time setting limits with their children; therefore, parents are more likely to ignore bad behaviour and to 'give in' against their better judgment when their child gets upset. The result is that they don't set or enforce age-appropriate expectations for behaviour".[43]

The first remedy of permissive parenting is to understand the importance of setting limits and boundaries to a child's security, self-worth and sense of safety. Some recommendations offered to permissive parents include:

i. **Agreement on the rules.** Family rules are clear statements about unacceptable behaviours. Parents should not fail to set limits because they feel uncomfortable that a child's feelings may be hurt. They should be willing to face this discomfort. A child's behaviour can be changed when there are clear consequences for breaking the rules.

ii. **Establish a routine:** Consistency and predictability are essential for creating a routine in the home. Routines and daily schedules help both parent and child to know what to expect each day. Routines can also improve your child's behaviour and your relationship with your child.

iii. **Never disregard bad behaviour:** Dangerous and destructive behaviours should never be ignored. For example, if children are hurting themselves, harming others, or destroying objects. This disorderly conduct should be stopped immediately.

"Children are the living messages we send to a time we will not see."

[John F. Kennedy, Former U.S. President]

UNINVOLVED PARENTING

Uninvolved or neglectful parenting is a style characterised by little knowledge of what the child is doing and a lack of responsiveness to the child's needs. This parenting style may meet the child's basic needs, but the parents are generally detached from the child's life and provide little to nothing in terms of guidance, structure, rules, attention or even support. These parents have curtailed time-sharing and interaction and expect children to raise themselves. In extreme cases, uninvolved parents make few to no demands of their children, and they are often indifferent, dismissive, or even wholly neglectful.

Parents who practice this parenting style were themselves generally brought up by dismissive and uninvolved parents. As adults, they may be replicating to some extent, the same scenario that characterised their upbringing. Other parents who model this style may be absorbed in their busy lifestyles that they favour a *laissez-faire* attitude. In certain instances, parents may be locked up in their problems (such as, being overworked, coping with distressing situations or grappling with substance abuse) that they are blinded to how uninvolved and neglectful they are with their children. In other instances, uninvolved parents might be utterly unable to provide the emotional and psychological support that their children need.

Few difficulties are presented for the family when both parents practice the same parenting style. Numerous research indicate that it is better for a child to have at least one parent who is authoritative than having both parents with the same, less effective style. Parenting should be considered from the perspective of mothers, fathers and children, while recognising that other factors not limited to parenting styles also influence child outcomes. Such factors include: the child's temperament and how it "aligns" with parental expectations; the school teacher's style of working with children and the degree of compatibility to parenting style. A child's peer, social or cultural group can also influence outcomes. These Baumrind parenting styles have not gone without the criticism of being *'americanised'* – viewed from a limited American perspective – and it is not clear how well these styles describe parents cross-culturally.

"I continue to believe that if children are given the necessary tools to succeed, they will succeed beyond their wildest dreams!"

[David Vitter, Former U.S. Senator]

IMPLICATIONS OF OVER-PARENTING

Parents are required to be caring and supportive. However, numerous negative consequences can result when parents exercise too much control. Those who are excessively involved in every aspect of their child's life (often seeking to remedy all their problems) end up suffocating the child's ability to function independently or solve his or her problems. Parents who overprotect – ostensibly in furtherance of children's safety (whether physically, emotionally, for security, academically, professionally or financially) also do so to promote their ego. These children grow up into adults still expecting to be continually instructed on what to do and how to do it and are bewildered by the prospect of having to fend for themselves as an actual independent human being would do. God help them when parents are gone. The pressures of over-parenting have evolved in ways that would have once seemed unreasonable, leading to the appearance of two types of related styles: the "helicopter" and the "lawnmower" parenting styles.

- **Helicopter Parents:** The term "Helicopter Parenting" was coined in 1969 by Dr Haim Ginott, a psychotherapist and parent educator, in his book '*Between Parent and Teenager.*'[44]

  Helicopter parents are those who give excessive attention to their children's experiences and always attempt to sweep away all problems and obstacles out of their path. As the name implies, such parents spend much of their time hovering like helicopters above their children, ready to swoop in to help or protect, even when it is not necessary. This takes place especially during the later stages of adolescence up to early adulthood at a time when the development of independence and self-sufficiency are essential for the child's future success.

- **Lawnmower Parents:** Lawnmower parenting is a term for parents who are one step ahead – ready to '*mow down*' and level obstacles in their child's path, so they do not experience adversity or discomfort on their track.

A common strategy of both helicopter and lawnmower parents includes interfering notably with their adult child's lives. These may involve complaining to employers when the child does not get a job, complaining to teachers when the child does not acquire good grades or complaining to the sports coach when the child is not selected. Obsessively facilitating a stress-free childhood does not contribute positively to children in the long term. Always hovering and doing things for children may also backfire. Continual interference is more likely to cause children to develop anxiety-related issues. Even though the link is not necessarily causal, being repeatedly rescued can reduce a child's confidence level. Meanwhile, when children play alone, they encounter challenges – and learn to solve problems, honing their creative skills in the process. Providing children with opportunities and a healthy environment helps them to gain valuable encounters and networks that are non-existent in more unfavourable settings. However, there is an essential difference between supporting children and swaddling them in gold-plated cotton sheets.

"My worst parenting moments, the ones I am least proud of, happened because I was trying to impress a bunch of strangers I'll probably never see again."

[Janel Mills, Librarian and Blogger]

LIMITATIONS OF PARENTING STYLES

Research on parenting styles has significant limitations – most of the studies were conducted with European and American families. These studies did not take into consideration the specificities of other cultures (see chapter 4). While evidence may show a link between a particular method and a specific pattern of behaviour, other indispensable variables such as a child's temperament can also play an essential role. In some cases, there is evidence that a child's behaviour can influence the style of parenting. A previous study found that the parents of children who display challenging behaviour began to exhibit less parental control over time. Such results suggest that children may not misbehave because their parents were permissive, but that, at least in some instances, the parents of difficult or aggressive children may be more likely to abandon trying to control their children.

Researchers have also noted that the link between parenting styles and behaviours are, in some cases, weak at best. In other cases, the expected child outcomes do not happen – parents with authoritative styles may have children who are obstinate or who engage in irresponsible behaviour, while parents with permissive styles may have children who are academically successful and self-confident.

When parents from predominantly (Central America, Asia and Africa) immigrate to the West, they bring their parenting styles with them, often authoritarian and collectivist. There is evidence, though, that the authoritarian discipline often seen in Asian American, Hispanic American, and African American families does not have the same negative consequences for young children's behaviour as it does in European American families. The difference is likely due to the fact that different disciplinary styles have different meanings in different cultures and subcultures. These findings remind us that it is important to evaluate parenting styles in their cultural context.[45]

WHICH PARENTING STYLE IS MOST EFECTIVE?

It is beneficial for a child to have parents practising different styles rather than both practising the same style. Every child is different, and each child requires a specific *"tailor-made"* parenting style. However, multiple studies in different countries have indicated that authoritative parenting is associated with observed positive outcomes which are predominantly related to healthy behaviours such as self-competence and self-esteem. However, it cannot be confirmed with absolute certainty that these behaviours result purely from this style.

There is no universally 'best' style of parenting, says author Douglas Bernstein in his book Essentials of Psychology. Bernstein further says authoritative parenting, which is so consistently linked with positive outcomes in European American families, is not related to better school performance among African American or Asian American youngsters.[46]

"Children are likely to live up to what you believe of them."

[Lady Bird Johnson, Former First Lady of the United States]

CONCLUSION

Effective parenting goes beyond conspicuous hazards like neglect, abuse, or debauchery. The National Academy of Sciences in its consensus study report delineates four primary responsibilities for parents: maintaining children's health and safety; promoting their emotional well-being; instilling social skills, and preparing children intellectually.[47]

Diverse studies suggest that the best-adjusted children are reared by parents who find a way to combine warmth and sensitivity with clear behavioural expectations. From a very young age, children will mimic parents and their behaviours. Parents may have 'off' days, make parenting mistakes from time to time, but remember that children are still watching. Moreover, what children learn through parenting style has the potential to affect every aspect of their lives – from their academics to their relationships with others.

"While we try to teach our children all about life,
Our children teach us what life is all about."

[Angela Schwindt, Home Schooling Mom]

CHAPTER 4

PARENTING BY CULTURE – BEAUTY IN DIVERSITY

> " *As iron sharpens iron, So one man sharpens
> [and influences] another [through discussion].*
>
> [PROVERBS 27:17 AMPLIFIED BIBLE] "

WHAT IS CULTURE?

he word culture has many different meanings. For some, it refers to a perception of good music, art, food, literature and ancestry. However, for anthropologists and other behavioural scientists, culture is the full range of learned human behaviour patterns. It has been said that only two kinds of information are transmitted across generations: culture and genes. Parents are the final common pathway of both.[48]

The term was first introduced in this way by English anthropologist Edward Burnett Tylor, regarded as the founder of cultural anthropology. His most famous work, *Primitive Culture* (1871), provides one of the earliest and most explicit definitions of culture, one that is extensively accepted and used by many present-day anthropologists. Tylor defined culture as:

"...that complex whole which includes knowledge, belief, art, morals, law, custom, and any other capabilities and habits acquired by man as a member of society."[49]

"Society is unity in diversity."

[George Herbert Mead, Philosopher and Sociologist]

CULTURE AND PARENTING

Culture, which expresses and perpetuates itself through parenting, provides the foundation by which parents generally learn parenting practices – both desirable and undesirable. These practices, which govern the beliefs and way of life of a group of people, are transmitted and shared from one generation to another. Parents bring certain cultural 'habits' into interactions with their children, and interpret even similar characteristics in children within their culture's frame of reference – parents then encourage or discourage characteristics as appropriate or detrimental to adequate functioning within the group.[50]

Parents typically organise and distribute their care giving along with specific characteristics that are considered important within their indigenous cultural belief systems and behaviour patterns. Certainly, culturally established beliefs can be so powerful that parents are known to act on them, setting aside what their senses might tell them about their children. Parenting in one culture is characterised, and distinguished from parenting in another by deep-rooted and widely acknowledged behaviours. Certain values and beliefs may be normative in one culture but not necessarily in the other. For example, parents in some cultures speak to babies and rightly see them as comprehending interactive partners long before infants produce language, whereas parents in other cultures think that it is pointless to talk to children before they are capable of speech.[51]

Culture embeds into parenting cognitions and practices, with similarities that are likely shared across cultures. Pivotal to the concept of culture is the expectation that different cultural groups possess distinct beliefs, behaviours and variations which are unique to their parenting. Although parents in any given country vary in their parenting style, each culture has a predominant style of parent-child relationships, emphasising certain values over others.[52]

Cultural parenting is generally considered as a set of distinctive patterns of parenting beliefs and behaviours that are acquired and shared by a group of people. These patterns serve as a fundamental role to regulate and shape parental cognitions that in turn, are thought to develop parenting practices. A child's upbringing experience within a cultural context consequently offers a supporting framework to become a culturally competent member of that society. For example, while European American mothers of toddlers use suggestions (rather than commands) and other indirect means of structuring their children's behaviour, Puerto Rican mothers use more direct means of structuring, such as commands, physical positioning, restraints and direct attempts to recruit their children's attention.[53]

Raising children in different cultures can be as varied as the regions from which they come because different cultures present different perspectives on parenting. Research shows that the majority of books concerning infancy and upbringing are rooted in western philosophy, which has resulted in the discarding of the parenting perspective of other cultures – and that of the West instead adopted. Such has been the case, especially with the eroding of Asian, African and Latino parenting styles and dispositions. It is imperative to glean from other cultures by encouraging a reciprocal paradigm shift. Expanding parenting literature to accommodate a complementary global perspective is a step in the right direction.

"No culture can live, if it attempts to be exclusive."

**[Mohandas K. Gandhi,
Indian Lawyer and Anti-Colonial Nationalist]**

CULTURAL PARENTING

Parenting beliefs and practices around the world can be conspicuously different. Adopting a culturally diverse mindset in parenting can help challenge the cultural status quo by bringing in new ideas – and even help to integrate new parenting styles adopted from other cultures.

Cultural parenting is a parenting style in which culture plays a pivotal role and forms the bedrock of parenting. It lays the ground rules, sets the limits, determines desirable qualities, establishes criteria for positive outcomes and defines social and moral norms. The culture – not necessarily the parents – plays a dominant role in achieving positive results. Cultural parenting is different from the other parenting styles (chapter 3) in that, while parents are a pre-requisite for the practice of the other styles, cultural parenting is not predicated on parents since they play a secondary role within the rules and boundaries as defined by the culture. As a result, even in the absence of parents, the culture provides a framework, respected by all, for standardized upbringing. This acts as a buffer to the effects of dysfunctional or deleterious parenting by providing systems that cannot be violated by such parents. For example, in some societies, marriage and inheritance, amongst others are determined by the established cultural norms and not by individual parents. In a sense, the children are being parented by the culture while parents are guides within that culture.

The nuclear family is the ideal structure for raising children in western societies. In many other parts of the world, extended family (and the community) takes a much more significant role in childcare and parenting. Most African societies regard parenting as a communal and extended family responsibility and not only for the biological parents. Communal parenting buttresses the ancient

African adage "*it takes a village to raise a child*" – an entire community of "*child investors*" (aunts, uncles, sisters, parents, neighbours, etc.) taking responsibility for the life and welfare of a child in the community. While the extended family system is rapidly eroding and failing to fulfil its primary role of socialisation and child upbringing; external pressures and 'political correctness' have diluted the rich parenting heritage of many communities.

The communal concept of parenting is bolstered by another African adage "*a single hand cannot nurse a child*", implying that although the biological parents have the responsibility of taking care of the child, the burden is being shared by all. Also, this system allows any older adult to reasonably discipline or correct a child. While some view this parenting style as something to be avoided; others are simply ignorant of the value of their cultural heritage – erroneously believing that to be culturally aware makes one uncivilised or outdated. This misguided mindset is the product of lack of appropriate knowledge. However, cultural practices that are not in the best interest of children or that fail to respect the dignity of children should be discouraged and discarded, especially if they lead to child abuse.

The Frances McClelland Institute in Tucson Arizona state that in traditional Chinese families (similar to African tradition), for example, parents emphasise respect for authority, devotion to parents and high achievement. Children are highly likely to put family first and remain obedient to parents.[54]

"Strength lies in differences, not in similarities."

[Stephen Covey, Author, Businessman and Speaker]

MODELS OF PARENTING – INDIVIDUAL VS COLLECTIVE

A widely debated issue in parenting is whether and to what extent a child's individuality should be developed. Marcia Carteret in *Dimensions of Culture* explains the two predominant ways in child-rearing – individualistic and collectivist. Individualistic cultures emphasise self-sufficiency, while collectivist cultures emphasise the dependence of individuals on the group of which they belong.[55]

Most western parents embrace the individualistic model, while parents in Africa, Latino cultures in Mexico, Puerto Rico and Central America and Asian cultures in China and India, for example, tend to be influenced by a collectivist tradition in which family and community interest are emphasised over individual goals.[56]

Group activities are dominant in collectivist cultures, responsibility is shared, and accountability is collective. Collectivism, cooperation and harmony among the group tend to be emphasised more than individual function and responsibility. Through this lens, the dissonance between parenting styles in the west and many parts of the world gives the impression of a profound difference. Collectivist cultures, by far the global norm, raise children in dependent behaviours including obedience, politeness, calmness and respect. Eventually, emphasis is placed on the conduct of children, who are expected not to bring shame to the family or community.

Children raised with Chinese and African values inculcate an accepted duty toward their family. As part of their child-rearing practice, Chinese parents are expected to instruct their children on how to live harmoniously with other people. Therefore, an individual emotional expression may be seen as harmful if it is a threat to preserving harmonious living. This, in turn, breeds a culture of "saving face," which produces shame on the child if society's expectations for dignity and propriety are violated.

Filipino families have similar concepts, such as hiya (referring to *'shame'* or *'sense of propriety'*) and pakikisama (living in harmony with others, even if it conflicts with an individual's desires). Again, if these principles are breached, rejected or violated, intense shame is attached to the act. According to Amy Chua in her book *'Battle Hymn of the Tiger Mother'*, (albeit some controversial points), children of Chinese parents are required to show respect and obedience; are not permitted to give up, and are not allowed to fail – including in their academics.[57]

The United Kingdom is renowned for its perfect nannies, namely Mary Poppins and Super Nanny. Although these examples are very stereotypical, they do reflect some of the values that parents in the U.K. endeavour to instil in their children. British parents rationalise with children; discuss their opinions and feelings; involve them in the problem-solving process. These children are expected to be polite and well-mannered and encouraged to express themselves and be authentic to their feelings.

From age seven, Japanese children, for example, are often allowed to travel on the subway by themselves. In like manner, the notion of children going to bed too early, say before 7:00 pm is unthinkable to Latino or Hispanic parents who place a high premium on children participating in evening family life. Cultural norms and standards can significantly impact which values parents deem essential and how they share those values with their children. Most European parents, for example, take a relatively relaxed view of sex and alcohol, while giving low importance to religion. Middle Eastern and Asian parents usually provide a high priority to traditional values of virtue and morality. South Asian immigrants in the United Kingdom avoid excessive verbal praise to prevent their children from becoming "spoiled" and "proud."[58]

In one study of Eastern European immigrants to the US, one Russian mother explained the difficulties such culture clashes can create. She said immigrant parents are teaching their sons that they have to respect other adults and anybody who is older than them. They are supposed to respect teachers, not to mention parents and grandparents. Well, what they have learned in the US is that they can state their opinion in front of anybody and in any way they want to. So, for immigrant parents, the downside of raising kids in the U.S. is that the first phrase they learn is, 'it's a free country.'"[59]

Though there are various parenting styles within the African context, there are ways in which the African parent brings up a child to integrate cultural values and become a responsible adult. Even ideas about nutrition, basic hygiene and health are often influenced by culture. When it relates to parenting values, the U.S. is a parenting cocktail, with views ranging from highly conservative to permissive. Also in the U.S. for example, Latino and Asian women are more likely to breastfeed and for more extended periods than African-American or white women.[60]

Meredith Small, anthropologist and expert on cultural variations in parenting, says that parents differ in who they go to seek parenting wisdom. In many traditional cultures, parents learn how to parent from their elders. In the U.S., parents are more likely to rely on the opinions of experts.[61]

Researchers have investigated cultural and historical differences in parenting practices for many years. Studies show that warmth, control and structure are three significant factors usually used to explain the differences in parenting style, viz: warmth versus hostility (how much warmth, love and affection parents show children); autonomy versus control (how much control children have over their lives); and structure versus chaos (how much structure and predictability regulates children's lives).[62]

"An individual has not started living until he can rise above the narrow confines of his individualistic concerns to the broader concerns of all humanity."

[Martin Luther King, Minister and Civil Rights Leader]

PARENTING EXCHANGE PROGRAMS

Exchange visits or study tours seek to improve the knowledge and experience of visitors and to integrate those experiences into professional development and a better understanding of global issues. The benefits of exchange visits include: gaining a better knowledge and understanding of other cultures; maturity through the challenges faced on an exchange: significantly improving current skills with a global standpoint: developing confidence out of familiar surroundings and "comfort zones"; developing increased self-confidence and a sense of self-reliance; and understanding the world through "new eyes".

The concept of exchange study visits can widen parenting practice. Parenting exchange visits can be defined as programs that seek to improve the parenting experience of children in a different culture and environment. It is a multi-faceted approach to an upbringing that encourages an array of different cultural and community perspectives. These visits offer the child the opportunity to experience a different philosophy of life and depending on the country of choice, learn new skills or improve old ones. For example, American children on 'parenting exchange visits' to China will experience parenting from the Chinese perspective, and vice versa. While in the U.S., they will be encouraged to develop traits of assertiveness and high self-esteem, which are crucial for personal and professional success in the U.S.[63]

Maturity and social poise, energised by the necessity to confront challenges outside a familiar comfort zone and support network make up the exchange program's unique experience for the children. British children on exchange visits to Africa or Latin America can learn authentic community living, while African children can learn from the U.K. how to be authentic to their feelings. While the strengths and weaknesses of each culture are generalisations; the concept of improving parenting through exchange visits needs further investigation. Notwithstanding, learning about cultural differences in parenting can illuminate our parenting practice and offer some positive alternatives for effective parenting. It is also the case that positive outcomes can be achieved by sending the child to live with another family in the same country without the necessity to travel internationally.

Parents can also create microenvironments at home so children can imbibe these qualities. A particular culture may be better at discipline while deficient in producing self-esteem. Parents need to weigh the options and make decisions in the best interest of children. Where possible, nuclear families should attach value to regular visits to their hometowns and connect with their extended families. Parents should frequently introduce their children to extended families on both sides.

While more could be done to encourage regular visits to environments that foster positive parenting, a reasonable alternative would be to visit other relatives or friends who can help children learn positive moral values. In some instances, these visits may be a solution to behavioural issues associated with a particular child. Parents must be aware of the possibility of abuse and make appropriate arrangements to safeguard their children's welfare.

"We are all different, which is great because we are all unique. Without diversity life would be very boring."

[Catherine Pulsifer, Inspirational Author]

CONCLUSION

Cultural diversity is a great asset and a source of parenting strength that should be respected, cultivated and preserved, while at the same time ensuring that all children have an equal opportunity to enter the social and economic mainstream. Most forward-thinking societies are not monolithic since they represent many different racial, ethnic and religious heritages.

Again, the media has taken precedence in families to the point that children are flooded with television programs and electronic gadgets, with limited information on the benefits of cultural values. Because of this, many children have lost touch with their rich cultural heritage, such as to give a helping hand to an adult or to offer up their seat to an elderly person, whether in private or public.

Even though it is constructive to understand the contribution culture plays in parenting, grading different cultures or categorising ethnic groups with 'best parents' does no one any approbation, particularly given the increasing diversity and multicultural nature of our world. It is evident that when it relates to parenting, there is no one-size-fits-all solution – especially when it involves raising a child in a diametrically different culture to the one in which parents grew up. Culture embeds into parenting cognitions and practices, with similarities that are shared across cultures. The blending of these cultures can make it easier for parents to learn something different about how it is done in other communities – to a greater extent, given the current socio-cultural and geo-political climate, this can only be worthy of commendation.

CHAPTER 5

AUTHENTIC FATHERHOOD –
RESPONSIBILITY BEYOND REPROACH

> " *Listen to your father's advice and don't despise an old mother's experience.*
>
> [PROVERBS 23:22, THE LIVING BIBLE] "

ABSENT FATHER SYNDROME

A UNICEF report (2007) shows that children in western countries, such as Canada, the U.K. and the U.S. rank extremely low regarding social and emotional well-being and happiness.[64]

Many propositions have been put forward to describe this primarily ignored and lamentable state of children. The prevalence and devastating effects of father absence in children's lives is rising to distressing and problematic proportions all over the world. The U.K. has 2.8 million families (15%) which feature a lone parent with at least one dependent or non-dependent child.[65]

In 2013, the U.K. Centre for Social Justice (CSJ) released a report titled: *'Fractured Families: Why stability matters'*. CSJ Director, Christian Guy, in the foreword alerts of the "tsunami" of family breakdown battering the nation – which he referred to as an "epidemic."

Guy said:

"There are many misguided reasons for such political paralysis. Some argue that it is no business of politicians to meddle in the personal family choices people make. Others suggest that rising family breakdown is just a modern process, an inevitable trait of human advancement. Others say family instability doesn't matter – this has to change. Our political discourse about family policy must mature. Family breakdown is an urgent public health issue. Backing commitment and setting a goal of reducing instability does not equate to criticising or stigmatising lone parents or those involved. Within this need for new maturity, we should also agree that marriage is not a right-wing obsession but a social justice issue: people throughout society want to marry, but the cultural and financial barriers faced by those in the poorest communities thwart their aspirations."[66]

Lone parent families are increasing at an alarming rate of more than 20,000 a year and will soon total more than two million. Further, it adds that around one million children grow up in the U.K. without a father or with no father contact. In some localities, fatherlessness has reached such a towering degree that they are virtual "men deserts".

As a result, the blame is laid on politicians for a "feeble" answer in response to this national "emergency".

The absence of fathers is associated with higher rates of teenage crime, pregnancy and disadvantage, the report says. The financial, social and human cost is "devastating" for children and adults alike. Findings from conducted polls show that 89% of people in the U.K. agree (with 52% strongly agreeing) that parenting is where to start if we have any hope of mending our broken society and family. The polls further show 81% of people think that children must grow up living with both parents.[67]

"Having kids – the responsibility of rearing good, kind, ethical, responsible human beings – is the biggest job anyone can embark on. As with any risk, you have to take a leap of faith and ask lots of wonderful people for their help and guidance. I thank God every day for giving me the opportunity to parent."

[Maria Shriver, Journalist]

Blackenhorn, the founder of the Institute for American Values, observes that:

"The United States is becoming an increasingly fatherless society. A generation ago, an American child could reasonably expect to grow up with his or her father. Today, an American child can reasonably expect not to; tonight, about 40 per cent of American children will go to sleep in homes in which their fathers do not live. Before they reach the age of eighteen,

more than half of our nation's children are likely to spend a significant portion of their childhoods living apart from their fathers. Never before in this country have so many children been voluntarily abandoned by their fathers. Never before have so many children grown up without knowing what it means to have a father.'[68]

These concerns are not unfounded. U.S. Department of Justice report titled '*What Can the Federal Government Do To Decrease Crime and Revitalize Communities?*' shows that children from fatherless homes account for higher rates of suicide, runaways, behavioural disorders, high school dropouts, juvenile detention, substance abuse and aggression.[69]

Father authority figures, for generations, were given a free pass, an unexamined prerogative. While some made positive contributions in their children's lives, others abused it. There is no cure for fatherlessness – there are only conciliatory. Single mothers, not by choice, should expose their children to the influence of male mentors – be they uncles, brothers, coaches and the like. The fatherless world needs substitute fathers – men who are willing to care about the lives of children who are not their own. Fathers who have neglected their parenting role for whatever reason should step up and get involved.

"Although father and mother usually play different roles in their child's life, 'different' does not mean more or less important."

[Richard A. Warshak, Author 'The Custody Revolution']

THE CHANGING FIELD OF PSYCHOLOGY

Ditta Oliker's article 'The Importance of Fathers,' published in *Psychology Today* succinctly chronicles the evolution of psychology in relation to understanding the role of the father.

Oliker writes:

"The world began to radically change with the social, economic and technical advances of the 20th century, and with those changes came a basic change in the structure and function of the family – with a consequent shift in the authority of the father. His influence was increasingly seen as minor, even negligible, and his importance was defined by how well he provided for the family. Another factor in the diminished role of the father was the then-new field of psychology. In fact, psychology became part of the problem. Research studies did not place much importance on the role of the father, and his influence on the development and growth of his child was reported as "insignificant." The term "parent" was often meant as a mother – and father, if mentioned, was equivalent to other influences. Only a small number of parent-child studies investigated the father's role, and the few studies that were done at that time focused on the father's involvement as reported by the mother. For example, in a number of studies that used over 2,000 parents who responded to questions about parenting, not one father was interviewed. An indirect result of the lack of research data on fathers was the implied assumption that they weren't interested in fathering.

The pendulum of the father's influence swung so far that the verse would have read: The fathers have eaten a sour grape that had an influence on the mothers, who chose not to offer them to the children. The pendulum slowly began to swing back in the 1970s, with newly designed studies beginning to support the impact of fathers. These days, neither the general public nor psychological researchers see the father as an equivalent to "other influences." The professional journals, as well as the Internet, are filled with articles reporting results confirming the importance of the father."[70]

"Children are our most valuable resource."

[Herbert Hoover, 31st U.S. President]

THE MYTH OF THE SUPERFLUOUS FATHER

Dr Wade F. Horn, former president and co-founder of the National Fatherhood Initiative, developed the phrase *"the myth of the superfluous father"* referring to the fact that too many fathers become persuaded that they are merely an extra set of hands to help around the house rather than irreplaceable in their children's lives. In his article published by Hoover Institution, Stanford University.

Horn comments:

"The greatest social tragedy of the last 30 years has been the collapse of fatherhood. Propelled by the twin engines of divorce and illegitimacy, the percentage of children growing up in a home without a father began to increase in the 1960s, gained momentum in the 1970s, hit full stride in the 1980s and tripled in the 1990s. Driving this collapse of fatherhood were three ideas about parenting, fathers, and children. Ideas do have consequences, and the cultural and social consequences of these ideas were

profound. Moreover, these notions became so entrenched in American culture that, until recently, they obscured the obvious cause of so many social disorders: absentee fathers. Once androgyny advocates established that most fathers were "doing it wrong," it became relatively easy to argue fathers were not really necessary to the "modern" family. Social scientists began to assert that there was a "nuclear family bias" in past research, and exhorted fellow researchers and practitioners to stop extolling the importance of a father – even a new nurturing father – to the well-being of children. By 1994, 24 million American children were living without their biological fathers. But not to worry, we were increasingly told, all family arrangements were equal and children could do just fine without their fathers. Put simply, the modern family might need a village, but it no longer needed a dad."[71]

By the early 1990s, findings from influential studies on family policy reached conclusions and recommendations on the role of fathers. One of the earliest of these was *'Putting Children First: A Progressive Family Policy for the 1990s,'* published in 1990 by the Progressive Policy Institute, which argued that the most important factor in the decline of children's well-being was the collapse of the family unit. The report identified 'absent fathers' as a primary culprit and recommended ways to bolster the two-parent family by reinforcing marriage and making divorce less common.[72]

The advocacy for the superfluous father had its intended effect. By 1982, psychologist Charlotte Patterson of the University of Virginia felt assured enough to state flatly, *"Children don't need a father to develop normally."* By 1994, 35% of men between 18 and 29 years old, and 62% of women in the same age group agreed with the statement, *"One parent can bring up a child as well as two parents."* Indeed, by repeatedly hearing that they were at best superfluous and at worst detrimental to the well-being of children, men could now claim that they are doing their children a favour by leaving them solely in the hands of the mother."[73]

The U.S. National Commission on Children, in its final report, *'Beyond Rhetoric: A New American Agenda for Children and Families,'* advocates for the family as the primary institution for supporting growth and development throughout childhood. Children do best when they have the personal involvement and material support of a father and a mother and when both parents fulfil their responsibility to be loving providers."[74]

"Fathers are essential to the wholesome growth of both girls and boys and provide the needed skills that complement a mother's contribution."

[Walter G. Vaux]

THE RISE OF ANDROGYNY

Writing in Hoover Institution on *'the myth of the androgyny ideal,'* author Wade F. Horn says the differences between men and women were widely recognized and even celebrated in much of the history of Western civilization. This biological difference produced behavioural differences that complemented and strengthened each other. However, beginning in the 1960s, gender distinctiveness gave way to the ideal of androgyny – advocacy that men and women are treated the same; should behave and parent in exactly the same way; mothers and fathers should parent so that a child would neither know nor care whether it was mom or dad in the room."[75]

Wade further reviews existing literature on the impact of divorce on children, highlighting the suggestions of some writers that divorce can be a self-actualizing experience for children. In their 1974 book *The Courage To Divorce*, authors Susan Gettleman and Janet Markowitz argued that "divorce can liberate children," and can lead to "greater insight and freedom as adults in deciding whether and when to marry" and to "break away from excessive dependence on their biological parents." Similarly, in his 1973 book *Creative Divorce: A New Opportunity for Personal Growth*, therapist Mel Krantzler stated that divorce provides "an ambiguous, expanded experience that moves kids to better adjustment in a society that is highly ambiguous and expanded."[76]

Major studies across the world disagree with the claim that divorce generally produces better outcomes for children. For example, in a 2002 book, *For Better or For Worse: Divorce Reconsidered*, Hetherington and her co-author, journalist John Kelly, describe a 25-year study in which Hetherington followed children of divorced parents and children of parents who stayed together. She found that 25 per cent of the adults whose parents had divorced experienced severe social, emotional or psychological troubles compared with 10 per cent of those whose parents remained together.[77]

A review published in '*Acta Paediatrica*' states that an active and regular engagement of fathers has positive outcomes on the behavioural and cognitive development of their children. This active father figure plays a prime role in reducing behaviour problems in boys and psychological problems in young women."[78]

Barack Obama, former U.S President – himself raised in a single-mother household, made a remarkable speech on Father's Day 2008. Obama said:

> "*Of all the rocks upon which we build our lives, we are reminded today that family is most important. And we are called to recognise and honour how critical every father is to that foundation. They are teachers and coaches. They are mentors and role models. They are examples of success and the men who constantly push us toward it. But if we are honest with ourselves, we'll admit that what too many fathers also are is missing – missing from too many lives and too, and the foundations of our families are weaker because of it*"[79]

THE 'IRREPLACEABILITY' OF FATHERS

"The fathers have eaten a sour grape,
and the children's teeth are set on edge."

[Jeremiah 31:29, English Standard Version]

For many centuries, this ancient biblical quote formed the framework for the power of fathers as the primary authority of the family. If the scientific study of fathers has taught us one thing, it is the data-driven reasons why children do better with father figures in their lives.

Today's culture undervalues the role of fathers, discounts the importance of men, and generally tends to dismiss the male gender as unnecessary. Stemming from the women's liberation movement that grew steadily in the late 1960s and early 1970s, the continuing and insidious concept which supposes that women do not need men and that they carry out almost every responsibility that a father does in a family, concludes that men are pretty much obsolete. Now with the science of artificial insemination, a woman does not even need a man for procreation; she only needs his sperm. Spurred on by radical feminist rhetoric, exemplified by Gloria Steinem's quip that "*a woman needs a man like a fish needs a bicycle,*" some even began to assert that children actually did better without fathers.[80]

The social psychology research pertaining to 'father-absent households' is reviewed in Barbara Cashion's study '*Female-Headed Families: Effects on Children and Clinical Implications*' published in the *Journal of Marital and Family Therapy*. The study shows that girls growing up without fathers have a higher IQ, good emotional adjustment, more independent and enjoy higher self-esteem than girls growing up with fathers. This, according to Cashion, is because the two-parent family is hierarchical with mother and father playing influential roles and children playing subordinate roles. Such division does not exist in the female-headed family. When women and children forgo much of the hierarchy and share more in their relationships, there is a general absence of conflict, and decisions are made more quickly and easily.[81]

Fathers, like mothers, are foundation pillars in the development of a child's emotional well-being. Fathers not only affect who we are on the inside but how we engage in relationships with other people as we grow into adulthood. The pattern a father sets in the relationship and the way a father behaves towards his child will impact and influence how the child relates with other people. Friends, lovers, and spouses will all be chosen based on how the child perceived the meaning of the relationship with his or her father. Fortunately, father participation has surged noticeably over the past few decades. Simultaneously the roles and responsibilities of fathers in their families have evolved from the conceptions of fathers as distant and remote breadwinners to a more sensible recognition that they are equal co-parents.

But there is still a broad chasm between research results and the actual acknowledgement of the value of fathers. Many fathers are still enunciating the feeling that they continue to be treated as second-class citizens in the world of their children's affairs. Books, magazines, and television shows are disproportionately inundated with information for mothers and maternal benefits. It is not long ago that domestic court, recognising the research findings on parenting and fathers, implemented equal child custody decisions. Helping men to understand the irreplaceable role they play can motivate them to make more significant commitments to their children. Linda Nielsen, a Wake Forest University professor of adolescent and educational psychology, analysed 60 studies over several decades and countries and concluded that shared parenting is better for children than single parenting on almost every measure of well-being.[82]

The Journal of the American Psychological Association published a paper titled *"Social Science and Parenting Plans for Young Children: A Consensus Report"* in 2014, with conclusions endorsed by 110 eminent authorities around the world. Authored by Dr Richard Warshak at the University of Texas, the paper concluded, "... shared parenting should be the norm for parenting plans for children of all ages, including very young children."[83]

In September 2017, *Acta Paediatrica*, a peer-reviewed medical journal in the field of paediatrics, published a paper by Swedish researcher Malin Bergstrom of the Karolinska Institute titled *"Preschool children living in joint physical custody arrangements show less psychological symptoms than those living mostly or only with one parent."* The study concluded that the mental health of children aged three to five with shared parenting is better on average than the mental health of those in the care of a single parent.[84]

The Journal of Epidemiology & Community Health in 2015 published a 150,000-person study titled *"Fifty moves a year: Is there an association between joint physical custody and psychosomatic problems in children?"* which concluded that shared parenting after divorce or separation is in the best interest of children's health because the arrangement lowers their stress levels.[85]

These studies validate the irreplaceable role fathers and mothers play in children's lives, particularly in the cognitive, behavioural, and general health and well-being of children. Having a positive male role model makes it easy for an adolescent boy to exhibit positive gender-role attributes and teenage girls are more likely to develop positive opinions of men and are better able to relate with other men. It is usually accepted under most circumstances that a father's presence and participation can be as critical to a child's well-being as a mother's.

Journalist Jonetta Rose Barras in her self-revealing book *'Whatever happened to Daddy's Little Girl?'* illustrates her pain of not having a father figure in her life. Writing from her personal experience and those of other women she interviewed, Barras writes about the emptiness and insecurity fatherlessness creates and the search to fill the void; the endless battles that are recreated with each new relationship – battles that are never won; the pain that resurfaces after the departure of each man in her life. Barras further says she wants women to understand the distinct patterns of sadness, insecurity, confusion and unresolved pain of those who experience a father's loss either through death, divorce, or abandonment."[86]

Nonetheless, some fathers who want to become more purposefully involved in their children's lives often face obstacles from their employers, the media, and even their wives – who may feel threatened by a child who attaches more to their father. Of course, fathers are not all the same. David Popenoe, Professor of Sociology at Rutgers University, writes:

"Fathers are far more than just 'second adults' in the home. Involved fathers—especially biological fathers—bring positive benefits to their children that no other person is as likely to bring.'[87]

"I'm a strong person, I'm a strong family man,
and I'm a strong husband and a strong father."

[David Beckham, Former Manchester United and England Captain]

FATHERHOOD – THE FAMILY GLOBAL POSITIONING SYSTEM (GPS)

The word "fatherhood" has all but lost its meaning in our modern cultural landscape which views fathers as an auxiliary person with little or no significance, rather than as a GPS that points children in the right direction. Journals, articles and scholars offer new and emerging body of "father facts," – insights which can improve fatherhood and inspire men. Fathers are a key factor in the evaluation of psychological indices concerning cognitive and emotional behaviours in children. With regards to research statistics, three separate international studies support the significant influence fathers have on their children. First, a study done by the Swiss government; secondly, a study by the Baptist Press and finally another study by MSNBC Television network.

Swiss Government Study

Switzerland's Statistics Office researchers Werner Haug and Phillipe Warner used statistics from the Swiss census which tracked multiple aspects of Swiss life including religious life. The study titled *'The demographic characteristics of the linguistic and religious groups in Switzerland,'* looked at the full spectrum of Switzerland's religious breakdown. Switzerland's population consists of over 7 million: 46% Catholic; 40% protestant; 9% of no religion and five other.

The study did not measure the influence of a particular religious practice, but rather revealed the influential role fathers play in transferring their faith in God. Haug and Warner discovered that the most critical factors affecting a child's future church attendance as an adult was the father's attendance. The study found that the religious practice of the father of the family, above all, influenced the children's future attendance at or absence from church.[88]

One of the reasons put forward for this difference was that children tend to develop their philosophy about domestic life from their mother while the conception of their worldview comes from their father. If a father takes faith in God seriously, then they transmit the message to take God seriously to their children.

Single mothers should not be discouraged since the study did not take into account the influence of "true faith in God, belief in prayer and other major doctrinal issues." In the epistle of 2 Timothy 1:5, the Apostle Paul acknowledges Timothy's mother and grandmother as significant spiritual role models in Timothy's faith life.

Baptist Press Study

The study shows that if a child is the first person in a household to become a Christian, there is a 3.5% probability everyone else in the household will follow; if the mother is the first to become a Christian, there is a 17% probability everyone else in the household will follow; but if the father is first, there is a 93% probability that everyone else in the household will follow.[89]

MSNBC Study

The study focused on a father's influence on the moral decisions of their children. The study concludes that teenagers whose fathers are more involved in their lives are less likely to engage in risky sexual activities such as unprotected intercourse. While a concerned mother can also help stave off a teen's sexual activity, fathers have twice the influence.[90]

Kathy Woodward, in her article 'Father Knows Best,' published in Western Standard, compares a father's leadership within the family with the law of gravity: you can try to wish it away; you can argue it's unfair, but walk off the edge of a building, and you plummet. Likewise, with fatherhood — try to ignore it, and your civilization collapses."[91]

"One father is more than a hundred schoolmasters"

[George Herbert, Poet and Priest

CONSEQUENCES OF FATHERLESSNESS

Extensive data show that children from fatherless homes are more likely to be poor, become involved in drug and alcohol abuse, drop out of school, and suffer from health and emotional problems. Boys are more likely to become interested in crime, and girls are more likely to become pregnant as teens. According to the U.S. Census Bureau, 19.7 million children, more than 25% live without a father in the home. Consequently, there is a father factor in nearly all social ills facing America today.[92]

Compared to living with both parents, living in a single-parent home doubles the risk that a child will suffer physical, emotional, or educational neglect. Absent father statistics show the following:[93]

- 43% of US children live without their father [US Department of Census]
- 90% of homeless and runaway children are from fatherless homes. [US D.H.H.S., Bureau of the Census]
- 80% of rapists motivated with displaced anger come from fatherless homes. [Criminal Justice & Behaviour, Vol 14, pp. 403-426, 1978]
- 71% of pregnant teenagers lack a father. [U.S. Department of Health and Human Services press release, Friday, March 26, 1999]
- 63% of youth suicides are from fatherless homes. [US D.H.H.S., Bureau of the Census]
- 85% of children who exhibit behavioural disorders come from fatherless homes. [Center for Disease Control]
- 90% of adolescent repeat arsonists live with only their mother. [Wray Herbert, "Dousing the Kindlers," Psychology Today, January, 1985, p. 28]
- 71% of high school dropouts come from fatherless homes. [National Principals Association Report on the State of High Schools]
- 75% of adolescent patients in chemical abuse centres come from fatherless homes. [Rainbows f for all God's Children]
- 70% of juveniles in state operated institutions have no father. [US Department of Justice, Special Report, Sept. 1988]

- 85% of youths in prisons grew up in a fatherless home. [Fulton County Georgia jail populations, Texas Department of Corrections, 1992]
- Fatherless boys and girls are: twice as likely to drop out of high school; twice as likely to end up in jail; four times more likely to need help for emotional or behavioural problems. [US D.H.H.S. news release, March 26, 1999]

Absent fathers' statistics in child custody access and support:[94]

- Two years after divorce, 51% of children in sole mother custody homes only see their father once or twice a year, or never.
- 42% of fathers fail to see their children at all after divorce.
- 90% of father disengagement is caused by obstruction of access by a custodial parent anxious to break the father-child ties.

"It is easier to build strong children than to repair broken men."

[Frederick Douglass, Abolitionist and Statesman]

CONCLUSION

Fathers and mothers bear the primary responsibility for meeting a child's emotional, physical and intellectual needs, and for providing direction and moral guidance. However, the breakdown of the family and deep-rooted moral crises of fatherlessness in our generation does not stand in isolation. They are inextricably linked to the intersecting interrelations of parents, family life, human behaviour and the holistic welfare of our children. Fatherless families must be treated as a matter of priority – ignoring the "elephant" in the room only perpetuates the problem. The question must be asked: How can society proactively make a difference in fatherless and broken homes?

- Firstly, as a society, we need to love and show concern for abandoned children and single mothers.
- Secondly, programs and policies should be initiated to mentor fatherless families.
- Thirdly, there should be an implementation of counselling to families, including fatherless children.
- Fourthly, deliberate adoption of fatherless children (numerous families cannot conceive naturally and adopting children locally and globally is a viable alternative to costly and controversial medical procedures).
- Fifthly, support orphanages both domestically and internationally by making them a part of relevant budgets.
- Sixthly, orphan hosting (both locally and globally) can be a viable alternative for those who cannot meet the necessary qualifications.
- Lastly, reconciliation and mediation between parents to enable the participation of both in the upbringing of a child.

While the perfect father syndrome is an unrealistic aspiration, it is commendable to aspire to be the good-enough father – one who, despite his many imperfections, shows an unwavering commitment to the welfare of the children – a renewed commitment to the importance of families and a resolute commitment to family relations that best nurture and support children in a rapidly changing world.

"The quality of a father can be seen in the goals, dreams and aspirations he sets not only for himself, but for his family."

[**Reed Markham,** *Former President - Board Trustees Regents College*]

CHAPTER 6

THE 7 PILLARS – PARENTING BY PRINCIPLES.

 Train up a child in the way he should go [teaching him to seek God's wisdom and will for his abilities and talents], Even when he is old he will not depart from it.
[PROVERBS 22:6 AMPLIFIED BIBLE]

TRAIN UP A CHILD

The above quotation is a seemingly simple, frequently quoted but overwhelmingly misunderstood verse. Many parenting views emanate from the various perspectives propounded (rightly or wrongly) from this verse. Firstly, some often use this verse as a guarantee that if you raise a child *"in the instruction and training of the Lord,"* he or she will always abide on the right path.[95] This interpretation can be problematic, especially for the "good-enough-parents" who despite their best efforts, still do not achieve the desired outcomes. Secondly, some view this verse as saying precisely the exact opposite. This verse is not a guarantee for parents, but rather a gentle warning. According to some scholars, the insertion of the word "should" in the English translation of this verse is not substantiated in the original Hebrew. The absence of the word "should" changes the essence – allowing children to go their way rather than the way they "should" go. In this view, the verse would, therefore, read as *"Train up a child in his way, and when he is old, he will not depart from it."*

Dave Miller from SBC Voices in an article titled: *'Train Up a Child: What Does Proverbs 22:6 actually Mean'*, suggest that this verse is not a promise to parents who raise their children properly but a warning to those who allow their adolescents to grow up without guidance, who raise them to go their own way.[96]

When children are left to remain in their own way, they are not likely to change; they will develop into adults who go their own way – the wrong way. Thirdly, some hold the view that this verse is not about the spiritual or moral direction of the child, but rather the gifts and talents of the child – about parents assisting children in discovering their path and purpose in life. Parents play a unique role in helping children learn how God has equipped them and how they can utilise their talents and gifts in positive ways as adults. Whichever view one takes, the common denominator of 'training the child' remains constant. All three perspectives, in a sense, complement each other. Training can guarantee future good behaviours, as well as endorse the warning that children left to go their way will face the consequences of irresponsible behaviour– which may not change in adult life. Training can never be adequate if a parent fails to encourage and nurture the child's God-given gifts, talents and potentials. Children do not attain the best character and conduct spontaneously without care and effort, but by natural growth and development. They need the guidance of parents who in most cases probably agree that training is essential, but face the challenges of lack of time, energy, resources, qualifications and support mechanisms to be able to provide quality training.

"We may not be able to prepare the future for our children, but we can at least prepare our children for the future."

[Franklin D. Roosevelt, 32nd U.S. President]

Kahlil Gibran, Lebanese born Poet and Author write;

"Your children are not your children. They are sons and daughters of life's longing for itself. They come through you but not from you. And though they are with you yet they belong not to you. You may give them your love but not your thoughts, For they have their own thoughts. You may house their bodies but not their souls; for their souls dwell in the house of tomorrow, which you cannot visit, not even in your dreams. You may strive to be like them but seek not to make them like you. For life goes not backward nor tarries with yesterday. You are the bows from which your children as living arrows are sent forth. The archer sees the make upon the path of the infinite, and He bends you with His might that His arrows

may go swift and far. Let your bending in the archer's hand be for gladness. For even as He loves the arrow that flies, so He also loves the bow that is stable."[97]

It hardly needs to be said that parenting is a tremendous responsibility. Training a child can be a fulfilling and joyful experience, albeit performed by parents who may have flaws themselves.

- First, training is necessary to assist and promote the natural development of children.

- Secondly, training also checks and eradicates negative hereditary tendencies derived from parents.

- Thirdly, training helps to accompany children on the journey of life as they counteract the undesirable effects of the temptations of the world.

THE CONCEPT OF BEHAVIOURISM

Behaviourism, also referred to as behavioural psychology, is a term given to a psychological approach based on the idea that behaviours can be acquired through conditioning - all behaviour is learned and shaped by the environment. Behaviourists hold the view that our responses to environmental stimuli shape our actions.[98]

Strict behaviourists believed that any person could potentially be trained to perform any task, regardless of genetic background, personality traits, and internal thoughts (within the limits of their physical capabilities). It only requires the right conditioning. According to this perspective, only observable behaviour should be considered – cognitions, emotions, and moods and independent activities of the mind are discounted. Behaviourism was formally established with the 1913 publication of John B. Watson's classic paper, *"Psychology as the Behaviourist Views It."*[99]

It is best summed up by the following quote from Watson, who is often considered the "father" of behaviourism:

> *"Give me a dozen healthy infants, well-formed, and my own specified world to bring them up in and I'll guarantee to take any one at random and train him to become any type of specialist I might select—doctor, lawyer, artist, merchant-chief and, yes, even beggar-man and thief, regardless of his talents, penchants, tendencies, abilities, vocations, and race of his ancestors."*[100]

Strict behaviourists like Watson advocates that any child or person could potentially be conditioned to accomplish any function or duty, notwithstanding considerations like genetic background and personality characteristics. All it takes is the right conditioning – an extreme 'nurture position'[101]

Critics of behaviourism argue that it is a one-dimensional approach to understanding human behaviour. It only accounts for what is observable and measurable, well, in fact, there are various unseen aspects of an individual that are very important in his or her personalities and learning capabilities. Behavioural theories ignore internal influences such as moods, thoughts, feelings, motivations and cognition. Even though these criticisms indicate the weakness of behaviourism, they agree that behaviourism has much to teach us about particular behaviours expressed by humankind.

How relevant is this theory to parenting? Does this theory answer the critical question that many parents often ask: can children become anything parents condition them to be? While behavioural conditioning as an isolated theory produces partial parenting results, optimum results can be reasonably achieved when complemented with other child development theories that consider all aspects of a child's life — persona, sense of responsibility, good and bad habits, character, the capacity to cope with difficulties and piety. Parents have the privilege of brief stewardship in their children's lives and are custodians of their teaching and training – a form of conditioning that produces desirable outcomes for children – in consideration of their welfare and wellbeing.

The Apostle Paul, writing to the Ephesians, uses the Greek word 'Paideia' to enumerate the duty of training.

"Fathers [or Parents], do not make your children angry, but raise them with the training..."[102]

Paideia relates to the upbringing that requires direction, teaching and instruction – as well as a certain measure of compulsion in the form of discipline or even chastisement. Teaching involves the establishment of specific rules. When there are no firmly set rules, a child's life is tossed about on the shifting tides of feelings and impulses. Parents need to set different rules for different ages. Children sometimes deserve some hours of free actions and some self–chosen pursuit. However, this must be supervised and monitored. Parents must never abandon their God-given oversight and always keep in mind that a child's desire for freedom runs ahead of his/her capacity for it. Parents have to determine the amount, kind and nature of freedom which a child's maturity can have and handle.

The behaviour of parents are children's first teachers, shaping their social skills and development. This is critical because children are born with an obvious tendency towards undesirable behaviour; consequently, if allowed to make independent choices for themselves, they are sure to choose wrong. Psychologists generally refer to this as the influence of parent socialisation – the process by which children learn behaviours and expertise in preparation for becoming successful members of society. Socialisation also includes inadvertent outcomes such as when harsh parental practices and poor home environments propel children on a detrimental trajectory of anti-social behaviour and poor achievement. Although most parents use similar ways to influence their children, differences can occur to the parenting style used.

A cursory glance at both biblical and historical heroes of faith shows that these men and women were not necessarily perfect parents. They were parents who acknowledged the necessity and inevitability of honesty and insight around issues of parenting. Strategies that work with one family may not necessarily work with another. While there is no recommended formula for bringing up successful children, studies have pointed to a handful of factors that forecast success. Empowering parents with the necessary tools needed for dealing with difficult situations should be the focus of parent-child policies.

THE SEVEN PILLARS OF POSITIVE PARENTING

Many researchers have proposed definitions of positive parenting, such as Seay and colleagues who in 2014 reviewed 120 pertinent articles and came up with the following definition:

> *"Positive parenting is the continual relationship of a parent(s) and a child or children that includes caring, teaching, leading, communicating, and providing for the needs of a child consistently and unconditionally."*[103]

The Committee of Ministers of Europe in their Recommendation 19 (2006) on *"Policy to Support Positive Parenting,"* defines positive parenting as:

> *"Parental behaviour based on the best interest of the child that is nurturing, empowering, non-violent and provides recognition and guidance which involves setting of boundaries to enable the full development of the child".*[104]

In this recommendation, the importance of children growing up in a positive family environment is endorsed, and the responsibility of the state to create the right conditions for positive parenting is emphasized. The paper further highlights that the goal of parenting is to promote positive parent-child relationship and optimize the child's potential development and wellbeing. Promoting positive parenting is of significant importance and requires a holistic approach that produces healthy development, responsible citizenship, economic productivity, lifelong health and wellbeing and healthy communities.

While there are various areas of interest in positive parenting, seven core pillars standout, namely; spirituality empowerment, financial responsibility, sensible discipline, attitude to charity, respect for authority, healthy relationships, and health/wellbeing.

SPIRITUAL EMPOWERMENT

"So keep these commandments carefully in mind. Tie them to your hand to remind you to obey them, and tie them to your forehead between your eyes! Teach them to your children. Talk about them when you are sitting at home, when you are out walking, at bedtime, and before breakfast! Write them upon the doors of your houses and upon your gates, so that as long as there is sky above the earth, you and your children will enjoy the good life awaiting you in the land the Lord has promised you."

[Deuteronomy 11:18-21, The Living Bible]

There has been a significant decrease in moral values and spiritual direction all around the world. Nations driven by pleasures seem to hold the view that science reigns supreme as the judge of all the crucial questions of life, thereby outgrowing the need for God. The nuclear family has mostly collapsed, and the stabilising impact of the extended family and close-knit communities has reduced. Increasingly, the '*me-first syndrome*' culture is selfish, materialistic, competitive and addicted to pleasures – characterised by substantial proportions of mental and emotional pressures, which have hugely impacted on families. Long gone are the days when families raised children to be morally upright and God-fearing. The true meaning and significance of life has evaporated in the crucibles of 21st-century revolutionary changes. Humanity is now at the brink of moral collapse. Unfortunately, children receive less direction on how they should behave and grow up to incorporate only murky ideas about what comprises right or wrong – the only remaining criteria for success seems to be material possessions and fame. Parents play an influential role in a child's spiritual development, just as they play a dominant role in every other aspect of the child's life. Research now shows that the spiritual faculty is inborn, fundamental to the human constitution and central in human physiology and psychology. Spirituality links brain, mind and body.[105]

Foundational to mental health and wellness is spirituality, particularly as it develops in the first few decades of the child's life. During this early stage of development, the child integrates his or her spirituality with other developing capabilities, including cognitive, social and emotional development, all of which are shaped by interactions with parents, family, peers and community. In a comprehensive and captivating compilation of current psychological and neurological research on the importance of spirituality, Psychologist Lisa Miller in '*The Spiritual Child: The New Science on Parenting for Health and Lifelong Thriving*,' explains the science and the power of spirituality. She observes that children raised with a well-developed spiritual life are happier, more optimistic, more thriving, feel more connected and less isolated, and better equipped to deal with life's traumas than children who are not. Miller further explains the clear, scientific link between spirituality and health and shows that children who have a positive, active relationship to spirituality are 40% less likely to use and abuse substances; 60% less likely to be depressed as teenagers; 80% less likely to engage in unprotected or dangerous sex and have notably more positive markers for thriving including a high sense of meaning and purpose, and increased levels of academic success.[106]

Extensive research shows that spirituality is a vast untapped resource in our understanding of human development, illness, resilience, health, and healing. Awareness of spiritual development creates opportunities to prepare teens for the important inner work required for individuation, identity development, emotional resilience, character, meaningful work and healthy relationships.[107]

"The greatest legacy one can pass on to one's children, and grandchildren is not money or other material things accumulated in one's life, but rather a legacy of character and faith."

[Billy Graham, Minister and International Speaker]

Bishop Alexander Mileant in 'The Upbringing of Children' states:

"The absence of a religious education unfailingly manifests itself in a person's character - a sort of fissure can be perceived in his spiritual makeup. A child is extraordinarily receptive to religious impressions and naturally drawn toward everything that opens up the beauty and meaning of life. Take this away from him, and his soul will become dulled, and he will feel lonely in a competitive and cruel world. Something similar happens with the physical appearance of a child. If he lives in gloomy, damp surroundings, he will grow underdeveloped, ailing and without joy. In both cases of the malady, physical or spiritual, the fault lies with the parents. On the other hand, when we consider prominent and successful people, people of high integrity and energy, we see that the majority of them came from large, hard-working families, brought up in religious traditions. Without spiritual guidance, a child will learn to pursue only his egotistical

interests and to reject any moral obligations. With time his conscience will become utterly indifferent to the means of reaching the desired goal.'[108]

While postmodern society is snowballing with disillusionment; parents must become intentional in their approach to teach children to develop a balanced worldview. Our worldview is our perspective, outlook or assumption on how the world functions and how we see and experience the world. A child is remarkably well disposed to religious views and attracted towards things that unfold the splendour, beauty, and meaning of life. The lack of a religious upbringing invariably reveals itself in a child's character – a type of rupture discernible in his spiritual disposition. Researchers from Harvard T.H. Chan School of Public Health examined the link between religious involvement in adolescence and well-being, health behaviour, mental health, physical health, and character strength. The study found that people who participated in weekly religious services or practised daily prayer or meditation in their youth reported greater life satisfaction and positivity in their 20s – and were less likely to subsequently have depressive symptoms, smoke, use illicit drugs, or have a sexually transmitted infection – than people raised with less regular spiritual habits.[109]

First author Ying Chen, said these findings are important for understanding health and parenting practices. The study further shows that religious upbringing can have a powerful effect on health behaviours, mental health, and overall happiness and well-being. The Christian Research Institute article '*Equipping the Next Generation*', first featured in Christian Research Journal, reveals that we are in danger of not passing on biblical faith to the next generation due to overexposure to worldly philosophy and an overdependence on church programs. Solutions proposed to counter this trend include:

- Firstly, defining what exactly we want from our children.
- Secondly, adopting a multigenerational perspective which provides opportunities for the older generation to impact a spiritual legacy to the next generation.
- Thirdly, all parents should transmit their faith to their children according to the Deuteronomy 6 model.
- Fourthly, fathers must take the lead as the spiritual thermostat of the home. Finally, the family and the church must be educated in sound doctrine, equipped in apologetics, and explained moral principles.[110]

The United Kingdom Education Reform Act (ERA) of 1988 identified five key areas that a complete education should address. It stated that a balanced curriculum should promote the spiritual, moral, cultural, mental and physical development of pupils at school and society; and prepare such pupils for opportunities, responsibilities, and experiences of adult life.[111]

The ability of parents to steer family discussions about real-life situations is an invaluable treasure. Parents should promote a stimulating environment at home where children are free at all times to ask questions and have conversations encompassing life and faith. Ideally, life and faith should be interconnected, so that there is very little contrast between the spiritual and the secular. Imperfectly, yet authentically living out the faith in front of children helps them develop biblical principles required for effective living. It may be the case that in later life, immoral behaviour may dilute faith developed in childhood. He starts failing to care properly for his convictions and impressions. When something unnerving befalls him, he begins to acknowledge his limitations and helplessness and starts to contemplate on the purpose of his life. Long forgotten feelings and instructions resuscitate within him and help him to connect back to God. Thus, the hallowed memories of childhood become very helpful.

"It is a fact that unless children are brought up in the nurture and admonition of the Lord, they, and the society which they constitute or control, will go to destruction. Consequently, when a state resolves that religious instruction shall be banished from the schools and other literary institutions, it virtually resolves on self-destruction."

[Charles Hodge,
Former Principal – Princeton Theological Seminary]

FINANCIAL RESPONSIBILITY

"But remember the Lord your God, for it is he who gives you the ability to produce wealth, and so confirms his covenant, which he swore to your ancestors, as it is today."

[Deuteronomy 8:18, New International Version]

In a fast-paced and materialistic culture bent on enticing children with trendiest fashions and newest gadgets; parents must cushion the seemingly insurmountable pressures by placing a high premium on knowledge in financial matters. Raising financially literate children involves giving them a diverse education on various economic issues – the value of money, integrity, investment, savings, management, generosity, hard work, entrepreneurship, and so on. In addition to the value of money, training children on fiscal responsibility will significantly assist them in the real world. Money management is a crucial life skill to be acquired, and it is never too early to teach children about economics, building their "financial DNA" before they become adults. Teaching children to be money-smart does not happen overnight since skills and behaviour develop over time.

A child's outlook on money will have a significant effect on his or her entire life. Learning how to make wise financial decisions is as paramount as deciding whom to marry and what career path to take. Beth Kobliner author of *'Get a Financial Life: Personal Finance in Your Twenties and Thirties'*, says to help the next generation avoid the mistakes of their elders, and to live financially fit lives, children need to be taught the essentials about money."[112]

Financial literacy is a principal constituent of healthy adulthood. Young people who know credit, loan, insurance, and other commercial products and those who eventually achieve financial independence are likely to have higher levels of economic well-being. The Journal of Financial Counselling and Planning, defines financial socialisation as: "*how young adults develop their financial values, attitudes, and behaviours.*[113]

While there are no universal formulas to financial literacy, the authors outlined suggestions to help promote financial literacy. These are: opening a childhood savings account; providing pocket allowance as a learning tool, no matter how small in value; cultivating parent-child dialogue about financial issues; and developing financial literacy through parental socialisation.

> *"I wish everyone could get rich and famous and have everything they ever dreamed of so they can see it is not the answer."*
>
> **[Jim Carrey, Actor and Producer]**

PRINCIPLES OF FINANCIAL SUCCESS

Teaching young children financial principles is stimulating and challenging and requires a radical paradigm shift from our 21st-century consumerism (a human desire to own and obtain products and goods more than one's basic needs) – to focusing on the essentials such as sufficient food, clothing, and shelter. Seven key areas of financial training include:

- **Delayed Gratification**
  "We do not want you to become lazy, but to imitate those who through faith and patience inherit what has been promised."[114]

- **A Culture of Savings**
  "The wise man saves for the future, but the foolish man spends whatever he gets."[115]

- **A Strong Work Ethic**
  "For even when we were with you, we commanded you this: If anyone will not work, neither shall he eat."[116]

- **Faithfulness in Little**

  "If you are faithful in little things, you will be faithful in large ones. However, if you are dishonest in little things, you won't be honest with greater responsibilities."[117]

- **Money Can't Buy Happiness**

  "Then Jesus said to them, Watch yourselves! Keep from wanting all kinds of things you should not have. A man's life is not made up of things, even if he has many riches."[118]

- **Keep Out of Debt**

  "The rich rule over the poor, and borrowers are servants [slaves] to lenders."[119]

- **Protect Your Name and Reputation.**

  "A good name [earned by honourable behaviour, godly wisdom, moral courage, and personal integrity] is more desirable than great riches; and favour is better than silver and gold."[120]

"Riches are not an end of life, but an instrument of life."

[Henry Ward Beecher, Minister and Social Reformer]

SENSIBLE DISCIPLINE

"To discipline a child produces wisdom, but a mother is disgraced by an undisciplined child."

[Proverbs 29:15, New Living Translation]

The concept of a 'liberal upbringing' of children has gained global popularity in the last few decades. This concept rejects all forms of restraint and discipline and insists that children are allowed to their own devices to develop and express their individuality freely. Can such an approach be beneficial for upbringing? "A child's heart tends to do wrong,"[121] says King Solomon and "*A child left undisciplined disgraces his mother.*"[122]

Human nature operates in two realms – spiritual and physical; parents, who only nurture the physical (or material) to the exclusion of the spiritual, produce children who grow up as "children of nature" and as slaves of wanton desires. Discipline, amongst many other things, primarily seeks to modify a child's behaviour, develop character, protect mental health and helps develop a close relationship with parents.

To valorise the importance of constraint in upbringing, Bishop Alexander Mileant in his article '*The Upbringing of Children*' implores parents to consider that a child's mind is not entirely developed to understand unmistakably in all circumstances what is right and what is wrong. Even when a child realises this, his will is lacking in power to resist all temptations and to direct his actions toward excellent but demanding tasks. A sensible and fair combination of guidance with punishment imprints on a child's character a sense of moral responsibility and good habits.[123]

Bishop of Constantinople, St. John, named Chrysostom (golden-mouthed) on account of his eloquence, on children, writes:

"To educate the hearts of children in goodness and virtuousness is the sacred duty of parents. The violation of this duty makes them guilty of spiritual infanticide. Some parents spare no efforts to make their children happy and wealthy, but for their children to be good Christians – for such matters, the parents have little need. This is a terrible short-sightedness! This is the very reason for the problems from which society groans. If the fathers strove to give their children a good upbringing, there would be no need for laws, or courts, or punishments. Prisons and executioners are necessary due to the lack of morality.[124]

American Academy of Paediatrics (AAP), published *'Guidance for Effective Discipline'* recommends certain conditions in the parent-child relationship that are essential in promoting positive child behaviour. These recommendations include: maintaining a positive emotional tone in the home; providing attention to the child; providing consistency with regular times for daily activities; responding consistently to similar behavioural situations; being flexible and involve the child in decision making, particularly with older children.[125]

AAP further recommended effective discipline strategies for parents and other caregivers to help reward desirable behaviours and reduce or eliminate undesirable ones. These include: a positive, supportive and loving parent-child relationship; using positive reinforcement strategies to increase desired behaviours; listening carefully and providing regular positive attention; helping them learn to use words to express their feelings; providing them with opportunities to make choices and helping them learn to evaluate potential consequences of their decisions; reinforcing emerging desirable behaviours with frequent praise and ignoring trivial mistakes; clarity on problem behaviour and the consequence the child can expect when this behaviour happens; delivering instruction and correction calmly and with empathy.

With such strategies, says the AAP, potential benefits and desired behaviours are more likely to become internalised. The newly learned behaviour will be a foundation for other desirable behaviours and the emotional atmosphere in the family will be more positive and supportive.

"Raising children uses every bit of your being - your heart, your time, your patience, your foresight, your intuition to protect them, and you have to use all of this

[Nicole Ari Parker, American Actress]

Lessons from Adonijah

"My child [son], listen to your father's teaching [instruction; discipline] and do not forget [neglect] your mother's advice [instruction]. [For] Their teaching [It] will be like flowers in your hair [a gracious garland on your head] or a necklace [beads] around your neck. "

Proverbs 1:8-9 Expanded Bible]

Adonijah, born to Haggith, the fourth wife of David, second King of ancient Israel, was a badly behaved son with a thirst for showmanship. After the death of King David, Adonijah attempted a coup plot to take over the kingdom despite not being the rightful heir. Ancient literature confirms that his misbehaviour was the result of the absence of parental discipline. King David indulged Adonijah by his omission of correction and training. Perhaps, David did not want to hurt his feelings. The result was a spoiled and disobedient son who eventually turned into a disturbed entitled young man. References of the texts state as follows:

> *"Now his father, King David, had never disciplined him at any time, even by asking, "Why are you doing that?"*[126]
> *"David did not want to hurt his feelings"*[127]
> *"Now his father had never corrected him"*[128]

This story exposes the challenges faced by professional parents in terms of time and patience – two ingredients required for sensible discipline. Overwhelmed by professional pressures, even the best-intentioned parents, over time, can develop a lacklustre approach to discipline. Factors contributing to the abdication of parental discipline include: reluctance to discipline children to avoid having conflict; unwillingness to devote energy and time to the task of discipline; feeling uncomfortable at a child getting angry; playing 'good cop' with their children, especially when competing for the child's affection with the other partner. Parent's ugly memories of being disciplined when they were children may favour making things easier on their children by relaxing the rules. Appropriate and measured discipline is not only good for children; it is vital for their well-being. Creating a work-life balance that takes child discipline onboard is the Eldorado of any parenting journey.

"A child who is allowed to be disrespectful to
his parents will not have true respect for anyone."

[Billy Graham, Minister and International Speaker]

The Sons of Eli

"The sons of Eli [Hophni and Phinehas] were worthless (dishonourable,
unprincipled) men; they did not know [nor respect] the Lord."[129]

David's total failure (in both word and action) to correct his child differs considerably from Eli's partial failure (in action only). An appropriate balance between firm words and appropriate actions ensure that discipline produces the best results. While verbal correction suffices for some children; others need firm actions to complement verbal corrections. No two children are the same. Every child's case must be dealt with on its own merits while taking into consideration the child's temperament, sensitivities, and psychological make-up. The Old Testament book of Samuel records the story of Eli as follows:

> *"Eli was very old. He heard about the bad things his sons were doing to the Israelites at Shiloh and how his sons were having sexual relations with the women who served at the door of the Meeting Tent. Eli said to his sons, "The people here told me about the evil things you have done. Why are you doing such things? Sons, stop that! The Lord's people are saying bad things about you. If you sin against other people, God might protect you. But who can help you if you sin against the Lord?" Eli's sons refused to listen to him"*[130]

Eli's form of discipline was exclusively verbal. Eli's failure to give equal weight to appropriate action as he did for verbal correction, eventually led his children to a disastrous end. Nevertheless, he deserves partial commendation, unlike David and many other parents who give a blind eye to the reprehensible activities of their children. The consequences of indiscipline cannot always be accurately predicted – it could lead to death, future job loss, breakdown in relationships, drop out from school, a prison sentence or generally produce undesirable consequences in the future of the child. When children consistently disobey verbal reprimands, they leave no other choice but firm action from parents, which if lovingly and tactfully applied produces positive results.

"I was a wonderful parent before I had children."

Adele Faber, Author and Adult-Children Communication Expert]

Discipline Vs Punishment

"Foolishness is bound up in the heart of a child; The rod of discipline [correction administered with godly wisdom and loving-kindness] will remove it far from him."

[Proverbs 22:15 Amplified Bible]

The distinction between discipline and punishment is straightforward, yet often lost in application. Discipline does not require a parent to penalise a child as payback for an offence, but it necessitates applying appropriate consequences to encourage a child to make better choices in the future. An observed distinction in the design of each is that one is retributive (punishment), while the other remedial (discipline). Punishment is a punitive measure undertaken to make the wrongdoers repay the debt they have incurred, and it is for the benefit of the offended rather than for the offender. Punishment may be physical such as in smacking, striking, or producing pain; it may be psychological as in disapprobation, isolation, or embarrassment. Punishment flows from anger, while discipline flows from love. Punishment focuses on past misbehaviour and provides little to assist a child in behaving satisfactorily in the future. When it is employed, the person who punishes the child becomes responsible for the child's behaviour. On the other hand, discipline is a corrective action carried out to change the harmful practice of the offender.

In contrast, discipline is a positive process that encourages and models appropriate behaviour. It teaches the child what behaviour is acceptable and what is not. The key to discipline is to instil self-control and responsibility.

	Punishment	Discipline
Purpose	To impose penalty for an offence	To train for correction and maturity
Focus	Past wrongdoing	Future correct acts

	Punishment	Discipline
Attitude	Hostility and frustration on the part of the parent	Love and concern on the part of the parent
Resulting emotion in the child	Fear and guilt	Security

Punishment, Discipline and Consequences

Our parents corrected us for the short time of our childhood as it seemed good to them. But God corrects us throughout our lives for our own good, giving us an invitation to share his holiness. Now all discipline seems to be more pain than pleasure at the time, yet later it will produce a transformation of character, bringing a harvest of righteousness and peace to those who yield to it."

[Hebrews 12:10-11 The Passion Translation]

In their book '*Boundaries*', authors Drs Henry Cloud and John Townsend differentiate discipline from punishment by their relationship with time. While punishment looks back and focuses on making payment for wrongs done in the past; discipline, however, looks forward.[131]

Mark Ballenger in an article titled '*The Biblical Difference Between Discipline, Punishment, and Consequences*', differentiates between punishment, discipline, and earthly consequences as follows: First, punishment is a punitive action done to make the offender repay the debt they have incurred. It is done for the benefit of the offended rather than for the offender; secondly, discipline is a corrective action done to change the harmful behaviour of the offender. It is applied for the benefit of the offender rather than for the offended; and finally, consequences are the negative, natural chain of events that occur because of our poor choices and actions.[132]

The significant difference between punishment, discipline, and consequences is about the past, present, and future. Punishments deal with the past while consequences often deal with the present and discipline looks towards a better future. Punishment is about condemnation, while discipline is about correction; punishment is about making the situation right while discipline is about helping the person get right; punishment flows from anger, while discipline flows from patience; punishment is a response when the relationship is broken while discipline is a response when a relationship is working towards restoration; punishment is about taking while discipline is about giving; punishment is a sign of hate, while discipline is a sign of love; punishment is easy to give but hard to get benefits from; discipline is hard to give but easy to get benefits back from.

Chip Ingram, CEO of Living on the Edge, writing in *Focus on the Family* gives a concise difference between punishment and discipline.

"Punishment produces some very negative characteristics in your children: guilt, shame, bitterness, resentment, regret, self-pity, fear, and more. Because it is focused on the past, children feel helpless. They cannot undo what they've already done, and they cannot change the circumstances that their behaviour has produced. Punishment doesn't give them a means to right their wrongs; the tools they need to understand redemption are not included in the

punishment package. It is simply retribution that leads to a lot of negative emotions. Discipline, on the other hand, is future-focused, always pointing toward future acts. It has nothing to do with retribution and everything to do with redemption. Whereas the purpose of punishment is to inflict a penalty for an offence, the purpose of discipline is to train for correction and maturity. Whereas the origin of punishment is the frustration of the parent, the origin of discipline is a high motivation for the welfare of the child. And whereas the result of punishment is fear and shame, the result of discipline is security. Discipline always holds the child's best interests, not the parent's anger, in the forefront. It is never out of control."[133]

In the biblical narrative, parents were not prohibited from discipline but were rather cautioned against brutality and child abuse. According to Craig Keener, the Apostle Paul was among the minority of ancient writers who opposed excessive discipline and brutality of children.[134]

Gordana Buljan Flander, Director of Child and Youth Protection Centre of Zagreb in an article titled '*International Day of Families: Four pillars of* parenting,' recommends that parents should agree on some family rules with the child in advance, to avoid a conflict with the child in some critical situation; rules should be formulated in favourable terms – in the form of some reward, and not a threat. She further recommends the use of natural consequences of the child's behaviour, such as, "If you go out without your jacket, you will be cold!" It is not good to emphasise some adverse consequences which may not happen and say for example, "If you climb that chair, you will fall and get hurt!" but "You might fall and get hurt!" Flander concludes that emphasis should be placed on praising good behaviours rather than only reacting to inadequate ones – a child is more likely to develop good behaviour after receiving praise, rather than stopping some behaviour which parents criticise.[135]

"Before I got married I had six theories about raising children; now, I have six children and no theories."

[John Wilmot, 2nd Earl of Rochester]

Do Not Provoke

"Fathers, do not provoke or irritate or exasperate your children [with demands that are trivial or unreasonable or humiliating or abusive; nor by favouritism or indifference; treat them tenderly with loving-kindness], so they will not lose heart and become discouraged or unmotivated [with their spirits broken]."

[Colossians 3:21 Amplified Bible]

Discipline should not be applied in a way that provokes and incites anger and rebellion. This is not merely referring to a child getting unhappy, for this is inevitable. It has to do with a wave of deep-rooted (or settled) anger that resides in the child and affects his character all through his life. Parents embitter and provoke their children to anger in various ways; these include: abusing their children or giving improper discipline; neglecting and not giving them attention and by not listening to them – listening is vital – let your child finish speaking before offering help; never encouraging good behaviour or failing to notice good behaviour and point it out in praise; and, showing favouritism toward other siblings.

"Give me five minutes with a person's check book, and I will tell you where their heart is."

[Billy Graham, International Evangelist]

Responsibility: Parents or Teachers?

The parent-teacher relationship has undergone various turbulent transformations from the turn of the century. Disregarding the traditional concept that a parent might defend the teacher and reprimand their rebellious child. The hard-pressed teacher of today has to make a conscious effort in dealing with a parent for whom discipline is an outdated notion. In 2008, the General Secretary of the Association of School and College Leaders, John Dunford, told its annual conference in Brighton:

"For some children, schools have had to take the place of the institutions that used to set the boundaries of acceptable behaviour - that was, fundamentally, the family and the church."[136]

He further suggested that the problems were more severe among working-class families.

"Schools can't and shouldn't replace the role of parents," Dunford said, adding: *"It is perhaps a sad indictment on the present age that we accept the need to help parents to play their part - to rediscover what being a parent means."*

A Harvard Graduate School of Education poll showed that 70 per cent of public school parents want schools to teach 'strict standards of right and wrong'; 85 per cent want schools to teach values."[137]

Are parents shirking the responsibility of discipline? Are teachers being turned into makeshift parents? Teachers are not surrogate parents on standby when parents fail in their responsibilities. Educators argue that parents have become too focused on being "friends" with their children and fail to implement boundaries. Through proper guidance, parents can help children better organise their learning time in and out of school. Some of the responsibilities parents have towards education include; spending time with the child, providing a supportive environment at home, connecting with school teachers and monitoring how the child learns. Schools cannot correct the wrongs of society and teachers cannot be transformed into substitute parents. A productive Parent-Teacher partnership fosters optimum pedagogic results. An Australian study found that three-quarters of Victorian teachers believe parents have unreasonable expectations about the school's role in raising children; nearly half of the teachers surveyed admitted that they had considered resigning over the past one year. Victorian Principals Association president Gabrielle Leigh says,

"Students are increasingly likely to be sent to school without adequate discipline from home. It's well beyond the duty of a teacher, but they can't ignore it."[138]

ATTITUDE TO CHARITY AND GENEROSITY

"Be generous, and you will be prosperous.
Help others, and you will be helped."

[Proverbs 11:25 Good News Translation]

When we speak of a life worth living, generosity is an indispensable part of that life. Generosity is the practice of giving without expecting anything in return. It is a rewarding lifestyle to model to children from a tender age. Parents are the primary agents to shape the worldview of children, including things such as money and possessions, and how to treat other people. Children are naturally egocentric, but parents can cultivate compassion in them. Generosity starts with empathy – the ability to understand and share the feelings of another. A study by the American Psychological Association found that giving to others increases life expectancy by at least five years.[139]

Douglas Henry of Institute for Faith and Learning at Baylor University writes;

"Generosity names not merely something we do, but an admirable quality of character, something we are. Undergirding the character of truly generous people is a special awareness of themselves, others, and God's gracious provision for the world and this understanding inspires genuinely generous activity."[140]

Psychologist Richard Weissbourd of Harvard Graduate School of Education runs the Making Caring Common project, which aims to teach children to be kind and to care about others and the common good. In a recent report, Weissbourd concludes that an intense focus on academic achievement has squeezed out serious attention to ethical character in many high schools and families. The report calls on parents and high schools to prioritise character and wellbeing above excessive academic pressure - only a small number of highly selective colleges will position students for success.[141]

About 80% of the young people in the Harvard study said their parents were more anxious with their achievement or happiness than whether they cared for others. The study also shows that the interviewees were three times more likely to agree that "My parents are prouder if I get good grades in my classes than if I'm a caring community member in class and school."

Research in human development shows that when children's concerns for others are cultivated, they are likely to be empathetic, caring, ethical, happier and more successful. Donald Altman in his book '*Living Kindness*', explores Jewish core concepts of generosity – concept of giving is essential – known as *tzedakah* or charity.[142]

In the *Mishneh Torah, Hilkhot matanot aniyim* ("Laws of Charity"), Chapter 10:7–14, Moses Maimonides, 12th-century Jewish philosopher defines 'eight levels of charity (*tzedakah*),' or 'eight levels of giving' with the lowest being level 8 and the highest being level 1.

- Level 8: Giving unwillingly and grudgingly.
- Level 7: Giving willingly but inadequately, but does so cheerfully.
- Level 6: Giving to the recipient only upon being asked.
- Level 5: Giving to the recipient without being asked.
- Level 4: Giving to a recipient you do not know, but who knows the donor.

- Level 3: Giving to a recipient you know, but who does not know the donor.
- Level 2: Giving when both recipients and donors are anonymous to each other.
- Level 1: Giving that enables self-reliance – which is the highest form of charity. This is giving to assist a person before they become impoverished or by providing a suitable loan, or by helping them get employment or establish a business to make it unnecessary for them to become dependent on others.

Parents as Role Models

"Like children who learn proper behaviour from their parents."

[Ephesians 5:1 The Message]

Children are more likely to be kind and generous when they have at least one parent who models that behaviour in front of them. Research by Mark Ottoni–Wilhelm of Indiana University shows the importance for parents having conversations with their children about generosity. The study found that adolescents were 18% more likely to donate money to a charitable organisation if their parents had made any donation of their own in the past year. It was also shown that if a parent had made a donation and talked with their child about giving, that child was 33% more likely to donate – an increase of 15%. The study concludes that adolescents whose parents did voluntary work were 27% more likely to volunteer themselves, and 47% more likely if their parents also talked with them about generosity.[143]

"Do not neglect to do good and to be generous,
for God is pleased with such sacrifices."

[Hebrews 13:16 International Standard Version]

Carol Weisman, author of '*Raising Charitable Children*', observes that children's selfish desires are fuelled by a barrage of consumer adverts which are antithetical to generosity, selflessness and compassion. In the introduction, Weisman notes that putting a cell phone in children's pocket and the 'right' shoes on their feet will never provide long-term happiness to fix children's cravings. It does not make any sense when parents talk to children about how much they are willing to pay for goods (and services), yet will not talk with children about how they give, how much they give and what they value.[144]

Writing on the attitude of generosity in the Epistle to the Corinthians, the author, Apostle Paul says: *"...but their joy was so great that they were extremely generous in their giving..."*[145]

Jesus Christ teaches: *"Whoever tries to keep his life will lose it, and whoever loses his life will preserve it."*[146]

Social scientists Christian Smith and Hilary Davidson in their book '*The Paradox of Generosity: Giving We Receive, Grasping We Lose*', note that those who give ten per cent or more of their income and those who volunteer their time are highly likely than others to report being very happy. Similarly, those who are generous in their relationships, offering their attention and emotions to others tend to be more satisfied than those who are less generous relationally. Generosity also produces health benefits. Those who are relationally generous, and who contribute more financially and volunteer their time, are more likely to be in very good health than others and also report a more definite sense of their purpose in life.[147]

Generosity has a positive effect on one's physical and mental health – it also reduces stress, supports physical health, enhances a sense of purpose, naturally fights depression, and increases lifespan.[148]

The Shepherd of Hermas – an anonymous early Christian writing – contains a series of pictures or visions, amongst which is an allegory of generosity and its benefits to the giver and receiver. This version of the text has been abridged and some parts modernised and rephrased to make it more reader-friendly. It reads:

"This is a similitude for the poor man and for the rich." "How so, sir?" said I; "explain the matter to me." "Listen," he said: "The rich man has much wealth, but is poor in matters relating to the Lord, because he is distracted about his riches; he offers very few intercessions to the Lord, and those which he does offer are small and weak, and have no power above. The poor man, with fewer distractions and greater needs, is often in prayer, and his intercession has great power with God. So, when the rich man refreshes the poor, and assists him without hesitation in his necessities, the poor man (being helped by the rich) intercedes for him, giving thanks to God for the one who bestowed gifts upon him. This moves the rich man to continue to interest himself zealously for the poor man, that his wants may be constantly supplied. For he knows that the intercession of the

poor man is acceptable and influential with God, and by it, he (the rich man) is blessed. Thus, both accomplish their work, and it is a great work, acceptable before God. Poor men, interceding with the Lord on behalf of the rich, increase their riches; and the rich, again, aiding the poor in their necessities, satisfy their souls. Both, therefore, are partners in the righteous work."[149]

"The measure of life is not its duration, but its donation."

[Peter Marshall, Scottish Clergyman]

RESPECT FOR AUTHORITY

*"Every person must submit to and support the authorities over him.
For there can be no authority in the universe except by
God's appointment, which means that every authority that exists has
been instituted by God. So to resist authority is to resist the divine order
of God, which results in severe consequences. For civil authorities don't
intimidate those who are doing good, but those who are doing evil.
So do what is right, and you'll never need to fear those in authority.
They will commend you for your good citizenship."*

[Romans 13:1-3 The Passion Translation]

It is increasingly fashionable to antagonise or question authority and to snub laws which we do not agree. Teaching children to respect authority and esteem the law is the hallmark of civil society –

respect for law and authority begins early with how parents teach and interrelate at home. Family rules are established, with the expectation they will be followed. How rules are set and enforced at home will set the pattern on how children engage with rules outside the home, at school, at work, and in the community. If parents permit the rules to be broken without consequence, they may unintentionally teach their children to disregard laws and authority. Do we ever openly disapprove when our children denigrate police officers, elected officials, or the elderly in society? When parents themselves show little or no respect for the law, they send the wrong signal to their children that such behaviour is acceptable.

In an era of mistrust, it can be challenging to teach children the obligation to respect authority, to welcome consequences for their actions and to stay away from responding with brutality. Our children will be more desirable citizens as we handle authority figures with esteem and as we train them on the importance of respect in a civil society.

"Authority exercised with humility,
and obedience accepted with delight are the very lines along which our
spirits live."

[C.S. Lewis, Writer and Theologian]

Should Children Question Authority

"Children, if you want to be wise, listen to your parents and do what they tell you, and the Lord will help you. For the commandment, "Honour your father and your mother," was the first of the Ten Commandments with a promise attached: "You will prosper and live a long, full life if you honour your parents."

[Ephesians 6:1-3 The Passion Translation]

With the wave of recently publicised examples of child sexual abuse, parents must teach children not only how to respect people in authority but also, in some specific circumstances, to question adult behaviour. Children need to grow and mature in their ability to read situations accurately, and adults need to be responsive to the concerns that children raise. Children should be encouraged to trust and take directions from authority figures, such as teachers, doctors, coaches, ministers and other professionals. Hopefully, most of the time, adults can and should be trusted; however, there are unfortunate moments where adults abuse or attempt to abuse those entrusted into their care. In such instances, children must be empowered to question the behaviour of adults.

Some adults act in a misguided fashion because they have predicaments of their own. Even adults who are supportive in some ways may conduct themselves inappropriately in other ways. If something feels wrong, then it indeed is. If an adult requests that a child participates in a particular behaviour and to keep it a secret, then something is almost certainly wrong. A Child should promptly treat any form of secrecy as a red flag and a warning sign. However, if those in positions of authority demonstrate menacing behaviour, then the appropriate action should be taken to safeguard the child. The key is persuading children that if they are experiencing suspicious behaviour from anyone, including relatives or family friends, that they will be listened to and supported.

HEALTHY RELATIONSHIPS

"Two people are better than one. When two people work together, they get more work done. If one person falls, the other person can reach out to help. But those who are alone when they fall have no one to help them. If two people sleep together, they will be warm. But a person sleeping alone will not be warm. An enemy might be able to defeat one person, but two people can stand back-to-back to defend each other. And three people are even stronger. They are like a rope that has three parts wrapped together – it is very hard to break."

[Ecclesiastes 4:9-12 Easy-to-Read Version]

Research from Harvard's 'Making Caring Common' project suggests that many teens and young adults are unprepared for romantic relationships.[150]

The key findings from the research show that a large number of teenagers and young adults are not prepared for caring and lasting romantic relationships despite the fact that they tend to greatly magnify the size of their *"hook-up culture."* The study also revealed that *mi*sogyny and sexual harassment are pervasive among young people – certain forms of gender-based degradation may be on the rise – yet the majority of parents do not talk about it.

Guidelines put forward in the findings include: helping young people understand the differences between mature love and other forms of attraction; helping young people to identify the difference between healthy and unhealthy relationships; exploring with teenagers and young adults the capacities and skills required to develop and maintain a healthy romantic relationship; discussing what it means to be an ethical person – treating others with respect and dignity; intervening when others are at risk of being harmed, and to advocate for those who are vulnerable. Psychiatrist Robert Waldinger, says fame and money do not make people happy and healthy as they go through life. As the director of a 75-year longitudinal Harvard study on adult development, Waldinger has unprecedented access to data on true happiness and satisfaction. The study found that healthy relationships are crucial to our overall happiness. While unhealthy relationships facilitate domestic problems, stress and financial difficulties, healthy romantic relationships foster healthier lifestyles and even higher wages. A YMCA *Eudaimonia* report concluded that people who surround themselves with healthy relationships have the highest uplift in wellbeing.[151]

Research findings published in the Journal of Youth and Adolescence found that adolescents who reported a positive family environment went on to have better relationship problem-solving skills and less-violent romantic relationships as young adults.[152]

"People who have good relationships at home are
more effective in the marketplace."

[Zig Ziglar, Author and Motivational Speaker]

Professional Relationships

"Whatever you do [whatever your task may be], work from the soul [that
is, put in your very best effort],
as [something done] for the Lord and not for men."

[Colossians 3:23 Amplified Bible]

Connected to the success of a company is the loyalty of its customers. While this customer-first mentality is necessary for the continuation of a company, employers sometimes forget to honour another vital element to company productivity and growth – the employee-employer relationship. Training to navigate this professional environment, and how to maintain healthy relationships and avoid toxic ones, is absolutely necessary. A healthy, harmonious and respectful relationship built on trust and understanding can improve morale and productivity, and ultimately, it can be a career booster. Children must learn the relational dynamics of the work environment. Healthy work relationships are vital for creating a strong organisational culture; poor relationship that lack cohesiveness will decrease productivity. Many companies have decent relational policies for staff members. While friendships are permitted, and even encouraged, romantic relationships are sometimes discouraged by companies, and there are valid reasons for this; if there is a relationship breakdown, then sexual harassment claims can be made against the manager or a claim made that the manager was asking personal favours in exchange for keeping the staff member on the job.

Work-Life Balance

"Do not let the love of money control your life.
Be satisfied with what you have. God himself has said, `I will never be
away from you. I will never leave you alone."

[Hebrews 13:5 Worldwide English - New Testament]

The modern-day workplace is becoming people-centred, with companies investing more in improving employee engagement and work-life balance – dividing time and energy between work and other important aspects of life. Work-life balance is the measure of how much time and energy a person gives their work-life versus other aspects of their personal life, such as, raising a family, hobbies, relaxation or anything else. While having a successful career is an integral part of many people's lives, maintaining a healthy work-life balance improves overall happiness and wellbeing.

Studies have found that *'only one-third of British employees are happy with the work-life balance.'* Astrid Hall, in the Independent writes that in an ideal world, employees said they would prefer to see adults dedicating just 30 per cent of their lives to work and the other 70 to life. Just one third believe they have already struck their perfect work-life balance. Work pressure and long hours were the most common factors cited as impacting work-life balance.[153]

The best way children inculcate a work-life balance culture is through imitation and observation of parents as they model this, which, according to developmental psychologists, have always been the effective way children learn.

"If you want your children to turn out well,
spend twice as much time with them and half as much money."

[Abigail Van Buren, Producer and Radio Show Host]

HEALTH AND WELLBEING

"Beloved, I pray that in every way you may succeed and prosper and be in
good health [physically], just as [I know] your soul prospers [spiritually]."

[3 John 1:2, Amplified Bible]

Health and wellbeing is generally affected by multiple socio-cultural, political and environmental factors. While the health of the UK population has improved in the last few decades, we nevertheless face daunting pressures of preventable diseases due to our shortcomings in focusing disproportionately on treatment rather than prevention. Healthy living involves health-improving lifestyle habits that promote overall health and wellbeing, and not just merely defined as the absence of ill health. Although old habits die hard, it is vital to identify less healthy habits and to replace them with new positive ones. According to the World Health Organization (WHO), a healthy lifestyle is a way of living that lowers the risk of being seriously ill or dying early. Health is not only just about avoiding disease. It is also about physical, mental and social wellbeing. When a healthy lifestyle is adopted, a more positive role model is provided to other people in the family, particularly children."[154]

A study from Harvard T.H. Chan School of Public Health concluded that adopting a healthy lifestyle could considerably reduce premature mortality and prolong life expectancy. Those who improve the quality of their diets, eating more whole grains, vegetables, fruits, nuts, and fish, and less red and processed meats and sugary beverages, may significantly reduce their risk of premature death.[155]

Frank Hu, professor and senior author of the study says that there is a long-term health benefits of improving diet quality with an emphasis on overall dietary patterns rather than on individual foods or nutrients.

A fast-paced, busy lifestyle has altered our feeding habits and our children have resorted to unhealthy eating habit as an alternative. This habit in childhood makes it harder to break later in life because childhood habits become established as a child grows into adulthood. The addictive taste of fast food makes it highly unlikely for future nutritional change. Harvard School of Public Health experts developed the Healthy Eating Plate, which gives full information to help people to make better eating choices. The Eating Plate has not gone without criticism; however, the main objective of The Healthy Eating Plate was to provide detailed guidance, in a simple format, to help people make the best eating choices.

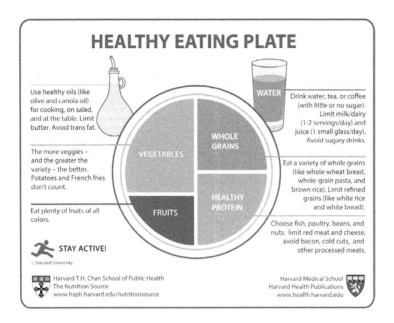

Copyright © 2011, Harvard University. For more information about The Healthy Eating Plate, please see The Nutrition Source, Department of Nutrition, Harvard School of Public Health, www.thenutritionsource.org, and Harvard Health Publications. www.health.harvard.edu

"Childhood obesity is best tackled at home through improved parental involvement, increased physical exercise, better diet and restraint from eating."

[Bob Filner, Politician and Former Mayor of San Diego]

Guidelines on healthy food choices include eating meals that constitute more of starchy carbohydrates; plenty of fruit and vegetables; a lot of fish – including regular portions of oily fish; reduction on the intake of saturated fat and sugar; a little salt – usually not advisable to be more than 6g a day for adults; active with regular physical exercises; maintaining a healthy weight; and, drinking plenty of water.

"I believe that parents need to make nutrition education a priority in their home environment. It's crucial for good health and longevity to instil in your children sound eating habits from an early age."

[Cat Cora, Professional Chef and TV Host]

EXERCISE AND PHYSICAL ACTIVITY

"[For] Training your body
[Physical exercise] helps you in some ways..."

[1 Timothy 4:8a Expanded Bible]

Parents should assist children develop a lifestyle of exercise and physical activity. The long-term health benefits include a reduction to the risk of developing several conditions, such as type 2 diabetes, cancer, and cardiovascular diseases. Most importantly, regular exercise can improve the quality of life, stimulate the body's own natural maintenance and repair system – bones, joints and muscles – especially the heart. A sedentary lifestyle in many ways increases health risks, which include: coronary heart disease, high blood pressure, strokes, breathlessness, little energy, flabby body, stiff joints, osteoporosis, poor posture and obesity. Staying healthy is not only about getting fit and feeling better, but it is about a holistic approach to wellbeing. Regular family medical checkups should be a priority.

Huffpost contributor Robert Reames, in his article, *'Parents Set The Example: Kids And Adults Should Exercise Together'*, writes that it is a well-established fact that consistent exercise and sensible eating habits will improve quality of life. A common denominator among people who successfully manage their weight and stay fit is that they exercise and make great nutritional choices as a matter of habit. The same holds true for kids. As parents, we must pay close attention and set an example. It is vital that we teach and encourage our kids to stay active. It's no secret that a life of overeating, lack of physical activity and being lazy can lead to a host of physical and potentially life-threatening problems. Exercising with our kids provides us as parents with a fantastic opportunity for mutual bonding. It establishes a great sense of camaraderie, companionship and a time for bonding. This is valuable time spent."[156]

"It's now vital that we recognise the importance of working towards achieving a healthy balance of physical activity, mental stimulation, and positive relationships – all which have a significant impact on our feelings of wellbeing. As a reduction in any of these can seriously undermine our ability to flourish."

[Rosi Prescott, Chief Executive of Central YMCA]

Effects of Smoking

"Do not love this world nor the things it offers you, for when you love the world, you do not have the love of the Father in you.
For the world offers only a craving for physical pleasure, a craving for everything we see, and pride in our achievements and possessions.
These are not from the Father, but are from this world.
And this world is fading away, along with everything that people crave.
But anyone who does what pleases God will live forever."

[1 John 2:15-17 New Living Translation]

The glamorisation of smoking in the media is of great concern as it is often associated with desirable attributes, but has a huge negative influence on children - who in some cases start smoking quite early. Children begin smoking for a variety of reasons –curiosity; peer pressure; a wish to assert a growing independence; copying parents or older siblings; the desire to appear grown-up and sophisticated; to imitate actors or models with appealing images. Smoking is the most significant cause of preventable deaths in England, accounting for nearly 80,000 deaths each year. One in two smokers will die from a smoking-related disease.[157]

Cigarette is a tobacco product that contains nicotine – a highly addictive stimulant as well as a depressant. Nicotine contains tar and other chemicals linked to lung diseases, cancer, increased heart and cardiovascular diseases. Life expectancy for smokers is shorter than for non-smokers and quitting smoking before the age of 40 reduces the risk of dying from smoking-related disease by about 90 per cent.[158]

The Centre for Disease Control and Prevention, in a 2016 report found that 41% of top-grossing US movies (which account for 96% of American ticket sales) showed people using tobacco.[159]

The reasons for smoking differ from one person to another. Some say they smoke to help ease the signs and symptoms of stress. Research into tobacco and stress has shown that instead of helping people to relax, smoking increases anxiety and tension. Nicotine creates a temporary feeling of relaxation, which soon gives way to withdrawal symptoms and increased cravings. The World Health Organisation (WHO) introduced a practical, cost-effective way to scale up the implementation of Tobacco control encapsulated in the acronym – MPOWER.[160]

The 6 MPOWER measures are:

M - Monitor tobacco use and prevention policies

P - Protect people from tobacco use

O - Offer help to quit tobacco use

W - Warn about the dangers of tobacco

E - Enforce bans on tobacco advertising, promotion, and sponsorship

R - Raise taxes on tobacco.

"A cigarette is the only consumer product which,
when used as directed, kills its consumer."

[Dr. Gro Brundtland, Former Norwegian Prime Minister]

Smoking and Pregnancy

The Centre for Disease Control and Prevention underscores the dangers of smoking during pregnancy. Smoking during pregnant puts mother and unborn baby at risk. It significantly increases the risk of pregnancy complications and health problems for developing babies. Additionally, e-cigarettes are not a safe option to use during pregnancy — flavourings used in e-cigarettes may be harmful to a developing baby.[161]

Smoking can prevent pregnancy. Pregnancy complication and erectile dysfunction rates are also increased with smoking. Women exposed to second-hand smoke are at risk of health conditions associated with smokers. Infertility rates in both male and female smokers are about twice the rate of infertility found in non-smokers, according to the American Society for Reproductive Medicine.[162]

Ruth Nyaboe, in her article titled 'World No Tobacco Day,' says:

"Babies who are exposed to tobacco smoke at home are at increased risk of sudden infant death. Young children who have one or more parents who smoke are twice as likely to suffer from chest problems in their first year of life. They will have more chest, nose, ear and throat infections than children whose parents do not smoke. They are also more likely to take up smoking themselves later in life."[163]

Quitting tobacco can be challenging, but it is possible. Quitting smoking is an important way to protect the health of mother and baby. Quitting early or before pregnancy is best, but it is never too late to quit smoking. Your doctor can play an essential role in helping you quit, including giving advice and support or connecting you with other resources. The National Institute for Health and Care Excellence (NICE) is the agency charged with providing national guidance, advice and recommendations on promoting good health and social care, and preventing and treating ill health. NICE guideline covers support to help women stop smoking during pregnancy and in the first year after childbirth. It includes identifying women who need help to quit, referring them to stop smoking services and providing intensive and ongoing support to help them stop. The guideline also advises how to tailor services for women from disadvantaged groups in which smoking rates are high.[164]

Biblical Perspective on Smoking

"Everything is permissible for me, but not all things are beneficial. Everything is permissible for me, but I will not be enslaved by anything [and brought under its power, allowing it to control me]"

[1 Corinthians 6: 12 Amplified Bible]

Although the Bible never directly mentions smoking, some principles certainly apply to smoking. First, we are not to allow anything to 'master' our bodies. Smoking is undoubtedly addictive, and it 'masters' us through its addictive ability. Can smoking be regarded as "beneficial"?[165] Can smoking genuinely enable us to honour God with our body?[166] Can a person sincerely smoke *"for the glory of God"*?[167]

Some people hold a contrary view by arguing that many people eat unhealthy addictive foods which also harm the body, such as caffeine. While true, it does not justify smoking? If the global smoking pattern does not change, more than 8 million people a year will die from tobacco-related diseases by 2030.[168]

Parental responsibility extends to teaching on the dangers of bad health choices, including smoking, even if parents have modelled the wrong example by smoking themselves. Parents who smoke not only find it an uphill task teaching their children but pose an unreasonable risk to their children's health through passive smoking — second-hand smoke from other people's cigarettes — a report by WHO warns that there is no safe level of exposure to second-hand smoke. Smoking-related diseases place a tremendous economic burden on society. Data from a variety of sources in the U.K shows that in 2015, £2.6 billion was the total estimated smoking-related cost to the National Health Service.[169]

"The only safer cigarette is your last one"

[Duane Alan Hahn]

Effects of Alcohol

"Wine and beer [strong drink; an alcoholic beverage made from grain] make people loud [mockers] and uncontrolled [carousers; brawlers]; it is not wise to get drunk on [be led astray by] them."

[Proverbs 20:1 Expanded Bible]

According to the National Health Service (NHS), alcohol is a potent chemical with a broad range of harmful effects on almost every part of the body, including the brain, bones, and heart. The NHS in its website outlines the risks associated with drinking and the long term effects of alcohol misuse. Some of the dangers related to alcohol misuse include accidents and injury; violence and antisocial behaviour; loss of personal possessions; unplanned time off work or college, and alcohol poisoning.[170]

The NHS is much concerned about the long term effects of drinking vast amounts of alcohol and the damage to many of the body's organs such as the brain, nervous system, heart, liver, and pancreas. Alcohol misuse also increases the risk of severe health conditions such as strokes, high blood pressure, liver disease, pancreatitis, cancer, dementia, depression and sexual problems, such as infertility, premature ejaculation or impotence. In addition to having an impact on health, alcohol misuse can also have long-term social and financial ramifications, such as family break-up and divorce, domestic abuse, unemployment, financial problems, and homelessness. New evidence has given us a better understanding of the link between drinking and some illnesses. There has been a revision of the previously held position, which suggested that some level of alcohol was beneficial to the heart.

It is now plausible to consider that the evidence on a protective effect from moderate drinking is less reliable than previously thought. "Low risk" drinking is not the same thing as "safe" drinking. According to NHS England, there is no safe drinking level. The important question to ask is not what might or might not be "personally permissible" to you – a self-centred approach – but the impact that your choices and actions have on other people.[171]

Alcohol and Pregnancy

According to the Centre for Disease Control and Prevention, there is no known safe amount of alcohol use during pregnancy or while trying to get pregnant. There is also no safe time during pregnancy to drink. All types of alcohol are equally harmful, including all wines and beer. If a woman is drinking alcohol during pregnancy, it is never too late to stop. Help can be obtained from local healthcare providers or alcohol treatment centres.[172]

In an updated guideline, the National Institute for Health and Care Excellence (NICE) advises that the risks of miscarriage in the first three months of pregnancy mean that it is particularly important for women not to drink alcohol at all during that period.[173]

Nonetheless, it is essential to understand that drinking alcohol carries risk throughout the whole pregnancy.

CONCLUSION

"Don't let your appetite destroy what God has done. All foods are fit to eat, but it is wrong to cause problems for others by what you eat."

[Romans 14:20 Contemporary English Version]

Parents should be realistic, open-minded, and supportive and guided by a child-centred approach – focusing on the child's needs and development. Parenting can be an emotional roller coaster, but the principles described in this chapter can help us take back control and focus on what is most important – the welfare of the child.

*"Children take more notice of what their parents do,
than what they say. Actions speak louder than words."*

[William Tiptaft, Writer and Minister]

CHAPTER 7

STRATEGIC POSITIONING – THE PRINCIPAL OBJECTIVE

> *Children are a gift from the Lord.*
> *Babies are a reward.*
> *Sons who are born to a young man*
> *are like arrows in the hand of a warrior.*
> *Happy is the man who has his bag full of arrows.*
> *They will not be defeated when they fight*
> *their enemies in court.*
>
> [PSALM 127:3-5 INTERNATIONAL CHILDREN'S BIBLE]

THE SPORT OF ARCHERY

Bows and arrows have been vital tools for hunting, warfare, and sport for thousands of years. Archery is the sport of shooting with a bow and arrow, especially at a target. Archery can be used in combat as well as for recreation. Even though archery equipment has advanced impressively over the last several centuries, the enterprise of shooting a bow has remained constant.

Once you fit an arrow onto the bowstring and pull it back, the muscles exert force on the string that bends the limbs of the bow backwards. Essentially, the greater the drawback force on the bowstring (known as the draw weight), the further back the bowstring goes (the draw length), and consequently, the faster the arrow will launch.[174]

In archery, it is common practice for the arrow not to be aimed straight at the target but deliberately aimed slightly off-target since the bow's trajectory follows a path that is different from its expected trajectory. Indeed, since the arrow eventually straightens out after being launched, it ends up striking the target, mainly if aimed by an excellent Archer.

"Archery does not get difficult or
hard to understand until the arrow misses."

[Lt. Col. Milan E. Elott, Army Officer and Author]

ARCHERY AND PARENTING

"Children are a gift [an inheritance] from the LORD; babies [the fruit of the womb] are a reward. Children who are born to a young man [of one's youth] are like arrows in the hand of a warrior [they help in the challenges and conflicts of life]. Happy [Blessed] is the man who has his bag [quiver]

full of arrows [them]. They will not be defeated [humiliated] when they
fight [speak to] their enemies at the city gate [the central place of commerce
and government]."

[Psalm 127:3-5 Expanded Bible]

Embedded in this timeless text is the critical link between archery and parenting – the principles of archery are akin to those of parenting. The skill to draw back a bow with precision and strength, take aim, and shoot straight to the centre of a target is akin to the skill required by parents. These skills, if comprehensively understood and applied, will determine the trajectory of children as parents aim them towards desired future targets in life. If parents do not help and point children in the right direction, someone else will. However, children suffer if parents are short-sighted, distracted and disabled by their challenges.

Modern arrows are usually made of rods or tubes of stiff, low-density material: aluminium, carbon fibre and wood shafts - fir, maple, cedar, bamboo and exotic woods such as bubinga – they all fly differently. The type of arrow used will determine how the arrow is aimed – high with a falling arc or straight ahead. The lack of strength and steadiness, in addition to the lack of accurate judgment of distance, risk sending the arrow onto a dangerous path.

Coercing children into a direction they were not prepared to travel can affect them physically, emotionally and psychologically. Finally, arrows, like children, may never reach their potential until they are fully released, avoiding the tendencies of over-parenting described in chapter 3. While releasing the arrow, compensation should be made to circumvent variables like air resistance, gravity, and other obstacles in its flight path as it strikes the target. The reason why the arrow is so thin is to enable it to prevent air resistance – small arrows easily slice through air. While air resistance hinders the forward speed of the arrow, gravity exerts a downward pull. These two forces can undermine the best intentions of an archer, causing the arrow to miss its desired target.

Arrows, like children, navigate through 'air resistance' and 'gravity' to successfully hit their targets. Consequently, parents should train children on how to overcome resistance, setbacks, disappointment, and situations that pull us down – like gravity. The irony is that some disappointments are beneficial for children – as long as they bounce back with coping mechanisms for disappointments and failures. Learning to deal with setbacks can help children develop key attributes required to succeed, such as vital coping skills, reasonable positive attitude, optimism, the ability to regulate emotions, creative thinking and '*bouncebackability*' – the capacity and ability to recover quickly from setbacks. Parents are children's guide and not their saviour. You cannot be there every time to tranquillize their feelings when they fall short at a task. Children must be prepared to manage setbacks. Showering a child with excessive compliments can do more harm than good. Over praised children become dependent on others for their validation. These children only feel valued through an avalanche of continued positive feedback. Psychologist Dan Kindlon, the author of *Tough Times, Strong Children*, says you get confidence from overcoming adversity, not from being told how great you are all the time.[175]

While parents cannot protect children from every setback, there are times when children need parental intervention, especially in situations whereby failure to intervene would cause children enormous humiliation, or where the child is in grave danger or the child is being bullied.[176]

Parents have the unique responsibility to model their children's worldview, and so should handle their disappointments with tact and wisdom. If parents panic every time something goes wrong, they are not demonstrating strong coping skills to the children. Children learn far more from what parents do than from what they say. By taking on new challenges where success is not instant, parents show children that it is okay to struggle. Parenting is about perfecting your archery skills: letting that arrow fly, knowing when to retrieve it when it misses the target, understanding mistakes and making the necessary adjustments. The act of focusing, taking aim and using the muscles of the body to hit a target requires self-discipline, patience, eye-hand coordination and balance. The good thing about archery, like parenting, is that confidence and skill levels improve quickly with knowledge and practice.

"You are the bows from which your children as living arrows are sent forth."

[Kahlil Gibran, Writer and Poet]

EVERY CHILD MATTERS (ECM)

Every Child Matters (ECM) – recently changed to 'Help Children Achieve More', is a U.K. government initiative launched in 2003 to improve outcomes for children and young people.[177]

The aim of ECM is that, irrespective of circumstances or socio-cultural background, every child should have the support they need to stay safe, healthy, enjoy and achieve economic well-being, and make a positive contribution.

S-H-E-E-P is a helpful acronym to remember these five aspects –every child shall be S-afe, H-ealthy, E-njoy, achieve E-conomic well-being and make P-ositive contributions.

ECM, as should parenting, focuses on the child as an individual.

There is a significant similarity between the principles of archery and parenting and ECM which focuses on the child as an individual. As with fingerprints, every child has a unique learning style. Research shows that what works for one child does not necessarily work for another – every child is different. In archery, all arrows do not follow the same trajectory even if shot from the same bow by the same archer.

"A good archer is known not by his arrows but by his aim."

[Thomas Fuller, Minister and Historian]

PRINCIPLES OF 'ARCHERY' IN PARENTING

"You are like a tree, planted by flowing, cool streams of water that never run dry. Your fruit ripens in its time; your leaves never fade or curl in the summer sun. No matter what you do, you prosper."

[Psalm 1:3 The Voice]

Great parents are often described as having 'a natural talent' for parenting even when they have spent years working hard on their parenting skills. Those who struggle with parenting believe they are held back by their lack of innate ability. So how do you become a successful parent? Is hard work and perseverance enough? Or do you need to possess the 'talent' first? Of course, natural talent still exists; the likes of Mozart, Michelangelo and Einstein demonstrate this. However, when we judge natural talent by the end result, we tend to forget the process and the hard work it has taken to get there. With or without 'natural talent,' the pre-requisite for successful parenting (archers alike) is hard work, focus, determination, intentional living and above all to love what you do.

While archery techniques may vary, they follow general principles which are alike to parenting. These include:

- **Focus**: The simple goal of hitting a target provides something real and stimulating on which to focus the mind.

  "Let your eyes look right on [with fixed purpose], and let your gaze be straight before you."[178]

- **Patience**: Like parenting, archery is easy to learn, but not easy to perfect; however, patience is essential for success. 'Rushing the shot' or 'punching the trigger' happens when you aim at the target then suddenly get nervous and prematurely release the shot – altering the aim and the flight of the arrow. Patience is needed to execute a smooth shot. This makes a better archer and consequently, a better parent.

  "We do not want you to become lazy, but to imitate those who through faith and patience inherit what has been promised."[179]

- **Coordination**: Shooting an arrow requires the coordination of the entire body including muscle memory. All body parts work in harmony to provide a strong foundation while keeping weight evenly balanced. Constant practice makes the coordination of all these body movements almost instinctive.

  "He makes the whole body fit together perfectly. As each part does its special work, it helps the other parts grow, so that the whole body is healthy and growing and full of love."[180]

- **Confidence**: Even in competition, the archer's most significant opponent is none other than himself. Identifying points of improvement and setting clear goals is easy – after all, results are all based on easily-measurable scores. As in parenting, progression breeds confidence, and there is no better sport to measure that than archery.

  "This is the confidence we have in approaching God: that if we ask anything according to his will, he hears us. Also, if we know that he hears us – whatever we ask – we know that we have what we asked of him."[181]

- **Distance**: Good archers and good golfers have a commonality: an extraordinary ability to judge distances. Deciding on the 'distance' they want children to cover in life will impact on the sacrifices parents are willing to make.

  "And you must think constantly about these commandments I am giving you today. You must teach them to your children and talk about them when you are at home or out for a walk; at bedtime and the first thing in the morning."[182]

- **Socialise**: Shooting can be a solitary endeavour. Notwithstanding, in between shots, archery, like parenting, is surprisingly a social activity – enabling friendships and social connections between individuals from all walks of life, who like you, find great satisfaction in the fine art of archery.

  "As iron sharpens iron, So one man sharpens [and influences] another [through discussion]."[183]

- **Strength**: While archery is not the most physically demanding sport in the world, it requires short bursts of energy from core muscles; the act of drawing a bow puts tension in the chest, hands, arm and large upper back muscles. Maintaining the strength to hold steady during the shot is quite challenging. The correct and continuous repetition of this movement strengthens the muscles making the task easy. Parenting, while equally challenging, requires an even greater level of energy, mental strength and emotional stamina.

  "Finally – let the mighty strength of the Lord make you strong."[184]

"In the long run, you only hit what you aim at."

[Henry Thoreau, American Essayist, Poet, Philosopher]

ARCHERS – PARENTS OR TEACHERS?

The home environment can prevent children (arrows) from hitting their academic 'targets' if they are stuck in front of computers or phone screens for hours every day. More often, children are worn out at the start of the school day, exhausted from excessively viewing unsuitable programmes. Children need parents to learn the rules of social behaviour. It is not the primary responsibility of the teacher, but of the parent to shoot the academic 'arrows' of their children. An increasing number of parents are realising their critical role in the educational future of their children. Parenting is much more than just meeting the everyday needs of the child and being contented over their enrolment into the best schools. Although commendable, these are no grounds to relinquish parental responsibilities - measured by 'time invested' in a child and not by 'things invested' for the child. In this way, what we do for our children will not be an excuse for what we are - or should be.

Research from North Carolina State University, the University of California, Irvine and Brigham Young University found that parental involvement is a more critical factor in a child's academic performance than the quality of the school itself. Toby Parcel, a professor of sociology and co-author of the study, says that parents need to be aware of how important they are and invest time in their children – checking homework, attending school events and letting kids know school is important.[185]

The partnership between teachers and parents is not always a straightforward one to maintain, but it is significant to the educational process. Parents can play a productive role by checking notes sent home by teachers, discussing with their child about school and attending school functions. Teachers can send back positive feedback about children, as well as letters about issues or problems. Regular calls to parents can develop a communication bridge that is beneficial to the child. The attitude of parents towards education can inspire children and show them how to be in control of their educational journey. In the end, the parents, and not the teacher, remain the bow from which the arrows are released.

We must remember that intelligence is not enough. Intelligence plus character – that is the goal of true education."

[Martin Luther King Jr., Minister and Civil Rights Leader]

ARCHERS – PARENT OR CHURCH?

*"Teach the wise, and they will become wiser.
Instruct those who live right, and they will gain more knowledge."*

[Proverbs 9:9 Easy-to-Read Version]

Healthy churches do not produce strong families; instead, strong families produce healthy churches. Nonetheless, healthy churches and strong families are needed to complement each other. The Church, while providing a safe environment for children, does not substitute the family; neither do church activities replace parenting responsibilities. The Church is not a panacea for parental shortcomings. Her purpose is not to raise children but to provide the necessary assistance and support to parents as they discharge their duties. There is a vast difference in time spent with children between parents and the Church. Parents spend on average from 2,000 to 3,000 hours a year with their children, if they live with them, whereas, the Church, on the other hand, has much less time with children per year – 100 hours if they show up for every weekly activity.

Despite its benefits, the tendency for parents to outsource parenting to Church and Sunday school teachers, is an unproductive concept, even though in certain circumstances, people in Church can play the role of "surrogate" parents especially if the parents are going through a major crisis and the children's lives are in danger. Nonetheless, parents, and not the Church, remain the main bows responsible for releasing arrows – children.

"When we let our children fly as arrows, we understand that we have been chosen by God to be the bow in their lives and point them in the right direction as we lead them to Jesus."

[Crystal McDowell, Writer, Speaker and Teacher]

CONCLUSION

"Train up a child in the way he should go [and in keeping with his individual gift or bent], and when he is old, he will not depart from it."

[Proverbs 22:6 Amplified Bible, Classic Edition]

First, parents should set proper goals for a child, taking into account the child's purpose, potentials and in some cases, skill set. Affluence, excellent schools, good churches and parental privileges can sharpen arrows; still, they cannot determine the travel distance or direction of the shot – the archer; likewise, the parent decides this, as well as the target. However, the absence of proper education produces a blunt arrow - it may strike a target but will fail to penetrate or create a positive impact. Secondly, as with some types of arrows, like survival arrows, fletching (adding feathers or other materials to the arrow shaft) helps to stabilise the arrow in flight. How parents fletch children to support them along life's flight path has been the focus of this chapter. Lastly, understanding that time is a crucial factor in a child's upbringing is important. The World Archery Federation (WA) governs modern competitive target archery. Olympic rules derived from WA rules. One of these rules states that archers have a limited set time in which to shoot their arrows. The urgency of parenting does not offer us the luxury of delay. Parents need to seize the opportunity while children are young and receptive. The time is limited, and the right time is 'as soon as practically possible'. The Apostle Paul, in his epistle to the Corinthians, writes, "For God says, *"At just the right time, I heard you. On the day of salvation, I helped you. Indeed, the "right time" is now. Today is the day of salvation."*[186]

"Children are a divine package with a unique earthly mandate."

[Jesse Song, Author 'Pillars of Parenting']

Notes

....
....
....
....
....
....
....
....
....
....
....
....
....
....
....
....

CHAPTER 8

SEXUALITY EDUCATION – RIDING WITH THE TIDE

Young people, it's wonderful to be young! Enjoy every minute of it. Do everything you want to do; take it all in. But remember that you must give an account to God for everything you do.

[ECCLESIASTES 11:9 NEW LIVING TRANSLATION]

BRIEF HISTORY

Sweden, with a long and established history of sex education, founded the Swedish Association for Sexuality Education (RFSU) in 1933. First, sexuality education has been compulsory in Swedish schools since 1955. Second, sexuality education in Sweden conveys facts about sexual and reproductive health. Third, it is included as a part of the general health objectives for public health work and often referred to as a vital part of 'sexually transmitted infections' prevention and promotion of sexual health. Fourth, there is hardly any opposition to sexuality education in Sweden.

The Swedish model, which has quickly gained popularity as the prototype for the western world is based on four premises, viz: teenage sexual activity is inevitable; educators should be value-neutral regarding sex; schools should openly discuss sexual matters; and sex education should teach students about contraception. This value-neutral approach to sex, which found its way into the western sex education philosophy, defends a view of sexual morality which holds that 'anything goes' as long as it is in private, between consenting adults and harms no-one else. This is asserted by the author of 'Curriculum Guide for Sex Education in California':

> *"'Right' or 'wrong' in so intimate a matter as sexual behaviour is as personal as one's own name and address. No textbook or classroom teacher can teach it."*[187]

A healthy approach to sex education is one that encourages the development of healthy sexual attitudes and behaviours in children.

"Sex education, including its spiritual aspects, should be part of a broad health and moral education from kindergarten through grade twelve, ideally carried out harmoniously by parents and teachers."

[Benjamin Spock, Paediatrician and Author]

SEX EDUCATION: GOVERNMENT OR PARENTS?

In 2017, the U.K. government announced that Sex and Relationships Education (SRE) is to be made compulsory in all schools in England. The announcement met with mixed reactions from supporters who claim it is a step in the right direction and critics who feared that it would weaken the influence of parents. In a BBC article *'Sex education to be compulsory in England's schools'*, author Katherine Sellgren, examines the reaction from supporters such as the Local Government Association, and critics such as Safe at School Campaign.[188]

Izzi Seccombe, chairman of the Local Government Association's Community Wellbeing Board, says:

> *"The lack of compulsory SRE in secondary academies and free schools is storing up problems for later on in life, creating a ticking sexual health time bomb, as we are seeing in those who have recently left school. We believe that making SRE compulsory in all secondary schools, not just council-maintained ones, could make a real difference in reversing this trend, by preparing pupils for adulthood and enabling them to better take care of themselves and future partners."*

Chief executive of the PHSE Association, Jonathan Baggaley, comments:

> *"This is a historic step and a clear statement of intent from the government."*

But critics like the National co-ordinator of Safe at School Campaign, Antonia Tully described the announcement as a tragedy. She says:

"Parents will be absolutely powerless to protect their children from presentations of sexual activity, which we know is part of many sex education teaching resources for primary school children. The state simply cannot safeguard children in the same way that parents can. This proposal is sending a huge message to parents that they are unfit to teach their own children about sex."

Christian Concern Chief executive Andrea Williams told the BBC that:

"Children need to be protected, and certainly when they're [still at primary school], we need to be guarding their innocence. We need to be protecting them from things, working with parents to ensure that what they might need to know - which will be different for every child, different in every context across the country - is properly looked at. But this is something that should be individualised, not something that the state can deliver wholesale."

"We need sex education in schools, but we need it at home first.
We need parents to learn the names of the teachers who are teaching their children. We need families to question day-care centres, to question other children and their own as to what goes on."

[Ron McKuen, American Poet]

WHAT IS SEXAULITY EDUCATION?

"Sex Education" addresses human sexual anatomy, sexual reproduction, sexual intercourse, and the mechanics of sexual behaviours. On the other hand, *"Sexuality Education"* addresses the

biological, socio-cultural, psychological, and spiritual dimensions of sexuality from the cognitive domain (information); the affective domain (feelings, values, and attitudes); and the behavioural domain (communication, decision-making and other relevant personal skills).

UNESCO – United Nations Educational, Scientific and Cultural Organization, defines sexuality education as:

"A curriculum-based process of teaching and learning about the cognitive, emotional, physical and social aspects of sexuality. It aims to equip children and young people with knowledge, skills, attitudes and values that will empower them to: realize their health, well-being and dignity; develop respectful social and sexual relationships; consider how their choices affect their own well-being and that of others; and, understand and ensure the protection of their rights throughout their lives."[189]

Children in some cultures are not given any information on sexual matters since such discussions are considered taboo. In other cases, many parents – because their parents struggled to talk to them – find it challenging to approach the subject with their children. Helping parents and guardians gain the confidence and skills to speak with their children about sex and relationships should not be a one-off lecture, but an ongoing conversation. Although aspects of sexuality education form part of the curriculum at many schools, it raises contentious questions at several levels – at what age should children start receiving such education; how much details and what topics should be covered. Significant areas of controversy are whether sexuality education is detrimental or valuable; the use of birth control and its impact on pregnancy outside marriage, teenage pregnancy, and the transmission of sexually transmitted infections.

According to Debra Haffner and Kate Ott, authors of the monograph '*A Time to Speak*', sexuality education for young people has four primary goals.[190]

- First, to provide correct information about human sexuality, including growth, development, and sexually transmitted diseases.

- Secondly, to allow the opportunity for young people to articulate their sexual attitudes in order to understand their family and religious values.

- Thirdly, to help young people develop interpersonal skills in the areas of communication, decision-making, peer refusal, and to learn to build satisfying relationships.

- Lastly, to assist young people to exercise responsibility regarding sexual relationships by discussing abstinence and resisting the pressure of sexual intercourse.

"Let's make sure that we are working
for age-appropriate sex education in our school system."

[Wendy Davis, U.S. Politician]

CRITICISM – DEPARTMENT FOR EDUCATION

In December 2017, the Department of Education opened its 'eight-week consultation' on changing SRE in England. The timing of the consultation was duly criticised by observers who claimed that the Department was using dubious tactics – parents and teachers had time constraints (due to Christmas festivities) to rigorously scrutinise the policy document. However, a higher number of respondents to the consultation disagreed with the government's proposals – a remarkable disquiet over the age-appropriateness of RSE content for both primary and secondary school pupils. In spite of the response, Damian Hinds, the education secretary, confirmed that he would move forward with only slight amendments to the reforms, which will come into effect in 2020. Some have called into question the Department's penchant for ignoring parents' views while favouring the agenda of special interest groups – perhaps for political gain.

KEY POINTS OF THE STATUTORY GUIDANCE

The Relationships Education, Relationships and Sex Education and Health Education (England) Regulations 2019, made under sections 34 and 35 of the Children and Social Work Act 2017, make Relationships Education compulsory for all pupils receiving primary education and Relationships and Sex Education (RSE) mandatory for all pupils receiving secondary education. Schools maintained by local authorities in England are obliged to teach Sex and Relationship Education (SRE) from age 11 upwards and must take into account the guidance from the Secretary of State on sex education published in July 2000 – Sex and Relationship Education Guidance (Ref: DfEE 0116/2000)

All schools must have an up-to-date sex and relationship education policy, drawn up by the governing body, and available for inspection by parents.

Introduction

- The guidance says the objective of sex and relationship education is to help and support young people through their physical, emotional and moral development. A successful programme, firmly embedded in PSHE (Personal, Social, Health and Economic Education), will help young people learn to respect themselves and others and move with confidence from childhood through adolescence into adulthood. (p.3, paragraph 2)

- Sex and relationship education should contribute to promoting the spiritual, moral, cultural, mental and physical development of pupils at school and society and preparing pupils for the opportunities, responsibilities and experiences of adult life. (p.4, paragraph 6)

- Effective sex and relationship education does not encourage early sexual experimentation. It should teach young people to understand human sexuality and to respect themselves and others. It enables young people to mature, to build up their confidence and self-esteem and understand the reasons for delaying sexual activity. It builds up knowledge and skills which are particularly important today because of the many different and conflicting pressures on young people. (p.4, paragraph 7)

What is sex and relationship education?

- It is lifelong learning about physical, moral and emotional development. It is about the understanding of the importance of marriage for family life, stable and loving relationships, respect, love and care. It is also about the teaching of sex, sexuality, and sexual health. It is not about the promotion of sexual orientation or sexual activity – this would be inappropriate teaching. (p.5, paragraph 9)

- The guidance says that pupils should "learn the importance of values and individual conscience and moral considerations; learn the value of family life, marriage, and stable and loving relationships for the nurture of children; learning to manage emotions and relationships confidently and sensitively; learning how to recognise and avoid exploitation and abuse; understanding human sexuality, reproduction, sexual health, emotions and relationships; the reasons for delaying sexual activity, and the benefits to be gained from such delay". (p. 5)

Developing a policy for sex and relationship education.

- The teaching of some aspects of sex and relationship education might be of concern to teachers and parents. Sensitive issues should be covered by the school's policy and in consultation with parents. Schools of a particular religious ethos may choose to reflect that in their sex and relationship education policy. Research demonstrates that good, comprehensive sex and relationship education does not make young people more likely to enter into sexual activity. Indeed it can help them learn the reasons for, and the benefits to be gained from, delaying such activity. (p.8, paragraph 1.7)
- The guidance reiterates the importance of suitable materials being used: "Inappropriate images should not be used nor should explicit material not directly related to explanation. Schools should ensure that pupils are protected from teachings

and materials which are inappropriate, having regard to the age and cultural background of the pupils concerned. Governors and head teachers should discuss with parents and take on board concerns raised both on materials which are offered to schools and on sensitive material to be used in the classroom." (p. 8, paragraph 1.8)

Specific Issues when Teaching Sex and Relationship Education

Parents and pupils may need to be reassured that the personal beliefs and attitudes of teachers will not influence the teaching of sex and relationship education within the PSHE framework. (p.14, paragraph 2.1)

Why parents are so important

- Research shows that children and young people want to receive their initial sex and relationship education from their parents and families, with school and other adults building on this later. But many parents find it difficult to talk to their children about sex and relationships. In particular, fathers rarely take responsibility for giving sex and relationship education to their sons. (p. 25, paragraph 5.1)

- Parents are the key people in teaching their children about sex and relationships; maintaining the culture and ethos of the family; helping their children cope with the emotional and physical aspects of growing up; and preparing them for the challenges and responsibilities that sexual maturity brings. (p. 25, paragraph 5.3)

- Parents need support in helping their children learn the correct names of the body; talking with their children about feelings and relationships; and answering questions about growing up, having babies, feeling attraction, sexuality, sex, contraception, relationships and sexual health. (p.25, paragraph 5.4)

- Schools should always work in partnership with parents, consulting them regularly on the content of sex and relationship education programmes. Reflection around parents' own experiences of sex education can often lead to a productive discussion in which teachers and parents can start planning sex and relationship education provision for their children. Parents need to know that the school's sex and relationship education programme will complement and support their role as parents and that they can be actively involved in the determination of the school's policy. (p. 26, paragraph 5.6)

"Answering questions is a major part of sex education. Two rules cover the ground. First, always give a truthful answer to a question; secondly, regard sex knowledge as exactly like any other knowledge."

[Bertrand Russell, Philosopher and Nobel Laureate]

INTERFAITH STATEMENT ON SEX EDUCATION

Those who introduce sex education programs into schools should not devalue it to mere exchange of information. These programs should recognise the fundamental moral principles enshrined within the noble heritage of western civilisation. In 1968, the National Council of Churches' Commission on Marriage and the Family, the Synagogue Council of America's Committee on Family and the United States Catholic Conference's Family Life Bureau issued an interfaith statement on sex education, affirming that human sexuality "is a gift from God, to be accepted with thanksgiving and used with reverence and joy." The 1968 statement calls upon communities of faith to provide resources, leadership and opportunities for sex education and recognises the vital role that schools play, reaching large numbers of young people who need to understand their sexuality and their role in society.[191]

For policymakers and stakeholders in education, the Interfaith Statement on Sex Education suggests the following guidelines:[192]

- First, such education should strive to create an understanding that decisions about sexual behaviour must be based on ethical and moral values, while also giving consideration to physical and emotional health.
- Secondly, such education should respect the backgrounds and beliefs of individuals, and recognise that sexual behaviour and development of each individual cannot take place in a vacuum but are connected to the other aspects of his life and his moral, ethical and religious codes.
- Thirdly, it should direct attention to how sex is distorted and exploited in our society and the heavy responsibility it places on the individual, the family and institutions to cope constructively with the problems created.
- Fourthly, it must recognise that sex education in schools

complement the education conveyed through the family or other family support structures. Sex education in the schools must make progress constructively, with understanding, tolerance, and acceptance of differences.

- Fifthly, it must stress the many points of agreement about what is right and wrong that are held in common by the main religions on the one hand and the generally accepted social, legal, psychological, medical, and other values held in common by society generally.
- Sixthly, where substantial differences of opinion exist on what is right and wrong sexual behaviour, objective and informed discussions on both sides should be encouraged. However, sponsors of an educational program or teachers should not give definite answers or represent their personal religious or moral beliefs as the consensus of society generally.
- Seventhly, throughout such education, human values and dignity must be stressed as the major basis for decisions of right and wrong.
- Eighthly, such education should teach that sexuality is only a part of the whole person.
- Ninthly, it should explain that people who love each other endeavour not to do anything that will harm each other.
- Tenthly, it should teach that sexual intercourse within a committed marital relationship offers the most significant possibility for personal fulfilment and social growth.
- Finally, such an education program must be based on unbiased content and must employ sound methods; it must be conducted by teachers and leaders qualified to do so by training and temperament.

"Young people are going to learn about sex and our question has to be where do we want them to learn? From the media? From their friends? Or do we want them to learn from an educated, responsible adult?"

[Tamara Kreinin, Health and Human Services Expert]

CHALLENGES WITH SEX EDUCTION CURRICULUM

The Scottish Government was sharply criticised in 2017 for proposing that children in nursery and primary schools should be learning about sexual consent.[193]

Critics spoke out that the Government had stepped the bounds by allowing the delivery of these lessons to underage pupils in primary school. Parents have also accused some councils of approving teaching materials that contain explicit descriptions and cartoons they say are inappropriate. Rather, these children should be learning generic principles about maintaining their boundaries and respecting others.

The Touching Myself section in the controversial 'All About Me' teaching programme issued as part of the sex education programme, instructs children aged six to ten about 'the rules of self-stimulation' - encouraging children aged between six and ten to touch their 'private parts' in bed and the shower. Campaigners had warned that the vague guidelines issued by the Department for Education meant that inappropriate sexual material could be given to children. Even politicians who were in support of the RSE legislation expressed concern. Tory MP David Davies said:

> *"I and many other parents would be furious at completely inappropriate sexual matters being taught to children as young as six. These classes go way beyond the guidance the Government is producing and are effectively sexualising very young children."*[194]

Piers Shepherd, of the Family Education Trust, said RSE guidance was too vague. He added *"it is even more concerning that parents may be denied the opportunity to withdraw their children from these lessons if the school brands them as relationship education classes rather than as sex education."*[195]

Other critics said that the programme exposed children to mature topics like masturbation, and some parents took their children off school for the week during which the programme was taught. One of such parent, Mr Seymour, told the Mail on Sunday:

> *"This sexualisation of our children is just totally inappropriate. They are calling it self-touching, and they won't use the term masturbation, but when you read it, that is exactly what they're talking about."*[196]

The teaching manual states that it is 'really very normal,' for children to touch their private part even though 'some people may get cross or say that it is dirty.'

Such cases are open for legal experts to determine if there has been any breach of Section 8 of the Sexual Offences Act 2003 which makes it an offence for a person intentionally to cause or incite a child under the age of 13 to engage in sexual activity.[197]

RECOMMENDATIONS FOR PARENTS

- First, parents should view the materials since most schools are required to provide the information.
- Secondly, arrange a face to face meeting with the head teacher. You can refer to the section of the guidance policy, which rules out inappropriate material. Always remember to be gentle and polite yet firm.
- Thirdly you can withdraw your child up until September 2020 after which legislation makes Relationships and Sex Education (RSE) compulsory for primary and secondary pupils.
- Fourthly, get in touch with the elected parent governors and express your views. School governors have ultimate responsibility for sex education in England.
- Fifthly, talk to other parents who share your concerns. A group of parents working together can be hugely influential.
- Sixthly, contact your elected official (local MP and Councillors) and the Local Press. Meet these officials in person or write a reasonable and temperate letter and raise your concerns about the SRE material. Write to the local press.
- Seventhly, raise an informal complaint first with the class teacher and head teacher. If not satisfied, contact the school governing body, then the local authority and ultimately the secretary of state. Request a copy of the school's formal complaints procedure.

"If children learn of sex as a relation between their parents to which they owe their own existence, they learn of it in its best form and in connection with its biological purpose."

[Bertrand Russell, Philosopher and Nobel Laureate]

THE FORGOTTEN LEGACY OF J.D UNWIN

In his monumental study 'Sex and Culture' (originally published by Oxford Press in 1934), the ethnologist and social anthropologist John Daniel Unwin at Oxford University and Cambridge University, conducted his landmark study of 86 known civilisations through 5,000 years of history and found a positive correlation between the cultural achievement of a people and the sexual restraint they observe.[198]

Aldous Huxley, the English writer and Philosopher described Unwin's *'Sex and Culture'* as a work of the highest importance, with conclusions that are based upon an enormous wealth of carefully sifted evidence".[199]

Humphrey Milford of Oxford University Press writes:

"This is a remarkable book. It presents in great detail and with the fullest documentation the results of an enquiry which the author conducted, not, he assures us, with any idea of proving a thesis, for he had none to proof."

According to Unwin, after a nation becomes prosperous, it becomes increasingly liberal about sexual morality and as a result, loses its cohesion, its impetus and its purpose. The process, says the author, is irreversible. The whole of human history does not contain a single instance of a group becoming civilised unless it has been absolutely monogamous, nor is there any example of a group retaining its culture after it has adopted less rigorous customs.

"I think sex education should include enhancing a girl's sexual self-image and self-esteem, and give her the tools to say "no", and ultimately "yes", when the time is right."

[Anita H. Clayton, Psychiatrist and Researcher]

CONCLUSION

Sex education has gone through recent major reforms – expanding to include a wide range of compulsory health and personal wellbeing topics. There is uncertainty across many countries about the role played, if any, by interest groups who seek to push their agenda into the sex education curriculum. As a result, some parents have actively engaged in defeating the concerted push for anything-goes SRE.

Sexuality is a sacred and blessed part of human life. Given the importance of sexuality education, it is advised that while coordinated efforts can often be enough to improve the implementation of SRE programs; more should be done to understand the life experiences that shape people's emotional universe – including socio-cultural, religious and ethnic backgrounds. Furthermore, it is possible to achieve a fuller, richer understanding of sexuality so that children can grow in an environment where men and women live and work together in harmony, cooperation, and love. While times have changed dramatically, for some, riding the tide of sexuality education is a journey of no return; however, the onus is on parents, not to stop the tide but to give direction to their ship.

"Educate your children to self-control, to the habit of holding passion and prejudice and evil tendencies subject to an upright and reasoning will, and you have done much to abolish misery from their future and crimes from society".

[Benjamin Franklin, One of the Founding Fathers of the U.S.]

CHAPTER 9

SINGLE PARENTING – THE BALANCING EQUATION

 I am the LORD, the God of all the peoples of the world. Is anything too hard for me?

[JEREMIAH 32:27 NEW LIVING TRANSLATION]

THE CHANGING LANDSCAPE

The breakdown of the traditional family structure and the soaring number of divorced and single parents – especially single mothers, has become one of the most significant social transformations experienced by Western societies in the last half-century. According to Joseph Chamie, former director of the United Nations Population Division:

"Of the world's 2.3 billion children, 14% – or 320 million – are living in a single-parent household, mostly in mother-only families. Governments and civil society need to adopt policies and establish programs providing the necessary assistance, support and opportunities to ensure that children in single-parent families are not penalized or disadvantaged, but can lead lives permitting them to develop successfully to their full potential, and thereby contribute meaningfully to overall society."[200]

The "single" parent classification is used to refer to different types of family structures with a child under the age of eighteen headed by a single, divorced or widowed parent. Single parents are overwhelmingly women. However, this phenomenon is becoming more diverse with single fathers on the rise. While parenting alone is hard for anyone, being a single father presents unique challenges. There were 2 million single fathers in 2016 according to the U.S. Census Bureau. About 40 per cent were divorced, 38 per cent were never married, 16 per cent were separated, and 6 percent were widowed.[201]

In the film 'The Pursuit of Happyness,' actor Will Smith portrays the character Chris Gardner, a single father who pulls himself and his young son out of homelessness by becoming a successful stockbroker. The movie plot is based on a true story, and we learn early on what drives Gardner when it comes to his son – he did not meet his father until he was an adult. He resolved that his children were going to have a good relationship with their father.[202]

After over a decade of the film's premiere, it is not uncommon for children in single-parent families to live with only their fathers.

Single-parents households are progressively becoming common in many countries, mainly due to the upsurge of divorce rates and having children outside of marriage. A 2011 Organisation for Economic Co-operation and Development (OECD) report, 'Doing Better for Families', projects that by 2025–30 the percentage of sole-parent families is expected to increase in all OECD countries (except Germany), from 8% for Switzerland and the USA to 29% for New Zealand. Most commonly, single mothers are heading these sole-parent families. However, families headed by single fathers represent a sizeable portion: about 2.6 million families in the USA, 330 000 in Canada and 300,000 families in the UK.[203]

It may be useful to make a difference between a single father and a divorced father. Men who do not offer full-time care to their children do not fall under the category of single fathers. They are considered divorced fathers. Single fathers are those who provide care for their children on a full-time basis, while divorced fathers are those who maintain a relationship with their children every other weekend and benefit from all kinds of freedom in between (and as such, do not act like fathers during that time). Many fathers assume that custody automatically goes to the mother, but this is not always the case. If either of the parents wants to be an involved and responsible parent, they have every right to request time with their child. According to the U.K. Office for National Statistics (ONS), there are around 1.8 million single parents – making up nearly a quarter of families with dependent children.[204]

Most people do not plan to be single parents, but unfortunately, circumstances can change family life, and the inevitable can happen – divorce, break-up, abandonment, hospitalisation, military deployment, incarceration, death, childbirth or adoption by a single person.

Frequent single parent challenges include: arranging custody and visitation; handling financial matters; helping children cope with loss and parental conflict, and obtaining childcare. Further challenges include the difficulty of being the only disciplinarian at home; the feeling of grieve when your child envies friends with two parents at home; new relationships may be complicated, mainly if a child is jealous or suspicious; the demands of income earning, child-raising and housework could constrict a single parent's time for themselves; a lonely parent may cling to a child for support and companionship, making it harder for the child to gain emotional independence eventually.

Single parenting can be challenging, overwhelming and stressful, but it can also be gratifying. Things work best when single parents have good relationships with their children and a secure support network, and if possible a reasonable working relationship with the other parent. While it is enticing to try to handle everything alone, it is highly recommended to look for trusted and vetted family members or friends to be role models for your children. Joining a single-parent support group can be very helpful to some single parents. The National Health Service (NHS) advices single parents to accept help from relatives, friends and to make arrangements with other parents to take turns to look after each other's children; and co-parenting on separation.

"There is no job more important than parenting. This I believe."

[Ben Carson, Author and Neurosurgeon]

UNDERSTANDING LIMITATIONS

"I am confident that the Creator, who has begun such a great work among you, will not stop in mid-design but will keep perfecting you."

[Philippians 1:6a The Voice]

The final 1991 report of the U.S National Commission on Children reflects our current 21st century single parenting landscape. The report observes that:

"The dramatic social, economic, and demographic changes have revolutionised the family system. Single parenthood has become increasingly common, and within many two-parent families there have been profound changes in traditional roles and relationships. Many values related to family life have been called into question. Yet the family remains the best institution for raising children and for giving them a sense of identity of their place in the world. The family is the basic social unit of our culture, and society suffers when families are weak and ineffectual. Unfortunately many children do not have two loving parents. Many single parents would not have chosen to raise the children alone. While the nation should strive to create a social and economic context in which strong, two-parent families can form and stay together, it must never fail to reach out and protect single parent families as well. Many single parents make extraordinary efforts

to raise children under difficult circumstances. Their success is a tribute to their commitment and hard work and to the loving attention they give their children. As parents, they deserve society's full support.'[205]

Children raised by single-parent mothers probably fare worse on many dimensions, including school achievement, social and emotional development, health and success in the labour market. They are at a higher likelihood of abuse and neglect (especially from live-in boyfriends), possibly become teen parents and are at a lower chance of graduating from high school or college.[206]

Not all children raised in a single-parent family suffer these adverse outcomes; it is merely that the risks are higher for them. Children who end up in a single-parent family as a result of the death of one parent do not show the same poor outcomes as children brought up by single parents due to divorce or born outside marriage. The presence of two parents in a child's life is vital as they both play critical complementary roles in the psychological and emotional development of a child. Joint custody, in recognition of the importance of both parents, is the most common order granted by family court judges.

Various helpful steps can be employed to mitigate situations where the other parent chooses not to be involved. First, ensure that the other parent has explicitly confirmed that they do not want to be involved and do not just assume their absence says this. Secondly, recognise that your behaviour may be a significant contributing factor to the alienation of the other parent. Thirdly, link the child to a positive role model other than yourself, so they have another person in their life. Fourthly, accept your limitations and recognise the fact that children benefit from good role models of both sexes.

Sociologists who have researched single mothers of different races, ages and classes have found that single parents are rarely mothers raising their children single-handedly. Instead, they have dedicated networks of friends and relatives and neighbours who care and assist them and their children and have been an integral part of their lives for years.

"Children are our second chance to have a great parent-child relationship."

[Laura Schlessinger, Author and Talk Show Host]

MANAGING CONFLICTS

"He heals the broken-hearted and binds up their wounds
[healing their pain and comforting their sorrow]"

[Psalm 147:3 Amplified Bible]

Parents must exercise self-control during conflicts or hostile situations or when relationships breakdown. Domestic violence and abusive behaviour are toxic and detrimental to children. Responsible parenting includes respectful and courteous interaction with the child's other parent. Unfortunately, some vengeful parents go as far as accusing their ex-partner of not being fit to be a parent, which may often lead to child protection investigations.

Child psychologist Penelope Leach in her new book '*Family Breakdown: Helping Children Hang on Both Their Parents*', describes vengeful mothers as those who tear fathers from their children's lives. She suggests that since children are desperate not to hurt parents going through a divorce, these children will say whatever they know she (as it is usually the mother) wants to hear. These children may even say they no longer want any contact with Daddy – when actually, they still love him.[207]

"Whenever you're in conflict with someone, there is one factor that can make a difference between damaging your relationship and deepening it. That factor is attitude"

[William James, American Philosopher and Psychologist]

PARENTAL BURN-OUT

"Don't be pulled in different directions or worried about a thing. Be saturated in prayer throughout each day, offering your faith-filled requests before God with overflowing gratitude. Tell him every detail of your life"

[Philippians 4:6 The Passion Translation]

Until recently, studies carried out on parental exhaustion focused on parents with sick children. Parenting is a tough grind, and to a greater extent when it involves a child with mental health issues. This type of parenting requires extra effort, especially if the child is at risk, struggling, or making less progress than other children. However, situations where exhaustion happens as a result of being physically and emotionally overburdened by one's parental role (regardless of the child's condition), is gaining soaring interest. This raises the question on how to keep going without becoming exhausted? The first traceable account of parental burn-out dates from 1983 in the testimony of Edith Lanstrom in her book *'Christian Parent Burn-out'*.[208]

When the daily stress of parenting becomes chronic it can turn into parental burnout, an intense exhaustion that leads parents to feel detached from their children and unsure of their parenting abilities, according to research published in *Clinical Psychological Science*. This type of burn-out can have serious consequences for both parent and child, increasing parental neglect, harm, and thoughts about escape.[209]

A study published in *'Frontiers in Psychology'*, surveyed responses from approximately 2,000 parents to check whether or not parental burn-out existed. The study examined the precursor of exhaustion and burn-out and provided practical advice to parents about how they can prevent burn-out. The study found that close to 13% of the parents surveyed, 12.9% of mothers and 11.6% of fathers had what the researchers called "high burn-out."[210]

The study further found that these parents felt exhausted, less productive, less competent and emotionally withdrawn – qualities that are similar to professional burn-out. The study also surprisingly found that burn-out was more strongly connected with highly educated parents, who may have, to a remarkable degree, very high expectations of themselves and their children.[211]

Avoiding parental burn-out requires efforts that increase resources and decrease risk factors. Experts noted that these efforts include consistent self-care, taking time out to relax, rest, and recharge, establishing secure support networks for yourself, and having a trustworthy therapeutic team for your child. Energise yourself with the most potent motivator – your love for your child.

"Burn-out is what happens
when you try to avoid being human for too long."

[Michael Gungor,
Award Winning Musician and Founder of Bloom]

MUTUAL PARENTING

Drawing from her work with families for nearly 40 years, Penelope Leach, on mutual parenting writes:

"Mutual parenting means that they are jointly committed to putting their children's wellbeing first and to protecting them as far as they can from the ill-effects of the family break-up. The most important word in that sentence is 'jointly'. Many mothers say that they put their children first, and many fathers say likewise – but not many of them credit each other with doing so. However much a mother may wish it weren't so, her ex is the children's biological father and should never be airbrushed out of their lives. The most difficult aspect of mutual parenting is that it requires frequent communication when you'd probably prefer to have nothing whatsoever to do with each other. One way or another, your joint

responsibilities will have to include making it possible - and enjoyable - for children to be closely in touch with each parent.'[212]

Leach further recommends the following questions to parents who are having trouble deciding if they can manage mutual parenting:

- Would you phone your ex-partner or expect him to call you in the middle of the night if there was an emergency?
- Would you discuss with him or expect him to discuss with you any worrying child behaviour?
- Would you do your best or expect him to do his best to make the transfer from one parent to the other at the beginning and end of visits easy for the children?
- Would you cover for him or expect him to cover for you if one of you had forgotten a sports day or school play and couldn't turn up?
- Would you pay attention to each other's views on critical educational decisions, such as choosing a school?
- Would you pay attention to each other's views on managing children's behaviour (such as how best to handle tantrums) and try to agree on routines (such as bedtimes) and limits?

A 'Yes' answer to all or most of these questions would indicate there is a foundation for mutual parenting.

"Every child is a different kind of flower, and all together, they make this world a beautiful garden."

[Author Unknown]

FINDING SUPPORT

As a single parent, you could accept help from trusted friends and relatives willing to lend a hand; suggest "swap" childcare arrangements with other parents; encourage older children to help with basic house chores; plan and organise in advance, especially for school items and significant shopping; learn new skills that could assist in your day to day life; do not discuss grown-up issues with children; get professional advice on your finances and what you are entitled to as a single parent; call a parenting helpline if necessary and talk with a professional. In responding to out of control children, single parents can get help and assistance from a variety of sources, including the child's school, local church or charity, social service agencies and mental health professionals. If they feel their life is spiralling out of control, they can seek assistance from organisations that offer help and support to single-parent families.

CONCLUSION

Single parenting has its unique challenges, but if a parent is managing the family without the other partner, it can prove particularly challenging. Single parents need help and support, and at the same time, they need an open mind and open arms to let others love them, and their child – with such backing, single-parent families can thrive.

At times, it can be hard managing the practical things in life, such as balancing work and home, different school runs, cooking and chores. You might not always get the parenting balance right. Do not be too hard on yourself. If your child is of sufficient maturity to understand, try to be honest with your discussions without going into unnecessary details. As a general rule, endeavour to keep grown-up issues out of bound with children. Some adult problems – like financial worries, infidelity or conflict with a former partner or the other parent – can make children feel very apprehensive. Use adult support networks, and talk things over with other adults, rather than use your children for 'adult emotional' support. Community institutions – schools, faith-based organisations, charities and employers have an important role in creating an environment that is supportive of single parents and children.

"You are the breadwinner, the head-of-household, the rule enforcer and the privilege-taker. You're the appointment-maker and prescription-filler, the grocery-getter and the chef, the mechanic and the handyman.
It's going to suck at first, honestly. Not gonna lie. Your list of to-dos is going to outnumber the hours in your day. But guess what?
Somehow, you figure it out. I don't know how it happens, but you just do. You find the extra thirty minutes you need, you scrape up an additional $100 at the end of the month, and you create a whole new realm of time management and you get stuff done."

[Jennifer Ball, Writer and Mom]

Notes

....
....
....
....
....
....
....
....
....
....
....
....
....
....
....
....
....

CHAPTER 10

MANAGING CONFLICT – BEST INTEREST PRINCIPLE

> *Grandparents are proud of their grandchildren, and children should be proud of their parents.*
>
> [PROVERBS 17:6 CONTEMPORARY ENGLISH VERSION]

BEST INTEREST PRINCIPLE

The United Nation Convention on the Rights of the Child (UNCRC) is a complete statement of children's rights ever produced, and the most widely ratified human rights treaty in history. The treaty, which is the basis of all of the work UNICEF does, sets out the political, civil, economic, social, health and cultural rights of all children, regardless of race, religion or abilities. Article 3 of the Convention places an obligation on member states to observe:

"The best interests of the child as a primary consideration in all actions concerning children, whether undertaken by public or private social welfare institutions, courts of law, administrative authorities or legislative bodies."[213]

Although the UNCRC does not offer a precise definition of 'best interests' or an explicit list of factors relevant to it, the Convention however states that 'best interests' generally refers to a child's general well-being, taking into account a wide range of factors including the need for a safe environment, emotional stability, family relationships, development and identity needs. Till date, there still exist covert and overt conflicts between professionals and parents about the definition of the best interest of children. The 'Best Interests' standard is child-specific and not necessarily a universal standard that can be applied across the globe since different conceptions of childhood exist across the world and 'best interests' is likely to change depending on the situation. According to a 2000 study by Pruett and colleagues, the very definition of *'the best interest of the child'* differs markedly between children and parents on the one hand, and legal practitioners and the judiciary on the other."[214]

The UK government previously maintained a reservation to the UNCRC by holding the view that the Convention applied only to UK children and not to foreign national children when regarding matters of immigration control. However, as of November 2008, this reservation no longer applies. The Immigration Act 2009 contains a mandatory duty in section 55 – an obligation on those making immigration decisions to safeguard and promote the welfare of children.[215]

Parenting is often the happiest aspect of many relationships. However, when divorce, unfortunately, becomes necessary, decisions about child custody can be the most difficult and heart-wrenching ones to make. A fundamental doctrine of family law is that judicial decisions are made in the *'best interests' of the child.* This ensures the protection of a child's best interests by all parties concerned during high-conflict child custody cases. When marriages break down, each family goes through the crisis in different ways. Some may deal with it effectively while others descend too quickly into long drawn out legal conflict.

*"History will judge us by the difference
we make in the everyday lives of children."*

**[Nelson Mandela,
Anti-apartheid Leader and Former South African President]**

THE JUDGMENT OF KING SOLOMON

The story of King Solomon's judgement is found in 1 Kings 3:16-28. An extract of the text reads:

"Then the king said, "Bring me a sword." So they brought a sword before the king. And the king said, "Divide the living child in two, and give half to one, and half to the other." Then the woman whose son was living spoke to the king, for she yearned with compassion for her son; and she said, "O my lord, give her the living child, and by no means kill him! But the other said,

"Let him be neither mine nor yours, but divide him." So the king answered and said, "Give the first woman the living child, and by no means kill him; she is his mother."[216]

The Judgment of King Solomon is a story that culminates with a ruling on a case brought before the royal courts by two women both claiming maternity of a child. During the hearing, both women made submissions to King Solomon claiming biological parenthood over the same child. Faced with the difficulty of identifying the actual mother of the child; the King commanded that the child be divided in two with a sword and then shared equally among them. One of the women spoke up, pleading with the King to spare the life of the child and to give it to the other woman. Solomon determined this woman, willing to forego her claim *'for the best interest of the child'*, was probably the parent. She preferred that the child should be given to her rival, rather than killed. The King reasoned that a biological parent would typically have a more significant concern about the welfare of their child than a stranger. After hearing the replies from the two women, Solomon knew that even if his assumption was wrong, he could make the correct decision according to the best interest of the child.

Since the days of Solomon, child custody battles have required extraordinary wisdom and insight. Issues of custody and parenting after divorce are similarly complicated, but in any event, the application of the 'best interest' principle of the child must be at the forefront of considerations. Sometimes the most disputable issue in a divorce is not how to divide the parties' cash or assets, but rather how custody over the children should be decided.

"If we don't stand up for children, then we don't stand for much."

[Marian Wright Edelman, Children's Right Activist]

BEST INTEREST AFTER SEPARATION

"See that no one pays back evil for evil,
but always try to do good to each other and to everyone else."

[1 Thessalonians 5:15 The Living Bible]

Decades ago, a misconception began to circulate that if parents are unhappy, the children are also unhappy. So divorce could benefit both parent and child. *"What is good for mother and father is good for the children,"* it was assumed. However, an enormous amount of studies on divorce and children point to the fact that behavioural and emotional issues are common in children when their parents are fighting or separating. Clinical Psychologist, JoAnne Pedro-Carroll in Encyclopaedia on Early Childhood Development, writes:

"There are a number of techniques that parents can use to protect children from the toxic effects of intense conflict. Among these are reframing their relationship into a respectful, business-like partnership for parenting. In so doing, parents agree to set clear boundaries and ground rules for interaction that include respecting the child's right to a healthy relationship with both parents, when it is safe to do so, establishing and abiding by an agenda for all meetings to discuss children and other matters pertaining

to the divorce, not using the children as messengers or informants, and
keeping children's transitions between parents safe and respectful"[217]

A report by the Early Intervention Foundation Published in
2016, found that:

"Unresolved conflict between parents has a potent influence on children's
early development, mental health and future life chances."[218]

The rate of divorce has increased exponentially since the early
20th century. In 1885, there were 300 divorces in England and Wales.
A century later, the figure was 160,000. In the UK today, around
42% of marriages end in divorce, and the peak for splits is between
the fourth and eighth years when couples are most likely to have
young children.[219]

A study by the University of York found that the children of
divorced parents are more devastated by the arguments that took
place during the marriage than by the separation itself. Watching
fights at home, means they are thirty per cent more likely to develop
behavioural issues following a divorce than those children with
married parents.[220]

A University of London research review on the impact
of divorce and separation on outcomes for children concluded
unequivocally that those children whose parents separate have
significantly greater risk factors than those whose parents
remain together, for a wide range of adverse outcomes in social,
psychological, and physical development. These factors include:
growing up in households with lower incomes and poorer housing;

experiencing behavioural problems; performing less well in school and gaining fewer educational qualifications; needing more medical treatment; leaving school and home when young; becoming sexually active, pregnant or a parent at an early age; reporting more depressive symptoms and higher levels of smoking, drinking and other drug use during adolescence and adulthood.[221]

Besides, some children do well despite parental separation; such as, when parental separation brings to an end an aversive family situation, for example when there is a high level of marital or relationship conflict or when the relationship between parent and child is of a poor quality.

Social science research points to the effects of family breakdown later in adult life. A child's position in a divorce is very different from that of parents. Once the parents decide to separate, their goal is to conclude the relationship and withdraw their emotional investment from one another. Divorce, however, does not dissolve a child's emotional ties with his or her parents. The process of recovery from divorce for a child involves the psychological re-structuring of the family, not its dissolution.

"Children are the living messages we send to a time we will not see."

[John F. Kennedy, Former U.S. President]

PARENTAL ALIENATION SYNDROME

Psychiatrist Richard Gardner developed the concept of *"Parental Alienation"* in 1985 to describe the process and result of psychological 'manipulation' or 'programming' of a child by one parent who is the object of a campaign of targeted hatred or denigration of the other parent.

A precursor to this manipulation is a phenomenon known as implacable hostility – first used by the court of appeal in 1984 to describe the mother's 'invincible opposition' to contact. It is defined as an attitude shown by one parent to another in denying access to, or contact with, their child after separation or divorce, or also defined as an effort to create unwarranted fear, disrespect or hostility towards the other parent and to interfere with the child's relationship with that parent. At some stage, children caught up at the centre of implacable hostility between parents may become resistant to make contact with the absent parent. The 'manipulated' child will present a seemingly genuine, strong wish not to have contact with the parent from whom they have been alienated.

Another precursor to this manipulation is the *'Malicious Mother Syndrome'*. Sometimes, partners stressed by divorce may become malicious in order to punish the other parent. Mothers who behave this way are said to have the *'malicious mother syndrome'* – a pattern of abnormal behaviour where one parent acts purposefully and vengefully towards the other during or following a divorce in an attempt to alienate children from the other parent, usually the father. This syndrome was first theorised in 1995 by Psychologist Dr Ira Turkat in a study published in the Journal of Family Violence.[222]

Since Turkat's 1995 paper, most psychologists and psychiatrists consider a more appropriate name – *'Parental Alienation Syndrome'* – since both mothers and fathers can be capable of such actions. Many psychologists have written about *"Parental Alienation Syndrome,"* but the phenomenon is still gaining popularity. While there is still a debate over the exact definition and measurement of parental alienation, there is a consensus that alienating behaviours sit on a spectrum of mild to severe with differing impact on individual children, the most damaging being the child aligns themselves with the alienating parent and rejects their relationship with their other parent without legitimate justification.

Dr Edward Kruk, in Psychology Today, reports that:

"The biopsychosocial-spiritual effects of parental alienation are devastating. For both the alienated parent and child, the removal and denial of contact in the absence of neglect or abuse constitutes cruel and unusual treatment."[223]

Anthony Douglas, the Chief Executive of the Children and Family Court Advisory and Support Service (Cafcass), issued a warning against the danger of *"parental alienation"* – responsible for around 80 per cent of the most challenging cases that come before the family courts. According to Douglas, divorced parents who *"brainwash"* their children against their ex-partners are guilty of *"abuse."* He further maintains that the deliberate and intentional manipulation of a child by one parent in opposition to the other parent has become so frequent in family breakdowns that it should be treated like any other type of neglect or child abuse. The way children are treated after a relationship has broken up, is just as powerful a public health issue as smoking or drinking.[224]

Ross Jones of Families Need Fathers, states:

"We see lots of cases like this. Such conflicts of loyalty for the children do seem to be a common feature of high-conflict separations. It's a huge problem for many users of our service and one which receives very little attention."[225]

Ross Jones further recognises that children who are in the centre of such extreme conflicts of loyalty between their parents may suffer short-term damage in anxiety and depression and long-term difficulties in education, mental illness, and their adult relationships.

A high proportion of children of separating or divorcing couples live with their mothers; so the controlling parent is likely going to be the woman and the alienated and undermined parent is highly likely to be the man. Nonetheless, it is possible, however, for women to be on the receiving end, in cases where the children live mostly with the man.

In a TED talk, Dr Harman at the University of Colorado says that parental alienation is a form of domestic violence.[226]

"Parental Alienation is an emotional act of violence that is aimed at an adult, but critically wounds a child."

[Steve Maraboli, Behavioural Scientist and Author]

Strategies of Alienating Parents:[227]

Sociologist and social worker, Edward Kruk in *Family Science Review* article '*Parental Alienation as a Form of Emotional Child Abuse*,' outlines some of the strategies on the part of the alienating parent to foster the child's rejection of the other parent. Such strategies include: bad-mouthing; limiting contact; erasing the other parent from the child's life and mind; forcing the child to reject the other parent; creating the impression that the other parent is dangerous; forcing the child to choose between the parents by threatening withdrawal of affection; belittling and limiting contact with the extended family of the targeted parent; forcing child to reject the target parent; asking the child to spy on the target parent; asking the child to keep secrets from the target parent; referring to the target parent by first name; referring to a step-parent as "Mum" or "Dad" and encouraging child to do the same; withholding medical, academic, and other important information from target parent; keeping target parent's name off medical, academic, and other relevant documents; changing child's name to remove association with target parent; undermining the authority of the target parent.

Despite the dominance of gynocentrism in our culture over the last few decades, a comprehensive agreement on children's needs between parents and the equal responsibilities of mother and father is now securely established in place in the U.K. and many other countries. The amendments to the Children and Family Act 2014 require that when making child arrangements orders, the courts should presume that the involvement of both separating parents improves the welfare of the child. Nevertheless, it is almost impossible to control a separating parent who is not interested in meeting the emotional needs of their child but is primarily focused to exacting revenge upon a former spouse or partner by frustrating and obstructing the other parent's relationship with their child.

Inter-parental relationships have a significant influence on children's long-term psychological outcomes. In most cases, a child's 'best interests' is closely intertwined with maintaining a close, loving and consistent relationship with both parents. What a child needs is to maintain a healthy and strong relationship with both parents, and to be shielded from parental conflicts. Objectively, every child should be striving towards maintaining a good relationship with both parents, albeit necessary deviations which may arise when issues concerning safety are involved. The National Society for the Prevention of Cruelty to Children (NSPCC) observes that separation may involve bad feelings between the parents (and their families). Children can pick up on this, which may make them confused or unhappy – or even blame themselves for the break-up."[228]

To support children during a separation, the NSPCC recommends that: parents remind them that they are loved by both parents; be honest when talking about it but keep in mind the child's age and understanding; avoid blame – don't share any negative feelings that adults have about each other; let them know they can talk about their feelings – whether sad, confused or angry, and listen more and answer questions will help them open up.

"Affirming words from moms and dads are like light switches.
Speak a word of affirmation at the right moment in a child's life and it's
like lighting up a whole roomful of possibilities."

[Gary Smalley, Author and Family Counsellor]

A Balance Perspective

Alienated parents feel the rejection and antagonism from their children who give the impression of being cold-hearted. Notwithstanding, it is of considerable significance to understand the hatred from the child's point of view. The children have the feeling that the targeted or alienated parent has abandoned them. They have been 'programmed' to wrongly believe that the parent they are rejecting is unloving, unsafe and does not care for them, and has rejected them. Accordingly, the primary responsibility of the alienated parent must consistently be one of emotional availability, absolute safety, and loving-kindness. Being there for the child and demonstrating unconditional love, is the first response that alienated parents can give their children, even in the face of the sad reality that this may not be enough to bring back the child.

"Other things may change us, but we start and end with the family."

[Anthony Brandt, Author and Editor]

VENGEFUL MOTHERS SYNDROME

Child psychologist Penelope Leach in *'Family Breakdown: Helping Children Hang on to Both Their Parents'* describes the unspoken scandal of vengeful mothers who tear fathers from their children's lives.[229]

Avoiding the vengeful parent trap is one of the best gifts to offer children. Penelope Leach, in her book '*Keeping Parenting and Partnership Apart*', observes that the best way to manage the break-up of a family with minimal long-term harm to children is to set yourselves to support the relationship each of you have with each of your children, and protect them from the failure of the relationship between the two of you. That's not an easy thing to do if you are overwhelmed with hurt and fury at the other parent. Although it may seem downright impossible, it is the most important effort you can make for your children because it will affect every aspect of their lives both during and after your separation and divorce.[230]

DESTRUCTIVE CONFLICTS

Inter-parental disagreements and conflicts are a normal part of intimate relationships – but if handled constructively pose few risks for children. However, frequent and intense conflicts can affect the ability of parents to form healthy and rewarding relationships with children. Repeated exposure to marital conflicts leads children to experience their parents as frightening, and older children are more likely to become more aggressive and learn poor behavioural and social skills.[231]

E. Mark Cummings and Patrick Davies in their book '*Marital Conflict and Children: An Emotional Security Perspective*', describe the child-destructive strategies that parents employ against each other, such as: verbal aggression like name-calling, threats of abandonment and insults; physical aggressive behaviour like pushing and hitting; silent tactics like avoidance, storming off/out, sulking, or withdrawing; and, capitulation – the action of ceasing to resist, which resembles a solution but isn't a genuine solution.[232]

When parents often use antagonistic strategies towards each other, some children may become troubled, anxious, worried, and hopeless. Other children may respond outwardly with anger, aggressive behaviour and develop character problems at school or at home. This stressful situation at home can interfere with their ability to pay attention, which creates learning and academic difficulties at school. Most children brought up in an environment of destructive conflict have problems forming healthy and balanced relationships with their peers. According to Cummings, when children observe mild to moderate conflict that involves support, compromise, and positive emotions at home, they learn better social skills, self-esteem, and emotional security, which can help parent-child relations and how well the child does in school. However, when children witness a fight and see parents resolving it, they are happier than they were before they saw it – this reassures children that parents can work things through. In conclusion, a University of Illinois study review found that children in high-conflict families, whether intact or divorced, tend to do worse than children of parents that get along. It also noted that children in non-conflict single-parent families fare better than children in conflict two-parent families. The battle between parents preceding divorce affects children negatively, while post-divorce conflict has a powerful influence on children's adjustment.[233]

BEST INTEREST: PARENTS OR CHILDREN?

"He will lead children and parents to love each other more,
so that when I come, I won't bring doom to the land."

[Malachi 4:6 Contemporary English Version]

Emotions run very high when parents engage in custody battles under the guise that it is in the child's best interest, but is that always true? According to the Encyclopaedia on Early Childhood Development, Clinical Psychologist JoAnne Pedro-Carroll, in the article *'How Parents Can Help Children Cope with Separation/Divorce,* **writes**:

"The three biggest factors that impact children's well-being during and after their parents' separation or divorce are potentially within parents' control: the degree and duration of hostile conflict, the quality of parenting provided over time, and the quality of the parent-child relationship. Underlying these, of course, are parents' own well-being and ability to function effectively. By learning how to manage their conflict, parent effectively, and nurture warm and loving relationships with their children, parents can have a powerful, positive effect on their children, even as they undergo multiple difficult changes in their own lives.'[234]

To foster their parental identity, some parents create an expectation that children choose sides. In more extreme situations, 'Parental Alienation Syndrome' and 'Malicious Parent Syndrome' could be deployed as tactics where children are manipulated by one parent to hate the other; the outcomes of such actions may lead to emotional combustion from which recovery for the child will prove very challenging even into adulthood. These often high-stress and contentious events can cause extreme undesirable behaviour on the part of those involved and the necessity of facing some of the less-attractive aspects of oneself such as revenge, bitterness and great anger. This cocktail of emotions can cloud a parents' ability to separate feelings and the needs of a child. Under such circumstances, parents may think it is impossible to cooperate. For many, it is the hardest time of their lives – but if they want their children's welfare, parents must create a tolerable situation in the best interest of the children, and not in their interest. Making quality decisions for the benefit of children is an integral part of parenting. While there is no suggestion that parents do not sincerely believe that what they want is in the best interest of their children, it is important to identify the best approach to help both parents and children. Parents should avoid conflict and keep a friendly relationship despite their disagreements, for the benefit of the children, and children should not be involved in loyalty conflicts between their parents. Children need the assurance that the care of each parent will not be interrupted and that their emotional, psychological, social, moral and spiritual needs are of paramount importance.

Every child has the fundamental human right to a healthy relationship with both parents. While it may be appropriate under extreme circumstances for parents to stay away from each other, alternative arrangements should be in place which guarantees the child's access to both parents. Parental interest should never trump the interest of the child. The same rule applies, such that denigrating one parent or fostering the child's rejection of the other parent will never be in the best interest of the child. Children are not weapons in parental conflicts, and should not be sacrificed on the altar of parental 'selfish' interest. Pedro-Carroll gives guidelines on how parents can strengthen their relationships with their children. These guidelines include committing to one-on-one time with each child, affirming their strengths and reinforcing positive behaviours; communicating well and frequently with children, especially listening to their feelings and responding with empathy; establishing new family rituals and routines that strengthen the bonds between parents and children; avoid rushing into new relationships.[235]

"It is easier to build strong children than to repair broken men."

[Frederick Douglass, Social Reformer and Statesman]

BLENDED OR STEP FAMILIES

*"If it is possible, as far as it depends on you,
live at peace with everyone."*

[Romans 12: 18, New International Version]

Blended families also called stepfamilies are on the rise globally. They are formed when two families come together with children from one or both of the parents' previous relationships. This new family has members from different backgrounds with different rules, histories, traditions, and expectations. Children need help as they go through this transition into a new blended family life. Cooperation, patience, and communication are essential in this transition. Blended families come with both challenging and rewarding experiences for both parents and children. Common challenges include different family traditions; helping kids adjust to change; sibling rivalry; compromising with parent disciplinary styles; and managing age differences.

Recommendations for Forming Step Families

- Do not to try to force your children to like your new relationship. They need time to come to terms with their new circumstance.
- Make time for your children who may have anxiety about not being as important as before. Help them feel secure by spending time with them.
- Reassure them that although the other children are valuable parts of their new family, they will not be replaced.

- Approach discipline with caution. As a general rule, do not try too quickly to assert yourself, instead, agree on ground rules with your new partner.
- Develop an equitable, loving relationship with stepchildren.
- Encourage and insist that children preserve regular, consistent communication with the parent living in the other home.
- Ensure that consequences and rewards are equal for all the children, no matter how it "used to work" before the two families got together.
- Politely inform your former partner (if any) about the change in your new family arrangements. Your former partner may need some time to adjust to the unique situation.
- Work together as a team and agree on your approach to parenting. This may involve agreeing on general rules about essential matters.
- No matter how difficult things seem at first, with plenty of love and patience, you can develop a successful bond with your new stepchildren.
- Finally, but most importantly, effective parent-stepparent relationships begin with healthy marriages.

There is no 'one size fits all' family dynamic. Stepfamilies are merely another type of family structure and bring strengths as well as weaknesses. It takes patience to develop a relationship with stepchildren and for parents to build a new family. Stepfamilies provide an environment where children gain a wider family with new friendships and grow into adult life with a considerable capacity to adapt. They can enhance their experiences by learning to be more tolerant of different family lifestyles.

The American Psychological Association article *'Making Stepfamilies Work,'* states that couples should anticipate parental changes and decisions by discussing the role that the stepparents will play in raising their new spouse's children, as well as household rule changes.[236]

Even when a couple lived together before marriage, the children are likely to respond to the stepparent differently after remarriage because the stepparent has taken up an official parental role. Successful stepparent-stepchild relationships are those where stepparents focus on the development of a warm, friendly and interactive style relationship with the stepchild. Once the foundations of mutual respect and affection are entrenched, stepparents who then try to take the role of a disciplinarian are less likely to meet resentment from the stepchildren.[237]

"The first happiness of a child is to know that he is loved."

[Don Bosco, Priest, Educator and Writer]

CONFLICT RESOLUTION IN RELATIONSHIPS

"Understand this, my beloved brothers and sisters. Let everyone be quick to hear [be a careful, thoughtful listener], slow to speak [a speaker of carefully chosen words and], slow to anger [patient, reflective, forgiving]"

[James 1:19 Amplified Bible]

Conflicts and disagreements are inevitable in life. They are an essential part of any type relationship – professional, family and marital. By design, men and women are 'wired' differently; more so, different family backgrounds bring different traditions, habits, temperaments and mannerisms into relationships. Through conflict, we test our commitment and also identify our strengths and weaknesses. When adequately resolved, conflicts can present opportunities for growth and improvement; however, when poorly managed, they can easily become a sword of Damocles. Suggestions to help resolve conflicts and disagreement include:

- Identifying the best time to talk – when both of you are well-rested and able to focus.
- Focusing on the main issue – speak calmly, factually and respectfully. Take one thing at a time and do not bring up unrelated issues.
- Avoid throwing accusations and pointing fingers – this will make the other person defensive.
- Listening actively – it helps you understand. Pay close attention to body language as it may reveal cues.
- Win the person and lose the argument – choose happiness over being right.

CONCLUSION

Happy Marriage for Happy Kids

In his study on families, David Code, drawing from the latest research in neuroscience, published his book *To Raise Happy Kids,*

Put Your Marriage First'. Code argues that an over-focus on children creates demanding, entitled children and anxious, exhausted parents, and those who desire the best for their children should spend less time seeking to be the perfect parent and make great effort to be the ideal spouse.[238]

Code's book addresses a typical, damaging pattern in marriages and helps couples reduce the distance in their relationship, thereby reducing the emotional baggage projected onto the children. Code observes that today's number one myth about parenting is that the more attention parents give their kids, the better they will turn out. But Parents have gone too far: over-focusing on children is doing them more harm than good. Parents today are too quick to sacrifice their lives and their marriages for their children. Most parents have created child-centred families, where the children hold priority over parent's time, energy and attention for each other.

Code holds the view that today's children are troubled because they receive too much attention. He writes:

"That's why children seem to have many more problems nowadays than we did, or our parents did. By killing ourselves to provide a perfect, trauma-free childhood for our children, we're wasting our energy. The greatest gift you can give your children is to have a fulfilling marriage yourself."

What if children have issues and problems that demand a parent's full attention? Code responds:

"Many parents believe the more attention they give their children, the better they will turn out. But our children are no healthier or happy that they were a generation ago. In fact, today's children are more troubled because

we have started 'marrying' our children instead of our spouses. We claim we are too busy to spend time with our spouses, but actually many parents have shifted their passion from their spouses to their children. We may be over-focusing on our children to escape an unhappy marriage. But if we find it easier to be with our children than with our spouses, our children pay a heavy price for that. As spouses grow more distant in their marriage, they project their distress and needs unto their children".

Although things may appear calm on the surface, children are mainly bearing the burden of misplaced stress from their parents' distant relationships. These children are under tremendous pressure to fulfil the emotional needs of their parents. Code further observes that the greatest gift parents can give their children is to have a fulfilling marriage themselves. Parents must regain the balance between tending their marriage and nurturing their children. When marriages meet intimacy needs, then parents can stop marrying their children. This frees up children to establish their own identity, learn self-reliance, and become more independent adults. The parent's marriage can also set a great example for their children's future relationships.

"Your children make it impossible to regret your past.
They're its finest fruits. Sometimes the only ones."

[Anna Quindlen, Author and Journalist]

CHAPTER 11

―――――― ◦ ☽⁄ ◦ ――――――

SOCIAL MEDIA – BLESSING OR CURSE?

> *Don't copy the behaviour and customs of this world, but let God transform you into a new person by changing the way you think. Then you will learn to know God's will for you, which is good and pleasing and perfect.*
>
> [ROMANS 12:2 NEW LIVING TRANSLATION]

WHAT IS SOCIAL MEDIA?

Social media generally refers to online platforms, websites and applications (apps) that people use to connect and interact with others, share media content, and form social networks. Some of the most well-known platforms include Facebook, Twitter, Whatsapp, Tumblr, Instagram, Pinterest, Skype, YouTube, Viber, and Snapchat. Facebook is the biggest and possibly most powerful social network in the world, with 1.55 billion active monthly users.

Online games also provide social media spaces for young people to communicate with others who share similar gaming interests.

Online social networking sites have become a central feature of daily life, with millions of social interactions being played out daily in the virtual space. It hosts a broad diversity of human experiences that affect parenting in many ways. Parenting in the social media age is not straightforward. It is not uncommon to focus on the negative aspects of social media – but there are many positives too. Social media allows us to connect with friends, make charitable donations, and receive information on global events. It enables professionals, businesses, and organisations that seek greater recognition and identification.

Before being carried away with the benefits that social media introduces into family life, there is need for precautionary measures to establish appropriate safeguards. A disturbing pattern has also emerged where parents use social media to shame their children as a form of punishment.

Alarming stories of cyber bullying, suicide, social media abuse, and cat-fishing may tempt parents to forbid their children from using it. Our screens can become damaging to our mental health as a result of spending too much time on these websites. However, social media offers huge benefits — it connects kids to peers and provides an outlet for exploring new ideas. Parents use social media for support and to connect with other parents, to ask for advice and help with parenting dilemmas. They also use it to unwind, relax, and for recreational purposes.

There are parenting benefits of using social media platforms. New research is proving that amazing things can happen when children connect, share and learn online. One study by UNICEF reports that spending some time on social media is beneficial and that digital technology seems to be good for children's social relationships.[239]

Social media has a broad and diverse use. These include:

- **Online profiles:** Most social media sites demand that users set up a profile, which usually requires personal details, address, e-mail, interests, and in some instances photos.

- **Friends:** Depending on the platform tool employed, users "follow" or "request" to be friends with people they know. They may also use it to discover new friends.

- **Messaging/Chats:** Using instant messaging over the internet or between smartphones to send messages (e.g., Facebook Messenger, iMessage, WhatsApp).

- **Walls and boards:** Sites on social media permit people to post or send messages in various ways. On Facebook, for example, messages are posted to a "wall". The user's privacy settings will determine whether some messages are visible to the public or whether they can only be visible to followers or friends.

- **Photo and video sharing:** Some social networking sites permit users to upload pictures and videos, including the option to share live videos.

- **Playing games:** Children visit online sites to play games, alone or with their friends. Some apps may contain product promotion or advertising.

Social media dynamics and the connected world of children can be challenging for parents because children do not interact online in the same manner and are not necessarily using the same platforms as their parents.

"The Internet is becoming the town square for
the global village of tomorrow."

[Bill Gates,
Philanthropist and Principal founder of Microsoft Corporation]

THE RISK OF SOCIAL MEDIA

"Making the very most of your time [on earth, recognizing and taking
advantage of each opportunity and using it with wisdom and diligence],
because the days are [filled with] evil."
[Ephesians 5:16 Amplified Bible]

The behemoth, referred to as social media, holds a dark side. It feeds profusely on the pervasive cravings for attention, recognition, love, excitement, and the human desire to connect with other people. After all, human beings are social animals. Excess and undisciplined social networking can produce loneliness and depression because cyber friends cannot fill the void of real people and one-on-one interactions. Apple CEO Tim Cook while attending a coding-related event at Harlow College, England, said to a Guardian reporter:

"I don't have a kid, but I have a nephew that I put some boundaries on... there are some things that I won't allow. I don't want them on a social network."[240]

Apple Founder, Steve Jobs once said he did not want his children to even own an iPad — the reason being that excessive use of digital devices and social media is harmful to the health of children and teenagers. A study in the journal Emotion, published by the American Psychological Association (APA), found that too much screen time is damaging to the mental health of children. Just one hour of screen time a day is linked to a rise in unhappiness levels in young people.[241]

Social media, like any other form of social engagement, does not come without risks. Some of the most basic risks include: spending unlimited time online and being detached from the real world; being the victim of cyber bullying; detrimental effects on your online reputation; having your private details shared online; being threatened, harassed or stalked by someone whose attention you do not want; and being the victim of an online scam.

The dangers of excessive use of social media (Facebook, YouTube, Twitter and Instagram) have been well documented. Studies have established a link between too much social media use and low self-esteem, feeling isolated, negative mental health and feeling increasingly unhappy. It has been found that social media promotes an environment in which people compare their realistic offline selves to the filtered, impeccable and edited online versions of others; thereby, damaging their mental well-being and self-esteem. They believe that other users are happier and more successful than they are, especially when they do not know them very well in real life.[242]

Facebook Director of researcher David Ginsberg and Social Psychologist Moira Burke in a report *titled 'Hard Questions: Is Spending Time on Social Media Bad for Us?'* acknowledged that social media could be harmful to the average user. A study by the California State University found that individuals who visited any social media site at least 58 times per week were 3 times more likely to feel depressed and socially isolated compared to those who visited social media fewer than 9 times per week.[243]

Researchers say internet addiction activates the same areas of the brain as drugs such as opioids – giving users the same feel-good effects as snorting cocaine or other dopamine-releasing drugs. Each 'Facebook like' or 'positive comment' activates the reward system and the brain releases dopamine[244]," says Dr Tara Emrani, a psychologist at NYU Langone Health. She added, "So, arguably, the feelings/ experiences of the brain, as a result of Facebook likes or comments, is similar to those resulting from cocaine, albeit less intense."[245]

According to Harvard University researcher Trevor Haynes, when you get a social media notification, your brain sends a chemical messenger called dopamine along a reward pathway, which makes you feel good. Dopamine is associated with food, exercise, love, sex, gambling, drugs – and now, social media.[246]

Former Facebook executives have admitted the network's decades-long erosion on traditional civil institutions. Former president Sean Parker stated that the social network provided "a dopamine hit and a social-validation feedback loop, which exploited vulnerability in human psychology." The former vice president for user growth, Chamath Palihapitiya, speaking at Stanford Graduate School of Business offered a more persuasive explanation, claiming that Facebook created tools that are ripping apart the social fabric of how society works." He further told people to take a "hard break" from social media, describing its effect as "short-term, dopamine-driven feedback loops."[247]

"We don't have a choice on whether we do social media; the question is how well we do it."

[Erik Qualman, Author and Motivational Speaker]

SIGNALS OF EXCESSIVE USE

Signals which indicate that a young person spends excessive time on social media include removing themselves from face-to-face or one-to-one social interactions; consistent stress, anxiety or feeling overwhelmed by ordinary routines; keeping away from real-life responsibilities, such as chores or homework; unresponsive to people in front of them; snub people next to them by looking down at their phone; and where their phone starts to create conflict in their closest relationships.

More than 100 child health experts, in an open letter to Facebook CEO Mark Zuckerberg, urged Facebook to withdraw the app 'Messenger Kids' - aimed at under-13s. The letter says:

"Younger children are simply not ready to have social media accounts. They are not old enough to navigate the complexities of online relationships, which often lead to misunderstandings and conflicts even among more mature users."[248]

The letter cites research which shows that teenager's social media use was linked to increased depression and anxiety. Other statistics, mentioned in the letter from a variety of research sources, include:

- Adolescents who spend 60 minutes a day chatting on social networks report less satisfaction with nearly every aspect of their lives.
- 10- to -12-year-old girls are more likely to have dieted due to concerns about their bodies."
- 78% of adolescents check their phones hourly.
- 50% say they are addicted to their phones.
- Half of parents say regulating screen time is a constant battle.

Social networking offers many positives, which can be a powerful force for good. While online communities help people, provide support and inspire action; caution is imperative because social media is addictive by nature and design. Millions of people worldwide are most likely addicts and do not even realise it. In the old days, it was termed 'gossiping' or being a busybody or a meddler in other people's affairs. Nowadays, it is called sharing, commenting, posting, following, liking, tweeting, retweeting and hashtag-ing. While most posts are presumably harmless, psychologists warn that others have the potential for causing harm. Posting personal details could jeopardise a child's life and expose the person to the risk of identity theft, or it could wind up in the hands of someone with improper motives.

"Social media is about sociology and psychology more than technology."

[Brian Solis, Digital Analyst, Speaker and Author]

PARENTAL MEDIATION

Parental mediation is defined as the parental management of the relationship between children and media, including simple restrictions. It involves the strategies parents employ in an attempt to manage the relationship between children and the negative effects of media use.

Types of mediation include:

- **Restrictive Mediation:** This is when parents set rules regarding the content allowed or the time to spend viewing media.

- **Active Mediation:** This refers to parent-child conversations about media, including parental attempts to provide children with critical viewing skills regarding media.

- **Co-viewing:** This is when parents view, use, or consume media with their children but do not necessarily discuss the content with them.

Parents should decide the type of mediation that best suits their parenting needs. They should engage children on an individual basis based on multiple factors, such as age and maturity of the child.

"The social media web is a very noisy one indeed and making sure that you are heard requires you to shout more effectively, rather than louder."

**[David Amerland,
Business Journalist and International Consultant]**

IMPORTANCE OF DIGITAL DOWNTIME

FOMO – 'Fear of Missing Out' – is fast becoming an 'addiction' for young people – checking their social media regularly to stay up to speed with recent happenings in their online circle. First, parents should keep a check on their use and set some practical house rules. For example, dissuade them from late-night use so that they can 'switch off' before bedtime and get sufficient sleep. Second, parents need to understand the relevance of technology in a child's life but also create a device-free family time – for everyone. Finally, parents should strongly encourage the child to invest time on other activities, such as hobbies, sports and face-to-face interactions with other people which reinforces the notion that satisfaction, achievement, and wellbeing can be produced from things outside social media, thereby, enhancing their sense of self-confidence and inner qualities.

In a 2019 Deloitte Global Millennial Survey, when asked about their personal use of digital devices and social media, 71 per cent of Millennials said they feel fairly positive or very positive. But a deeper dive into the data reveals a more complex picture – nearly 64 per cent of Millennials said they would be physically healthier if they reduced the time spent on social media, and six in 10 said it would make them happier people; 55 per cent said, on balance, that social media does more harm than good; 44 per cent said not being able to check social media for a day or two would make them anxious; 4 in 10 wish they could stop using it completely.[249]

DISTRACTED PARENTS

'Social Media Parents' are those parents who stroll with their children while chatting on their smartphones rather than with their little ones. These parents answer calls or text messages in the middle of a parental conversation with their child. Not only have we seen such parents, but some of us have also even been those parents. Distracted parenting is not distinctive to the digital age. Generations of children have been brought up by "distracted parents" – parents who come home with work, who unnecessarily interrupt the dinner to answer phone calls and who ignore their child's recount of the day to catch up their favourite TV show.

Many parents have graduated from a normal distracted state to a state of absolute digital dependence. Smartphones and other devices have evolved into bedfellows, 'second partners' and dinner associates. While parents are annoyed and frustrated with their children for "always being on their devices," parents might want to take an honest moment to evaluate their own social media obsession, which they have perhaps modelled for their children. Either verbally or non-verbally, distracted parents communicate that the distraction is more important than the child's needs.

"Children have never been very good at listening to their elders,
but they have never failed to imitate them."

[James Baldwin, Novelist, Playwright and Activist]

FAMILY PRIVACY POLICY

"Finally, my friends keep your minds on whatever is true,
pure, right, holy, friendly, and proper.
Don't ever stop thinking about what is truly worthwhile
and worthy of praise."

[Philippians 4:8 Contemporary English Version]

Media psychologists are warning of the risks of parents disclosing too much information about their children on social media. Does broadcasting a parenting experience on social media come at a cost? An attempt to answer this question introduces the concept of *'performative* parenting' – a phenomenon whereby parents share and trade generally or their parenting specifically, to get something in return – the feeling of praise and validation. Performative parenting is a version of parenthood that positions itself before an audience to seek a reward. It uses the internet to define an identity that goes beyond parenthood itself. With an arsenal of whitewashed walls and hashtags, performative parents attempt to find a tangible reward in the doldrums of parenthood.

What about the indiscriminate sharing of children's pictures on social media? It has become second nature for parents to post photos of their children online – and some have even transformed it into a profit-making venture. Is it always unethical to mix kids and social media? London School of Economics (LSE) report 'Preparing for a Digital Future,' found that three-quarters of parents who use the internet at least monthly share photographs or videos of their children online.[250]

The project conducted interviews whereby even small children wished their parents would share fewer photos of them and consult them more. The project observed in a few families that children were learning to tell their parents to stop. However, insofar as this sharing is to bring families together, even when geographically dispersed, there are also advantages and children appreciate those too. It is a matter of respect and consent, and protecting that is important, more than the fact of sharing itself. Dr Jenny Radesky, a paediatrician, specialising in child development, studied parental behaviours while out on dinner with her children. She noticed that as soon as parents were seated at the dinner table, many of them retrieved their phones and started using them. Dr Radesky says that it is a big mistake because face-to-face interactions are the primary way children learn. If children are not interacting with their parents, they are not learning how to have a conversation and are *"missing out on important development milestones."*[251]

Furthermore, undisciplined mobile phone use can cause gross inattention which produces profound emotional consequences for the child, as this tells children that "they do not matter and are not as important as anything else", so they feel that parents are not sufficiently interested in them and may at the slightest ping or bleep, interrupt time with them.

"What you post online speaks VOLUMES about who you really are. POST with intention. REPOST with caution"

[Germany Kent, Activist and Philanthropist]

SCREEN TIME AND BRAIN WHITE MATTER

A new study found that children age 3 – 5 years who exceeded the recommended screen time of one hour a day without parental involvement had lower levels of development in the brain's white matter — an area key to the development of language, literacy and cognitive skills. The study based on a sample of 47 healthy children — 27 girls and 20 boys has also suggested that children with higher periods of screen time on mobile phones or portable devices also have lower scores on language and literacy. Twenty-eight (60%) of the 47 children had a portable device of their own.

These findings were published by the Journal of the American Medical Association on 4 November 2019 under the title *'Associations Between Screen-Based Media Use and Brain White Matter Integrity in Preschool-Aged Children'.*[252]

Lead author Dr. John Hutton, a paediatrician and clinical researcher at Cincinnati Children's Hospital, in a media release says *"screen-based media use is prevalent in the home, childcare and school settings at ever younger ages. This is significant because the brain is developing the most rapidly in the first five years."* He added that this period is when brains are very plastic and soaking up everything, forming these strong connections that last for life. Hutton further says the findings *"highlight the need to understand effects of screen time on brain development in early childhood so that policymakers and parents can set healthy limits."*

RECOMMENDATIONS

Children "growing up digitally" need help to learn useful concepts of digital use and citizenship. Parents play an indispensable role in teaching these skills. The American Academy of Paediatrics (AAP) provides recommendations to help children develop and manage healthy media use.[253]

- The use of screen media should not be encouraged for children younger than 18 months, except for video-chatting.
- For children aged 18 - 24 months, parents who want to introduce digital media should choose high-quality programmes and co-view or co-play with them– this encourages social interactions, bonding, and learning.

- Children should not use the media by themselves.
- Limit media use to no more than 1 hour or less per day of high-quality programming for children older than two years.
- At least 8 hours of adequate sleep should be a priority for teenagers, with at least 1 hour of physical activity.
- Designate media-free family times together (such as dinners) and media-free zones (such as bedrooms). All electronic devices in children's bedrooms should be switched off, including TVs, computers, tablets and smart phones.
- All applications for children should be properly researched to ensure they are age-appropriate.
- Parents are encouraged to create personalized media plans based on each child's age, personality, health and developmental stage. This should be clearly communicated to other caregivers, so that media rules are followed consistently.
- Technology can help as an emotional pacifier in keeping children calm and quiet, but should not be used as the only tool.
- Parents must strictly warn children about the importance of privacy and the dangers of predators and 'sexting', includes texting of inappropriate photographs.
- Children will make mistakes using media. Parents should handle errors with empathy and turn a mistake into a teachable moment.

Media and digital gadgets are an integral part of our current world. The benefits of these devices, if used moderately and appropriately, can be significant. However, research shows that face-to-face time with family, friends, and teachers plays a fundamental role in promoting learning and healthy development.

CONCLUSION

There have been investigations into how social media platforms like Facebook handle users' data and privacy. Children should learn to protect their privacy by agreeing:

- not to share personal details like phone numbers, house address and date of birth with strangers online, or with people, they do not personally know; not to add personal information, such as date of birth or phone numbers to private profiles;

- to regularly check privacy and location settings, especially on mobile phones and tablets;

- keep passwords and log-in details secret and not share these with other people including with friends; and log out after using public computers.

It is nearly impossible for parents to avoid social media – which has become an integral part of many children's social life. Minimising the risk associated with social media should first start with parents curtailing their own consumption – setting a good and healthy example through their online behaviour can achieve significant results in helping their children use social media safely.

"Don't say anything online that you wouldn't want plastered on a billboard with your face on it"

[Erin Bury, Technology Expert and Entrepreneur]

CHAPTER 12

CELEBRITY CULTURE – THE PARADOX OF OUR TIME

Therefore see that you walk carefully [living life with honour, purpose, and courage; shunning those who tolerate and enable evil], not as the unwise, but as wise [sensible, intelligent, discerning people], making the very most of your time [on earth, recognizing and taking advantage of each opportunity and using it with wisdom and diligence], because the days are [filled with] evil.
[EPHESIANS 5:15-16 AMPLIFIED BIBLE]

THE PARADOX OF OUR AGE

Dr Bob Moorehead, pastor of Overlake Christian Church in Redmond, Washington for 30 years, is credited for *The Paradox of Our Age*, and published in Words Aptly Spoken.

The firebrand Dr Moorehead says:

"We have taller buildings but shorter tempers; wider freeways but narrower viewpoints; we spend more but have less; we buy more but enjoy it less; we have bigger houses and smaller families; more conveniences, yet less time; we have more degrees but less sense; more knowledge but less judgement; more experts, yet more problems; we have more gadgets but less satisfaction; more medicine, yet less wellness; we take more vitamins but see fewer results. We drink too much; smoke too much; spend too recklessly; laugh too little; drive too fast; get too angry quickly; stay up too late; get up too tired; read too seldom; watch TV too much and pray too seldom.

We have multiplied our possessions, but reduced our values; we fly in faster planes to arrive there quicker, to do less and return sooner; we sign more contracts only to realise fewer profits; we talk too much; love too seldom and lie too often. We have learned how to make a living, but not a life; we have added years to life, not life to years. We have been all the way to the moon and back, but have trouble crossing the street to meet the new neighbour. We have conquered outer space, but not inner space; we have done larger things, but not better things; we have cleaned up the air, but polluted the soul; we have split the atom, but not our prejudice; we write more, but learn less; plan more, but accomplish less; we make faster planes, but longer lines; we learned to rush, but not to wait; we have more weapons, but less peace; higher incomes, but lower morals; more parties, but less fun; more food, but less appeasement; more acquaintances, but fewer friends; more effort, but less success.

We build more computers to hold more information, to produce more copies than ever, but have less communication; drive smaller cars that have bigger problems; build larger factories that produce less. We have become long on quantity, but short on quality. These are the times of fast foods and slow digestion; tall men, but short character; steep in profits, but shallow relationships. These are times of world peace, but domestic warfare; more leisure and less fun; higher postage, but slower mail; more kinds of food, but less nutrition. These are days of two incomes, but more divorces; these are times of fancier houses, but broken homes. These are days of quick trips, disposable diapers, cartridge living, throw-away morality, one-night stands, overweight bodies and pills that do everything from cheer, to prevent, quiet or kill. It is a time when there is much in the show window and nothing in the stock room. Indeed, these are the times!"[254]

"The United States has degenerated into a social order that is awash in public stupidity and views critical thought as both a liability and a threat. Not only is this obvious in the presence of a celebrity culture that embraces the banal and idiotic, but also in the prevailing discourses and policies of a range of politicians and anti-public intellectuals who believe that the legacy of the Enlightenment needs to be reversed."

[Henry Giroux, Scholar and Cultural Critic]

THE DOMINANT INFLUENCE

"Large crowds followed Jesus as he came down the mountainside."
[Matthew 8:1 New Living Translation]

Media-propagated, celebrity-driven culture is a dominant influence on children. The days of collectivist role models of scientists, doctors, police officers or teachers and engineers have now given way to more individualistic role-models of elite athletes, the super-rich or merely those who are famous for being famous. We have a general tendency to idolise – an irresistible urge to follow the daily lives of celebrities, from their tragic experiences, like their heartbreaks and deaths, to the monotonous, like the type of dinner they had that evening. Self-absorption with personal image is approaching extraordinary proportions: Instagram, since its launch in 2010 has 700 million users with more than 40 billion photos shared, with around 95 million uploaded daily by its 700 million users. Unfortunately, celebrity culture deposits on our children the relentless desire for popularity and to emulate their celebrity idol. Many children learn this through media relations, such as magazines, reality TV, music videos, DVDs and internet sites.

Fame – the principal motivation that drives celebrity culture is connected with status, wealth and the perception of the 'perfect' body. In the article 'Celebrity Culture,' published in *Society*, author Frank Furedi writes that although the idea of a celebrity has been around for a long time, its mutation into an important cultural force is a relatively recent development. In recent decades, the meaning of a celebrity has altered and is now often applied to those who are famous for being famous. The ascendancy of the celebrity has been fuelled by Society's uneasy relationship with the question of authority. Often, being a celebrity provides an alternative source of validation. The tendency to outsource authority to the celebrity represents an attempt to bypass the problem of legitimacy by politicians and other figures.[255]

TV series, talk shows, and social media have fostered a celebrity-driven environment in which children irresistibly fixate on famous music stars, athletes or TV celebrity presenters from a very young age. A series of commercials attract children to a life that seems more colourful and attractive than their own. Shockingly, children imitate, copy and are captivated by the images on the screen interpreting them as reality. It becomes laborious to change their opinions about celebrities due to the fixation of seeing their idols as primary role models.

A 2007 study by University of California, Los Angeles (UCLA) Children's Digital Media Centre published in *Cyberpsychology*, found that fame was the number one value communicated to pre-teens on popular TV ranking higher than achievement, community feeling and benevolence.[256]

First author Uhls observes that:

"Preteens are at the age when they want to be popular and liked just like the famous teenagers they see on TV and the Internet. With Internet celebrities and reality TV stars everywhere, the pathway for nearly anyone to become famous, without a connection to hard work and skill, may seem easier than ever."

Co-author Greenfield says the rise of fame in preteen television may be one influence in the documented rise of narcissism in our culture.

Growing into a celebrity appears to be seen as a career choice – it is perhaps unsurprising that long-term achievements like following a path of education diminish in comparison with instantaneous TV opportunities. A survey commented in *Teen Vogue* shows that over 30% of 14 to 18-year-olds were reported to be thinking that they were possibly going to be famous one day.[257]

However, for other children, celebrity influence and obsession are shaped and modelled by their parents' perception of celebrity life. With the excitement adults share in celebrity shows, it is not surprising that their children want star-status. When parents model a high-value system on celebrity culture themselves, they should expect no less from their children who may be emulating their examples. On the other hand, a scarier phenomenon rising in popularity worth is the VIP syndrome – a word coined by Dr Walter Weintraub in 1964. This occurs when famous or wealthy VIPs exert adverse influence on medical professionals or institution to make unorthodox decisions under the pressure or presence of the VIP.

Popular culture attacks children at the most basic level – the values that guide their lives. It promotes vices and disguises them as valid entertainment. Nevertheless, not all stars have a gloomy impact on the world of their young fans. There are many celebrity personalities who use their popularity to create awareness and to support charities, as well as many sports stars that inspire children by their life stories to achieve success. These stars are a huge inspiration and excellent role models to children and in some cases, are positive influences on their academics. In particular, with the younger celebrities, it is highly recommended to keep a close watch on their activities and public engagements and to brief children about any changes in their social behaviour at the earliest opportunity.

"If you look at the footballers, you look at our celebrity culture;
we seem to be saying, 'This is the way you want to be'.
We seem to be a society that celebrates all the wrong people."

[Iain Duncan Smith,
Politician and Former Conservative Party Leader]

BODY IMAGE

"And I praise you because of the wonderful way you created me.
Everything you do is marvellous! Of this, I have no doubt."

[Psalm 139:14 Contemporary English Version]

Celebrity culture and Social media – Twitter, Facebook, Instagram, Snapchat – have created a highly-charged 24/7 cycle of unrealistic body images that teenagers, unfortunately, aspire to emulate. Direct messages associated with body weight are indeed conveyed to teenagers in the media by fashion models and celebrities. Their body weight, appearance, and beauty are related to their popularity, wealth and VIP status. The quest by teenagers to reach perfection has led to a rise in a condition of dissatisfaction with body appearance – Dysmorphia.[258]

Body image is a person's perception of the aesthetics or sexual attractiveness of their own physical body, involves how a person sees themselves and how they feel about their body in comparison to others and the standards set by society. Positive body image is a clear, accurate perception of one's physical shape

– body satisfaction, while, on the other hand, negative body image involves a distorted perception for one's shape – body dissatisfaction (including feelings of shame, anxiety, depression, isolation, low self-esteem, and eating disorders).

Research shows that body image is influenced by many factors, including friends and family; the environment where the teen lives; socio-cultural background and celebrity pictures. When young people view these '*attractive*' images on social media, they often compare their appearance to those images and think they are less attractive than the images they see.

A Young Men's Christian Association (YMCA) survey on '*the expectations young people face to look perfect,*' found that of more than 1,000 young people aged between 11 - 16 years-old who were asked about body image expectations, 58% said that celebrities were responsible, while 52% blamed social media. The pressure to look 'perfect' is especially prevalent among older young people, with 62% of 15 to 16 year-olds admitting that pressure about their looks emanated from individuals on social media, compared to 43% of 11 to 12 year-olds.[259]

Studies show that adolescents who worship celebrities do not just imitate their style, but make a choice for plastic surgery more often than those who do not venerate celebrities.[260]

The American Society of Aesthetic Plastic Surgery approximates that between 33,000 to 65,000 children below 18 receive cosmetic surgery each year, with nonsurgical cosmetic procedures stretching from 91,000 to 190,000 each year.[261]

Denise Hatton, Chief Executive for YMCA and founding partner of the *Be Real Campaign*, says that we have all been guilty of posting our most flattering pictures on social media. While there is nothing wrong with wanting to show yourself from your best angle, it is important that we still like ourselves when we are not looking our best, which is probably the majority of the time for most of us. The beauty standard of today is entirely unobtainable, leading us to continuously feel bad about our bodies and how we look. This is particular with young people, and can have severe effects on their mental and physical wellbeing.

Writing in Psychology Today, Jim Taylor, a specialist in sports and parenting, masterfully summarises popular culture:

"Popular culture is like a network of saboteurs that infiltrate your family's lives with stealth and deception, hiding behind entertaining characters, bright images, and fun music. Popular culture is also an invading army that overwhelms your children with these destructive messages. It attempts to control every aspect of your children's lives: their values, attitudes, and beliefs about themselves and the world that they live in; their thoughts, emotions, and behaviour; their needs, wants, goals, hopes, and dreams; their interests and avocations; their choices and their decisions. With this control, popular culture can tell children what to eat and drink, what to wear, what to listen to and watch, and children have little ability to resist.[262]

"Being a celebrity does not make someone an authority.
Take it all in, but do the due diligence, vetting and fact-checking before you
buy into the hype that may be truly popular but is entirely false."

[Loren Weisman, Business Consultant,
Speaker and Author]

HEALTHY MEDIA DIET

"Only pay attention and watch yourselves closely so that you do not forget
the things which your eyes have seen and they do not depart from your heart
all the days of your life. Make them known to your children and your
grandchildren [impressing these things on their mind and penetrating their
heart with these truths]"

[Deuteronomy 4:9 Amplified Bible]

Parents may also have to assist children in dealing with borderline-pathological conditions, which includes a condition where an individual has delusions that someone of a higher social status, very often a celebrity, is in love with them – *erotomania.*[263]

Drs. Derenne and Beresin advocate that parents need to limit children's exposure to media, promote healthy eating and moderate physical activity and encourage participation in activities that increase mastery and self-esteem.[264]

In 2016, the American Academy of Paediatrics (AAP) introduced new recommendations for Children's Media Use to help families maintain a healthy media diet. These recommendations include:[265]

- **For children younger than 18 months:** Avoid the use of screen media other than video-chatting.

- **For children between 2 to 5 years of age:** Limit screen uses to 1 hour per day and only allow high-quality programs.

- **For children between 6 years of age and older:** Place consistent limits on the time spent using media.

- **Designate media-free times together:** Time together, such as dinner, as well as designating media-free locations such as bedrooms.

- **Have ongoing communication:** Ongoing communication about online citizenship and safety, including treating others with respect online and offline.

The American Academy of Paediatrics (AAP) in an article *"Children, Adolescents and the Media,"* highlights that the digital age is the ideal time to change the way we all address media use. According to the lead author of the report, Victor Strasburger, for nearly three decades, the AAP has expressed concerns about the content and amount of time children and teenagers spend on the screen. The authors explained that parents should promote a healthy *'media diet'* that minimises potential health risks and fosters appropriate media use. Co-author Marjorie Hogan says parents, educators and paediatricians should participate in media education, which means teaching children and adolescents how to make good choices in their media consumption.[266]

"Celebrity is the chastisement of merit and the punishment of talent."

[Emily Dickinson, American Poet]

GUIDELINES FOR PARENTS

The AAP Committee on Public Education in its article titled 'Children, Adolescents, and Television' advises Paediatricians to recommend the following guidelines to parents to help mitigate the harmful effects of media.[267]

1. Limit the total media time (including entertainment media) of children to 1 – 2 hours of quality programming per day.
2. Remove television sets from children's bedrooms.
3. Discourage television for children younger than two years, while encouraging more interactive activities that promote proper brain development, such as talking, singing, playing and reading together.
4. Monitor programs children and adolescents view.
5. View television programs with children, and discuss their content.
6. Use controversial programs as a stepping-off point to initiate discussions about family values, sex, violence, and drugs.
7. Encourage alternative entertainment for children, such as reading, athletics, creative play and hobbies.

The AAP published two articles in the Journal *Pediatrics*: "Media and Young Minds" recommendations for infants, toddlers, and Pre-schoolers; and "Media Use in School-Aged Children and

Adolescents". The conclusion of both articles is that parents should approach the screen-time issue with a strategy. Families should proactively think about their children's media use and talk with children about it. Report author Jenny Radesky observes that too much media use can mean that children don't have enough time during the day to play, study, talk, or sleep. What's most important is that parents be their child's 'media mentor.' That means teaching them how to use it as a tool to create, connect, and learn."[268]

"Children are very quick observers; very quick in seeing through some kinds of hypocrisy, very quick in finding out what you really think and feel, very quick in adopting all your ways and opinions. You will soon discover that, as the father is, so is the son."

[J. C. Ryle, First Anglican Bishop of Liverpool]

LURE OF GANG CULTURE

"Do not be so deceived and misled! Evil companionships (communion, associations) corrupt and deprave good manners and morals and character."
[1 Corinthians 15:33 Amplified Bible, Classic Edition]

The American Academy of Child and Adolescent Psychiatry defines a gang as a group of children, adolescents and young adults who share a common identity and are involved in wrongful or delinquent activities.[269]

According to the charity organisation *Family Lives*, a group may be classed as a gang if it fulfils certain condition, namely, if it has a name; controls a defined territory; uses a specific colour in clothing; uses specific hand gestures or signs and uses symbols shown in tattoos or graffiti.[270]

Gang membership is likely made up of people from diverse races, cultures and socioeconomic backgrounds. However, recent trends show that younger children, as early as primary school age, are gaining membership. Conventionally, gang activity has been concentrated in cities, but they also exist in rural areas and much smaller towns. The majority of young people have no involvement in gangs and do not want to associate with it. However, the behaviour of a minority who are involved has a significant impact on their families and associates, as well as themselves and the wider community. The UK Home Office in a published leaflet, *'Advice to parents and carers on gangs: Helping young people make the right choice'* helps parents identify and respond if their children are affected by gangs.[271]

Young people (if not adults) join gangs for reasons which make sense to them. Factors that enable young people to join a gang include:

1. Growing up in an area with substantial gang activity.
2. A history of gang involvement amongst family members.
3. A history of violence in the home.
4. Too little adult supervision.
5. Unstructured free time – after-school hours and weekends.

6. A lack of positive role models.

7. Exposure to media (television, movies and music) that glorifies gang violence.

8. To gain status, respect and a sense of belonging.

9. To win friends, to find a substitute family

10. Peer pressure.

11. Feeling of hopelessness about the future because of limited educational or financial opportunity.

12. Underlying mental health issues

13. Behavioural disorders.

14. Power, protection and money.

15. Thrill and Excitement

"Gangs are a group reaction to helplessness."

[Jesse Jackson, Minister and U.S. Civil Rights Activist]

GIRL AND GANGS

"Keep company with the wise, and you will become wise. If you make friends with stupid people, you will be ruined."
[Proverbs 13:20 Good News Translation]

Girls can be affected by gang culture, but their involvement may be harder to detect. They may be asked to conceal weapons or act as drug mules. They can also be targets of male gang members in revenge attacks or gang initiations. Girls connected to gang members (such as friends and relatives), including female gang members themselves, are in danger of emotional, physical and sexual abuse. Most girls involved with gangs are convinced that their activities are reasonable, and it may not be apparent to them that what is happening is illegal. They may be scared of the consequences of telling anyone, or they may be of the view that no one will believe or protect them.

SIGNS OF GANG MEMBERSHIP

"When peer pressure compels you to go with the crowd and sinners invite you to join in, you must simply say, "No!". When the gang says—"We're going to steal and kill and get away with it. We'll take down the rich and rob them. We'll swallow them up alive and take what we want from whomever we want."

[Proverbs 1:10-12 The Passion Translation]

Gangs often use signs to indicate their presence, and your child might adopt some of these signs either as an associate or as a gang member. Tactfully discuss any abrupt changes in the child's lifestyle if you observe any of the following signs:

1. Having unjustified money, expensive new items, or clothing.
2. Wearing clothing that is all one type, style, or colour or changing appearance with unique haircuts, tattoos or other body markings.
3. Using hand signs, particular slangs or words with hidden messages, or having gang graffiti-style tags on possessions.
4. Associating with known gang members.

5. Withdrawing from family, not obeying curfews, staying out unusually late, changing or worsening attitude with adults and peers.

6. Using or possessing drugs and alcohol and carrying weapons.

7. Talking differently – new slang or language with an aggressive tone; Poor school results or skipping school.

8. Interest and enjoyment in music which glorifies weapons/gang culture

9. Physical injuries (which may indicate violence from others), and refusing to seek medical help for such injuries.

10. Fearful or withdrawn or prone to unexplained outbursts of anger.

"Even gang members imagine a future that doesn't include gangs".

[Greg Boyle, Priest and Director of Homeboy Industries]

REDUCING RISK OF GANG INVOLVEMENT

"But test everything that is said to be sure it is true, and if it is, then accept it. Keep away from every kind of evil."
[1 Thessalonians 5:21-22 Living Bible]

Prevention is undoubtedly better than cure when it concerns gang membership. Guidelines for decreasing the risk of joining a gang include:

1. Closely monitoring the child's daily and weekly movements.

2. Talk to the child, listen and keep lines of communication open.

3. Motivate them to get involved in positive activities and think about their future employment.

4. Require their participation in extracurricular activities such as afterschool programs, or athletics, art, community organisations or religious groups.

5. Meeting the friends of the child and their parents.

6. Assist them in managing pressure and offer guidelines on how to deal with conflict without violence.

7. Speak to them about the consequences of irresponsible or criminal behaviour.

8. Help them to understand the dangers of gang life and help find constructive alternative ways to use their time.

9. Monitor their internet activities and ask questions if you notice anything suspicious.

10. Provide them with basic needs to reduce their chances of seeking them elsewhere.

11. Employ methods of discipline that do not involve anger or violence.

12. Work with other parents and schools to observe their behaviour.

13. Contact local voluntary organisations that provide mentoring and other support services for young people.

14. Any gang-related gestures, graffiti, marking, signs or symbols, are out of bounds.

15. Give them your full affection and make them feel loved and wanted.

16. Let them know the unfortunate consequences of being a gang member – injury, jail or death.

"A team is where a boy can prove his courage on his own.
A gang is where a coward goes to hide."

[Mickey Mantle, Professional Baseball Player]

IF YOUR CHILD IS ALREADY INVOLVED

"You must not do wrong just because everyone else is doing it.
If you are a witness in court, you must not ruin a fair trial.
You must not tell lies just because everyone else is."

[Exodus 23:2 New Century Version]

You may be worried to find out that your child is involved in a gang. Confronting a child suspected of gang activity is very challenging – the child may not want to talk about it or scared to disclose gang activities. Parents and children may fear gang retaliation. They may worry about giving up benefits they receive because of the child's gang involvement. The Home Office advice leaflet recommends:

- Parents and carers should stay calm, ask questions, but listen too.
- Not be afraid of confrontation, but try not to approach them with anger and accusations.
- Try to understand the situation from their point of view and why they have joined the gang.
- Ask them what you can do to help.
- Try to agree about what they should do next.

- Work with them to find solutions and choices.
- Parents and carers should also seek help from local community organisations or youth services that offer specialist support and programmes to help them leave the gang.
- Contact local support networks such as faith groups or neighbourhood police officers connected to your local school.

CONCLUSION

"Don't be afraid. I am with you. Don't tremble with fear.
I am your God. I will make you strong,
as I protect you with my arm and give you victories."

[Isaiah 41:10 Contemporary English Version]

Confronting a child suspected of gang activity is not an easy task. Parents may have to handle the legal consequences of a child's past behaviour while also being actively involved in protecting the child from violence, drugs, and criminal activity. If you suspect your child participates in gang activity, seek help from anti-crime and community youth agencies.

Many cities run youth clubs and local gang prevention projects. Some police departments have officers familiar with gang behaviour, who are willing to meet with parents for early gang intervention. Parents also have the option to seek help from trained mental health professionals who can evaluate and remedy mental health problems that may have contributed to gang involvement.

"Joining a gang is like sky diving without a parachute.
Oh, at first it's all fun, as you take on gravity in a thrilling and
exhilarating free fall towards earth. The truth is, anything that is risky
and dangerous always starts out as fun. But the odds are always stacked in
gravity's favour, for you will eventually come face to face with the earth, and
mother earth always wins those battles.
The same thing can be said about being in a gang."

[Drexel Deal, Speaker and Author]

CHAPTER 13

PARENTING WITHOUT GUILT – THE ULTIMATE PATHWAY

*The father of godly children has cause for joy. What a
pleasure to have children who are wise*

[PROVERBS 23:24 NEW LIVING TRANSLATION]

THE REALITY OF PARENT GUILT

P arent Guilt is the feeling that you, as a parent, are not doing
a sufficient job and that you could be doing more in raising
your child. This natural fear comes from within and lurks
in mind. It manifests on a continuum from mild to moderate to
severe. Comparisons with other parents and the pressures of good
parenting from social media have not made it any easy for Millennial
parents. Most parents genuinely provide their children with a decent
and healthy upbringing, but mistakes do happen. In hindsight, they

wish they had done things differently, and a fear that they may have already inflicted damage on their children. You cannot reverse the hands of time. Alleviate your guilt by understanding that no parent is perfect and focus on doing better next time.

Is parental utopia possible to achieve? This question crystallises one of the most challenging aspects of parenting – to lead a productive, fulfilling adult existence while raising happy, successful and well-adjusted children. If we define parenting as caregiving, then the best parent is not the one who parents to the maximum, and certainly not the one who parents to the minimum, but the one who parents to just the correct measure. Some parents feel guilty about everything that goes wrong for their children. Parenting does not have to be perfect; it has to be just good enough by focusing on the well-being of the child. The critical thing about parenting is the fact that at some point, most parents will experience guilt, which may cause parents to develop unhealthy discipline habits, like succumb to children when it is not in their best interest. While this strategy may temporarily ease a parent's guilt, it could be harmful for children.

The inability to create a sensible balance between family and career is an excellent source of the feeling of blame experienced by both men and women. In our survey of over 1,300 parents nationwide conducted for the book 'Mommy Guilt' - 96% reported feelings of guilt associated with some aspect of parenting.[272]

So, statistically speaking, mommy guilt is a universal feeling. The survey authored by Julie Bort and Colleagues explain that parents today try too hard to be superhuman, often sacrificing their well-being – and relationships with friends, family, even their spouses

– to meet the escalating demands of their children's lives. As might be expected, such efforts inevitably fall short, and parents blame themselves. Mommy Guilt encourages parents to avoid unobtainable (and ill-advised) goals in favour of parenting philosophies that concentrate on the whole family."

Mommy Guilt, to a moderate extent, is different from Daddy Guilt. Fathers are more likely to feel guilty over specific occasions when their behaviour fails to achieve their expectations. Mothers often bundle up all their adverse reactions into more generalised "mommy guilt." However, a father's guilt does not get talked about much. The stereotype of masculinity subtly says that guilt is not something men should feel. After all, they are supposed to be strong physically and emotionally. However, is "father guilt" a reality? Do fathers also, in equal measure, experience some level of remorse for not investing more in their children? Or for working too much for long hours? Or for taking the wrong discipline method? Or for not showing enough love?

Throughout history, fathers were generally considered to be distant providers, while mothers did all the caretaking, but today, fathers take a much more engaging role in family life. A Pew Research Centre Survey on how working mothers and fathers in two-parent households balance their jobs with family responsibilities and how they view the dynamics of sharing childcare and household responsibilities. They found that about 40% of working mothers said they do not spend enough time with their children; 18% of part-time working moms and 11% stay-at-home mothers said the same.[273]

For their part, working fathers are strikingly more likely than working mothers to say they spend very little time with their children – half of the full-time working fathers say this is the case. According to an online survey of 1,200 men from Fatherly and Today.com: about one in five (19%) fathers said that they felt guilty about not being "present" enough with their children, and 17% reported that they suffered from "dad guilt" as a result of working too much. About one in four (28%) said they felt guilty about not providing enough for their family the way they would have wished to.[274]

In *'Parental Guilt: A Silent Epidemic'*, Robin Grille comments that:

"Parents everywhere agonise in secret: 'Where did I go wrong? Will my child be damaged because of what I did, or because of what I failed to do?' And so, we worry in private about how we rate as parents, how our actions will affect our kids. So painful is this festering guilt, we tend to keep it buried; a conversation we have with ourselves in the quiet of the night. Rarely do we show one another how vulnerable we sometimes feel. The result: most of us tend to live in an illusory world where parents all around us look as if they are coping so much better than we are. I know of no better antidote to the "guilts" than finding out that parenting is an ever-evolving work in progress. A quick glance at the evolution of parenting through the ages does wonders to liquidate our sense of guilt, and replace it with humility and excitement for learning and growing as parents.[275]

The media is flooded with multiple accounts of 'successful' professional men who have sacrificed home life to climb to the ladder of success. Cracks are beginning to appear in this universally accepted narrative. In *'Dying for a Paycheck'*, author Jeffrey Pfeffer argues that a lot of modern management commonalities such as long work hours, work-family conflict, and economic insecurity are harmful to employees – and destroying people's physical and emotional health. We must rise to the dangers and enormous costs of today's workplace.[276]

Discipline is another common source of parental guilt. Parents will often express feelings of guilt about being too lenient with their children and "caving in," or 'techno-guilt,' which involves the sense of unease about using phones and other devices to distract toddlers and Pre-schoolers.

"Guilt is always hungry, don't let it consume you"

[Terri Guillemets, Author and Quotation Anthologist

ARE YOU A GUILTY PARENT?

Psychology Today contributor, Ann Smith in the article *'Are You a Guilty Parent,'* examines the causes of guilt. According to Smith, guilty parents regret the following: that they were not there enough; they did not listen and were too focused on work; they were not affectionate enough; they were critical and yelled, hit, and blamed; they were a bad role model; they did not take time to understand their children; they were not consistent; they pushed too hard or did not push enough; they spanked; they drank; they were depressed; they fought with the other parent; they got divorced; they said hurtful things; they were selfish; they ignored the child; and they did not protect their children.[277]

"Guilt is an emotion, not a reality or a life sentence"

[Ann Smith, Clinical Social Worker and Therapist]

THE 'GOOD ENOUGH' PARENT

"Lord, how you have helped me before! You took me safely from my mother's womb and brought me through the years of infancy. I have depended upon you since birth; you have always been my God. Don't leave me now, for trouble is near and no one else can possibly help."

[Psalm 22:9-11 The Living Bible]

Over 50 years ago, a British paediatrician and psychoanalyst Donald Woods Winnicott introduced the concept of the *"Good Enough Mother."* He demonstrated that loving parents who provide a stimulating environment, set clear boundaries and did not worry about doing enough, had children with the best outcomes. A parent who is too interfering impedes the child's separation and development of selfhood, but a parent who is too detached (i.e. not good enough) produces anxiety in the child. In either case, the absence of good-enough parenting can hamper the development of a child's sense of self, and as an adult, the ability to form meaningful relationships.[278]

Inspired by the writings of Winnicott, Bruno Bettelheim's in the 1987 book *A Good Enough Parent* generalised Winnicott's concept of the 'good enough mother' to include both genders – father and mother. . Bettelheim in the preface of the book writes:

"To raise a child well, one ought not to try to be a perfect parent, as much as one should not expect one's child to be, or to become, a perfect individual. Perfection is not within the grasp of ordinary human beings. Efforts to attain it typically interfere with that lenient response to the imperfections of others, including those of one's child, which alone make good human relations possible".[279]

The book reassures parents of the excellent job they are probably already doing. Towards the end of the book, Bettelheim writes that parents are not perfect; they are indeed good enough parents if most of the time they love their children and do their best to do well by them.

Good enough parents believe that the child's universe does not spin around the parents. Children's actions are not primarily motivated by a desire to please or to hurt parents, but by desires that have to do with their attempt to discover their place in the world. Good enough parents do not focus on taking much credit, nor much blame for children's actions; they focus on understanding and helping where help is required.

"Guilt is to danger, what fire is to gunpowder; a man need not fear to walk among many barrels of powder, if he has no fire about him."

[John Flavel, Author and Clergyman]

PARABLE OF THE PRODIGAL SON

"Don't worry—I am with you. Don't be afraid—I am your God.
I will make you strong and help you. I will support you with my
right hand that brings victory."

[Isaiah 41:10 Easy-to-Read Version]

There are no guarantees in the parenting journey. This parable, traditionally known as the story of the prodigal son, is the reality of many parents. No matter how much efforts some parents undertake to raise their children in the right way of life; and no matter how much they love, pray and provide for their children, some choose to turn it all down! Even in God-fearing families, children sometimes rebel and run away from their moral foundation!

This parable from the gospel of Luke reads:

"Then Jesus said, "Once there was a father with two sons. The younger son came to his father and said, 'Father, don't you think it's time to give me the share of your estate that belongs to me?' So the father went ahead and distributed among the two sons their inheritance. Shortly afterwards, the younger son packed up all his belongings and travelled off to see the world. He journeyed to a far-off land where he soon wasted all he was given in a binge of extravagant and reckless living. "With everything spent and nothing left, he grew hungry, for there was a severe famine in that land. 15 So he begged a farmer in that country to hire him. The farmer hired him and sent him out to feed the pigs. The son was so famished, he was willing to even eat the slop given to the pigs, because no one would feed him a thing "Humiliated, the son finally realized what he was doing and he thought, 'There are many workers at my father's house who have all the food they

want with plenty to spare. They lack nothing. Why am I here dying of hunger, feeding these pigs and eating their slop? I want to go back home to my father's house, and I'll say to him, "Father, I was wrong. I have sinned against you. I'll never be worthy to be called your son. Please, Father, just treat me like one of your employees." "So the young son set off for home. From a long distance away, his father saw him coming, dressed as a beggar, and great compassion swelled up in his heart for his son who was returning home. So the father raced out to meet him. He swept him up in his arms, hugged him dearly, and kissed him over and over with tender love.

"Then the son said, 'Father, I was wrong. I have sinned against you. I could never deserve to be called your son. Just let me be—'"The father interrupted and said, 'Son, you're home now!' "Turning to his servants, the father said, 'Quick, bring me the best robe, my very own robe, and I will place it on his shoulders. Bring the ring, the seal of sonship, and I will put it on his finger. And bring out the best shoes[g] you can find for my son. Let's prepare a great feast[h] and celebrate. For this beloved son of mine was once dead, but now he's alive again. Once he was lost, but now he is found!' And everyone celebrated with overflowing joy.

Now, the older son was out working in the field when his brother returned, and as he approached the house, he heard the music of celebration and dancing. 26 So he called over one of the servants and asked, 'What's going on?' "The servant replied, 'It's your younger brother. He's returned home, and your father is throwing a party to celebrate his homecoming.' "The older son became angry and refused to go in and celebrate. So his father came out and pleaded with him, 'Come and enjoy the feast with us!' "The son said, 'Father, listen! How many years have I been working like a slave for you, performing every duty you've asked as a faithful son? And I've never once disobeyed you. But you've never thrown a party for me because of my faithfulness. Never once have you even given me a goat that I could feast on and celebrate with my friends like he's doing now. But look at this son of yours! He comes back after wasting your wealth on prostitutes and reckless living, and here you are throwing a great feast to celebrate—for him!'

'The father said, 'My son, you are always with me by my side. Everything I have is yours to enjoy. It's only right to celebrate like this and be overjoyed because this brother of yours was once dead and gone, but now he is alive and back with us again. He was lost, but now he is found!'[280]

This text presents a compelling story that has been performed on stage, in music and art, and most remarkably, has been relived in innumerable lives and families all over the world. The author draws us into the very human situation by rendering the feelings of the father and his son in an intensely felt manner. Respect for one's father is paramount in the cultural context of the story; the younger son's request for his inheritance from a father who is still alive constitutes an unimaginable transgression. Notwithstanding, the father approves it!

This story is a classic example of a parent whose roles and responsibilities are beyond reproach, yet the child still turns out on the negative path of life. Rather than allow parental guilt to flood his soul, the father stays serene with a calm assurance knowing that he had done everything humanly possible as a responsible parent. Timothy Keller, the author of *'The Prodigal God,'* suggests that the two brothers signify the two fundamental ways human beings attempt to make life work. The younger son who views life from a different perspective is on a course of "self-discovery" – a quest for self-realisation, even if some people get crushed along the way. The older brother's focus is to a more socially exemplary way of being in the world –the path of "moral conformity" on earning the approval of his community and his father.[281]

Should the father in this story feel guilty for his actions since he could have easily denied inheritance to the younger son, or forcefully compelled him to stay? But why did he not go against his son's wishes? These are all questions that do not have a straightforward answer, as every case is different. Should the father be held responsible for the son's actions? Certainly not. In such cases, parents should not be made to feel guilty when children are experiencing the consequences of their actions.

Something dramatic happens when the son returns to his father. The father sees him from the horizon and with compassion welcomes him home – far from the humiliation that the son was expecting based on his previous impudent lack of self-control and disrespectful treatment of his father. This story presents the father's love and tenderness as the motivating factor that propelled the younger son to go back home – an attribute that should govern every parent-child relationship. Irrespective of the acts committed by children, broken relationships can be mended when true repentance is reciprocated with love, forgiveness and acceptance.

"Children need love especially when they don't deserve it."

[Harold Hulbert, Author and Psychiatrist]

COMPETITIVE PARENT SYNDROME

Competitiveness in children is often considered a dirty word. It evokes the image of an aggressive child who cannot tolerate losing or failing, and who is focused on being the 'best' and 'first' in everything. Competitiveness is not a negative thing; it encourages children to achieve their potential. However, competitiveness can become a problem when the goal of winning is all that counts or when your child is prepared to do anything – cheat, lie and take advantage of others – to achieve that goal.

Competitive or comparing parents are those who in addition to boasting and bragging about their child's achievements, also feel guilty and look down upon themselves when their child does not achieve a high level of success. From the outside, it may look like other parents are doing a better job at raising their children This comparison attitude could lead to stress, frustration, and sense of failure and guilt in some parents, especially amongst 'Kyoiku mamas,' 'Soccer moms' and 'Stage mothers'.

- *'Kyoiku Mama'* is a Japanese pejorative term that translates literally as "education mother" – referred by some in the western world as 'pushy mothers.' The Kyoiku mama is a stereotyped figure in modern Japanese society portrayed as a mother who relentlessly drives her child to study, at the expense of the child's social life, physical development and emotional wellbeing. These mothers compete with each other to get their children into the most prestigious schools.

- *'Soccer Moms'* are those who schedule every moment of the child's spare time with sports and other activities. These parents should be 'realistic' about the child's physical ability and stage of development, and not drive the child beyond his or her capacity. Parents should avoid 'becoming wrapped up' in how well their child performs and must remember the need to develop good sportsmanship.

- *'Stage Mothers'* like Kyoiku mamas and soccer moms, stage mothers get their sense of social value through their children. Aside from gaining social recognition, the stage mother often makes her living from the success of their children. Sometimes, women who themselves have longed for fame, but were frustrated in their attempts to achieve it, are highly likely to become stage mothers.

According to psychologists, the above three *'mother phenomena'* can undermine a child's psychological health and wellbeing. Parents should not bear the guilt of their children's inability to enter their preferred school, or join their anticipated sports club or win a state medal. When a child's sense of approval hinges on performance (whether academic, athletic, or artistic), it can lead to a vulnerable sense of self-esteem – being rewarded only for good performances can produce children who are unable to accept themselves unless they perform to extraordinary standards.

Parents should not feel guilty about encouraging children to succeed, but it should not be done at the expense of their mental and emotional health; it should not hinder the physical, mental and psychological development of children and the friendly relations with fellow parents. Finally, parents are advised to measure their levels of parental pride by asking whether their self-esteem depends on their children's performance.

GUILT- FREE LIVING

The LORD's love never ends; his mercies never stop.
They are new every morning; LORD, your loyalty is great."

[Lamentations 3:22-23 New Century Version]

The strategies for guilt-free living revolve around seven principles:

1. **Parenting guilt is normal:** First and foremost, at some point, every parent will experience guilt.
2. **Let go of perfection:** Having realistic expectations can make a big difference. The capacity to always correctly solve every problem effortlessly and without stress is often not possible.
3. **Channel thoughts and feelings into action:** Guilt can have a dual effect; it can weigh or hold parents down, or it can be the motivation that starts a change for the better.
4. **Seek out reliable, evidence-based parenting advice:** An objective search for programs and resources that offer practical parenting advice.
5. **Create a beneficial network with other parents:** Build a network with other parents for the sharing of mutually helpful experiences.

6. **Avoid treating parenting as a competitive sport:** Raising children is not a competitive game. Avoid being swept into the competition, and this will reduce worry and stress about parenting decisions.

7. **Guilty of Guilt?** Feeling guilty is a habit that may not be easy to break. Do not feel guilty about feeling guilty. Just do not feel guilty. You cannot go back. Concentrate on doing better next time.

"As a parent, I can empathize with how difficult raising children can be. There are challenges, especially within the framework of divorce, when parental guilt can sometimes blur what should be the best decision."

[LZ Granderson, U.S. Journalist]

FAMILY HISTORY

Does parental history always repeat itself? One of the worst fears of most parents is for their personal 'history' to repeat itself in their children. As the sayings: the apple does not fall far from the tree; He's just like his father; Like father, like son; A chip off the old block; She is definitely her mother's daughter.

What role does the knowledge of family tree play in parenting? A family tree is not exclusive to medical conditions; it may well involve other issues – psychological, mental, emotional, marital, financial, and so on. Should parents feel guilty when children develop problems that tend to run in the family? A particular issue or disorder could be reported as 'running in the family' if more than one person in the family has the problem.

Guilt may develop when parents think they are the cause of a child's predicament – medical or emotional. While some conditions can be inherited (passed down from parent to child), others are the result of environmental factors or a combination of genetic and environmental factors. A professional can use a person's family history (a record of medical information about several generations of the family) to help decide whether a disorder has a genetic component or environmental component.

Advances in medical research mean doctors now have the tools to understand how certain diseases, or increased risks for certain conditions (heart disease, high blood pressure, stroke, certain cancers, and diabetes), pass from one generation to another. While medical history helps us understand the risk of particular health concerns, having family members with a condition does not mean that an individual will develop that condition. On the other hand, a person with no family history of a disorder may still be at risk of developing that disorder. The risk of developing certain conditions in children is considerably reduced when both parents know their family histories. While frequent screening, check-ups and lifestyle changes can help mitigate these conditions; in extreme cases, not having children with a particular person for medical reason is highly advised.

CONCLUSION

"Therefore, put on the complete armor of God, so that you will be able to [successfully] resist and stand your ground in the evil day [of danger], and having done everything [that the crisis demands], to stand firm [in your place, fully prepared, immovable, victorious]"

[Ephesians 6:13 Amplified Bible]

Parenting is a very emotional experience. Interactions with children can trigger feelings of helplessness, frustration and disappointment. Dealing with stubborn and disobedient children is challenging for parents, and sometimes, children adopt positions that are hard to understand from an adult's perspective. The Apostle Paul in the epistle to the Ephesians writes:

"Having done everything [that the crisis demands], to stand firm [in your place, fully prepared, immovable, victorious]."

While this advice may seem counterintuitive to those parents crumbling under parenting pressures; it can offer relief in the most challenging moments – when parents are stuck at the crossroads. Parents should take an inventory of their lives and discuss their failures with their children while providing advice to prevent them from making the same mistakes. There is no guilt in being open and transparent with children. Sometimes we do stupid things; other times we do things we should not have done. Notwithstanding, we get better as long as we learn from our mistakes. Regardless of the stage in your parenting life, you can be proud of your achievements. Raising children is not about going from one point to the next.

The parenting life is about the journey – and the key to loving life is to enjoy the ultimate ride.

When you have done everything that could possibly be done, the only thing that remains is what you could still do if you only knew it."

[Carl Jung, Psychiatrist and Founder of Analytical Psychology

CHAPTER 14

HONOURING PARENTS — RISING ABOVE ABUSE

> *"Children, obey your parents in the Lord [that is, accept their guidance and discipline as His representatives], for this is right [for obedience teaches wisdom and self-discipline]. HONOUR [esteem, value as precious] YOUR FATHER AND YOUR MOTHER [and be respectful to them]—this is the first commandment with a promise— SO THAT IT MAY BE WELL WITH YOU, AND THAT YOU MAY HAVE A LONG LIFE ON THE EARTH."*
>
> [EPHESIANS 6:1-3 AMPLIFIED BIBLE]

HONOURING PARENTS

rom young to the old, parents face the challenge of disobedient children. The central point is that disobedience is not just a child issue – we all are born with a propensity for defiance.[282]

Disobedience left unchecked can influence a child's future relationship with those in authority – teachers, employers, and even friends. To honour father and mother is not a mere suggestion – it is a command that places a demand on children towards their parents – appreciate them; accept their authority; treat them with great respect, and provide for them. Before we jump into criticising our children for failing to honour us, maybe as parents, we should carry out an appraisal of our relationship with our parents, as a starting point, by asking the question "how much honour do I show my parents?" What is commonly referred to as the law of Karma – law of cause and effect – "you reap what you sow!" is in effect a cardinal biblical principle penned down by the great Apostle Paul, which says,

"Make no mistake about it, God will never be mocked! For what you plant will always be the very thing you harvest."[283]

Are parents reaping now what they sowed as children themselves? As the idiom holds "as you make your bed, so you must lie on it" – meaning you must live with the consequences of your actions and take responsibility for them. While this may be true in certain circumstances, it is not a universal rule as events in life are more complicated than a simplistic explanation of cause and effect; other factors such as abusive parents, cultural and socio-economic background all play an essential role in the deviations observed from the law of cause and effect. Stepping up and taking full or partial responsibility for a past action is a commendable way forward. However, attributing too much responsibility is not praiseworthy. It is one thing to own your actions and their consequences, but where difficulties emerge is when we allow these past actions to shape our identity. It can lead to a form of voluntary suffering that interferes with our true identity. King Solomon in the book of proverbs teaches the necessity of correcting disobedience, which if left unchecked will lead a child to destruction.

"Correct your children while there is still hope; do not let them destroy themselves".[284]

To pretend not to notice insubordination is to be irresponsible towards a delinquent child. Obedience to parents is the duty of children – as long as what the parents require does not violate moral codes of ethics and responsible citizenship.

PARENTAL ALIENATION – A FORM OF CHILD ABUSE

Parental Alienation as a form of child abuse involves a set of abusive strategies on the part of a manipulative parent to promote the child's rejection of the other parent and the child's unjustified campaign of demonising the targeted parent.[285]

Abundant research suggests that parental alienation is a severe form of both emotional child abuse and a kind of domestic violence. Parental Alienation leads to:
1. Emotional child abuse.[286]
2. Psychological child abuse.[287]
3. Family violence.[288]

A child witnessing these forms of violence against a parent is in itself, a form of child abuse. There is considerable research on the devastating effects of alienation on targeted parents. A "suicide epidemic" has been identified among divorced fathers without their children in their lives.[289]

"Child abuse casts a shadow the length of a lifetime."

[Herbert Ward, British Sculptor, Illustrator and Writer]

ABUSIVE PARENTS

"If any of you lacks wisdom [to guide him through a decision or circumstance], he is to ask of [our benevolent] God, who gives to everyone generously and without rebuke or blame, and it will be given to him."

[James 1:5 Amplified Bible]

Children have a special place in our universe. When Jesus' disciples tried to prevent children from coming to Jesus, He reprimanded them and welcomed the children saying:

"Let the children come to me, for the Kingdom of God belongs to such as they. Don't send them away! I tell you as seriously as I know how that anyone who refuses to come to God as a little child will never be allowed into his Kingdom. Then he took the children into his arms and placed his hands on their heads, and he blessed them."[290]

It will be straightforward if children are required to honour parents only if they are reasonable, loving and kind. There is a considerable number of children, many with valid reasons, who find this instruction a bitter pill to swallow. Should we honour an abusive or alienating parent? Moreover, where do we set a limit on what we are willing to do or accept?

Children can be brought up with all the privileges that life can afford, yet desperate for the smallest demonstration of love and affection. Finally, they grow into adulthood, crippled by the emotional disconnection from their parents. So, child abuse and mistreatment can be very subtle and occurs in several different ways, all of which are abhorrent. There is abuse which damages a child's psyche at an early age – even though he suffers no physical abuse; there is, of course, the more evident type – when a child is neglected, beaten, sexually abused or molested. The harm can last long into adulthood. Is it still possible to honour such abusive parents under such circumstances? The first step for an abused person is forgiveness – the act of pardoning an offender. The willingness to forgive is an honour to both God and the parent. The biblical Greek word translated *"forgiveness"* signifies *"to let go,"* as when a person does not demand payment for a debt. Jesus used this comparison when he gave the ardent teaching to his followers to pray:

"Forgive our sins as we ourselves release forgiveness to those who have wronged us."[291]

Experts suggest that forgiveness does not mean:
* Pretending that the offence did not take place;
* Denying, condoning or excusing the crimes;
* Allowing other people to take advantage of you;
* Releasing people from legal accountability.

While anyone with information that a child is going through abuse should report to the appropriate authority, those who have experienced abused can begin their journey to wholeness by talking to qualified professionals – Counsellors, Pastors, Therapists, Doctors and other public child healthcare professionals. There are also many organisations, charities and community support groups that can offer assistance.

How do you honour an abusive parent in real life? Factors to consider include:

- Be willing to forgive even if they refuse to apologise or admit to what they have done
- Substitute your disappointment with acceptance of who the person is.
- Cultivate an attitude of compassion for the right things they did.
- Show gratitude for any slight efforts they make to show love.
- Desist from making derogatory statements about your parent.
- Establish wise boundaries when in communication with your parent to reduce the likelihood of any undesirable issues.

Forgiveness and honour are not synonymous to remaining a prisoner in a dysfunctional family. Families with destructive cycles are dangerous, and children who break free need to find safety elsewhere. There is no guilt in distancing oneself from abusive parents, as long as vengeance or retribution is not the motivation. You can honour your parents from a distance. Sadly, some parents do not value their children enough to maintain a relationship.

"Parenthood…it's about guiding the next generation and forgiving the last."

[Peter Krause, Actor]

CHILD – PARENT ABUSE

*"The proverbs of Solomon: A wise child brings joy to a father;
a foolish child brings grief to a mother."*

[Proverbs 10:1 New Living Translation]

Child on Parent Violence (CPV), more often called parent abuse, is not as popular as child abuse or partner on partner domestic abuse. Nonetheless, this does not mean it is an uncommon occurrence. In the article 'Is parent abuse a form of domestic abuse", published in *Social Policy and Society,* author Paula Wilcox writing on abuse says:

"It's one of the biggest taboos in family life. It happens – we know that – but no one talks about it. And there's really no one to talk to about it – mothers (who are most often on the receiving end) don't tell their friends and there isn't the network of support organisations to help you deal with it the way there are for women battered by partners. Whilst it is common for adolescents to demonstrate healthy anger, conflict and frustration as they transition from childhood to adulthood, anger should not be conflated with violence.'[292]

What is Parent Abuse?

Parent abuse is any behaviour used by a young person to manipulate, intimidate, control, dominate, threaten or coerce parents – to exert control and have power over the parent. It takes many forms and includes emotional abuse, financial exploitation, severe physical assaults, destruction of property and psychological manipulation.

Barbara Cottrell, in her book *When Teens Abuse Their Parents'*, defines parent abuse as *"any harmful act of a teenage child intended to gain power and control over a parent."*[293]

Parent abuse is not limited to a defined social group; it has an equal impact on two-parent and single families. However, it is usually the mother (or the primary caregiver) who is most affected, but others in the family and fathers can also be affected.

Signs of parent abuse include, but not limited to: threats of physical violence; intimidation; constant disobedience; swearing and name-calling; bullying; criminal financial activities; deliberate destruction of property; emotional blackmail; denigrating parents in public; drug/alcohol abuse in the home. It is not uncommon for children to 'moderately' oppose parents, however, when this rebellion crosses the 'red' line and turns violent, parents must stand their grounds in authority and set proper limits and boundaries. Parents must make it clear that abuse is never accepted and never tolerated. If faced with threats and bullying, don't threaten or bully back but rather de-escalate the conflict by taking some time out to calm down. Parents who stay united and strong in parenting decisions will prevent children from playing the 'divide and rule' game.

Factors to consider when dealing with adolescents who abuse parents include: a history of domestic abuse within the family unit; an abusive intimate relationship; being coerced into abusive behaviours; displaying heightened sexualised behaviours; association with violent groups; difficulties in forming relationships; mental health issues; disengagement from education; substance abuse and misuse; obsessive use of violent games or pornography.

"Child abuse and neglect is sometimes the result of a parent who reaches the end of their frustration and tolerance level. If we can give parents tools to deal with an infant who is particularly challenging with their crying, we will have taken an important step toward our prevention mandate."

[Gary Kleeblatt,
Connecticut Department of Children and Families]

THE CASE OF ABSALOM

The important stories of the Old Testament are not fairy tales of the past. Instead, they contain valuable lessons about historical places, events and people.

"Now, all these things serve as types and pictures for us—lessons that teach us not to fail in the same way by callously craving worthless things"[294]

"Everything that was written in the past was written to teach us. Those things were written so that we could have hope. That hope comes from the patience and encouragement that the Scriptures give us."[295]

A major compelling piece of evidence for the reliability of the sacred text of the Bible is the impartial manner in which it portrays the lives of its characters. The weaknesses and errors of its heroes, as well as its villains, are resolutely revealed. The life of David, ancient Israel's greatest king, is depicted in like manner, even though he was an influential statesman, an accomplished musician, a first-class poet, and an extraordinary leader. His third son, Absalom, reflects an example of child-parent abuse when he put together a coup, a plot, to overthrow David's leadership. The conspiracy became stronger, and at the opportune time, Absalom, backed by a huge military force, proclaimed himself to be the new King.[296]

For fear of his life, David assembled some of his servants and fled the capital, not before giving clear orders to his military officers to "deal gently" with Absalom – in spite of his treason. Unfortunately, the coup plot did not last; Absalom died in the process.

While in some circumstances, it is quite challenging to navigate the conflict between parental expectations with children's aspirations, rebellion and parent abuse is not the solution. This is playing a game that children cannot win. They may have the upper hand for some time, and get done what they wanted to be done, but at the end, it will lead to pain and hurt, not just for parents, but to the children as well. They may not end up like Absalom, but such actions will produce harmful effects in their life.

"Those who cannot remember the past are condemned to repeat it."

[George Santayana, 19th-century Philosopher and Poet]

PARENT ABUSE: RECOMMENDATIONS

"He heals the broken-hearted; And binds up their wounds [healing their pain and comforting their sorrow]."

[Psalm 147:3 Amplified Bible]

The charity organisation Family Lives in an article *Teen Violence At Home'* provides the following recommendations on what to do if you are experiencing violence from your teenager.[297]

1. **Look after yourself** – This is important to develop a coping mechanism to deal with the anger and aggression from your teen. You probably feel exhausted, demoralised and are likely to be making considerable efforts to get a tiny amount of control.

2. **This is not your fault** – No parent can avoid making mistakes, life itself is an imperfect process full of disappointments, and difficulties and children need to be able to cope with these.

3. **Choose your battles** – You cannot tackle everything at once, put some issues on the back-burner for appropriate future action.

4. **Try not to take it personally** – If your child is struggling, it is often because of a range of other issues that may have been beyond your control. Once you are aware of them, you can give support and help to address their fears and worries.

5. **Separate the behaviour from your teen** – You can still love your teen but not like their behaviour. It is not a package, and it is essential to try to view their behaviour as a stand-alone issue.

6. **Use language that separates the behaviour from your teen** – Avoid using a negative language of blame.

7. **Ignoring the behaviour will not make it go away** – It is tough to go through this, but playing it down will not help it go away. If it is not properly addressed, the violence could increase and become a life-long pattern.

8. **Keep yourself safe** – This is so important and ensures you and other members of the family are safe. If you can spot the signs of the conflict turning into violence, have a safety plan for those times. Try to go to a place of safety while you decide what to do next. Call the police if you need to.

9. **Calling the police** – You may feel reluctant to call in the police as you may not want your child to get into serious trouble or for other reasons. The police have been working with many families on adolescent-parent violence and abuse and understand the impact. If you are in fear for your safety or you are feeling threatened, it is the right thing to call the police to help diffuse the situation.

10. **Redress the balance** – Often, the only attention you will be giving your teen is in response to harmful behaviour. If you feel able to, find moments where you can show your appreciation when they are doing well.

11. **Be aware of your responses and reactions to conflict** – You might be inflaming the situation without meaning to, for example, by shouting or responding with aggression. Keep yourself calm. Leave the room for a while if you need to. Respond rather than react.

12. **Acknowledge their feelings** – "I know you are outraged", recognises the fact without criticism. "What would help you now?" "I will see what I can do, and we will talk about it later." A gentle look, a kind touch can convey this without hostility and before trying to talk about what is wrong.

13. **Try to find the root of the anger** – School pressures, bullying, friendships, mental health, family breakdown, illness can all be

trigger factors that add to a child's stress levels. They are not excuses, but there may be reasons for it. Talking through the pressures, listening to your teen attentively, without judging, interrupting or directing them can help them to offload their feelings and release the tension constructively.

14. **Help them develop self-strategies** – Helping your teen to understand the triggers and what to do when they are angry is crucial to help them overcome this. When things are calm, have a chat and find out what they think would work for them. It may be a case of trial and error, but it is good to help them manage their emotions and find a different outlet for expressing their angry feelings. They might want to use calming down strategies for their anger, or an alternative option is a meditation to help them quieten down. Let them know that you are there for them.

15. **Give them space** – Recognise that your teen is taking anger out on you and may not know how else to deal with painful feelings. Once they have calmed down, you may be able to talk to them about what has happened and suggest they let you find them some help.

16. **Do not fight fire with fire** – Avoid using violence with your teen. If you are hitting your teenager in response, then you are giving them the message that it is acceptable to use force to solve disagreements. By avoiding the use of violence, you are setting a positive example of what you find acceptable.

17. **Get support for yourself** – Know what assistance you need, and pick and mix from your friends and relatives to get the best fit that you can. Contact supports services for help and advice.

Linda Herman's thought-provoking book 'Parent to the End: *How Baby Boomers Can Parent for Peace of Mind, Foster Responsibility in Their Adult Children, and Keep Their Hard-Earned Money'*, proposes the bill of rights of Parent – ten rights that contribute to the overall health and well-being of parents.

These include:[298]

- The right to be free from abuse.
- The right to be guilt-free.
- The right to peace of mind.
- The right to have reasonable expectations.
- The right to be imperfect.
- The right to decide what to do with your own money.
- The right to decide what to do with your time.
- The right of selective association.
- The right to retirement; the right to say "No"

"Tradition holds that children ought to obey their parents, but modernism holds that parents ought to obey their children."

[Jesse Song, Author 'Pillars of Parenting']

IMPORTANCE OF SOCIAL SERVICES

"Speak up for those who cannot speak for themselves; ensure justice for those being crushed."

[Proverbs 31:8 New Living Translation]

In an incredibly complex society filled with injustices and pressing challenges, we need dedicated social workers who bring positive social change in the community, helping individuals and being an advocate for those who have lost their voice - especially children. The primary goal of the social worker is to assist needy people in addressing, managing and resolving various social problems. They are available to use their skills and knowledge to help families going through difficult challenges in life – whether it's abuse, addiction, poverty, disability, mental illness, criminal behaviour, or anything else. Without social workers, countless children would have gone without the support and guidance they need to lead healthy and fulfilling lives.

Families often feel apprehensive at the possibility of the involvement of social services because they are afraid that their children will be taken away, or they may have heard of the experiences of other families. These fears are rational, but a child will only be removed if there is undeniable proof that they are at risk of serious harm. If the welfare or safety of a child is at stake, they will conduct what is called a Section 47 enquiry - an investigation when there is reasonable cause to suspect that a child has been abused, neglected, abandoned or is likely to suffer significant harm in the future unless concrete steps are taken to safeguard the child's welfare.

Social services can get involved with families in several ways. You or a family member who is concerned can approach social services, the police or contact the National Society for the Prevention of Cruelty to Children (NSPCC). Referrals can also be made by other professionals who are working with your family or children, including schools, GPs, health visitors, religious leaders and more.

"Social Work is the Art of Listening and the Science of Hope."

Unknown Author]

HOW TO HANDLE FALSE ACCUSATIONS

Child abuse is any action that causes or is likely to cause significant harm to a child. It can be physical, emotional or sexual, alongside child cruelty and neglect. There does not have to be strong evidence to trigger a referral to Social Services. Sometimes it is merely an opinion or a suspicion that a public employee has, although it has to be 'evidence based.' There have been some cases where families were accused of physical abuse with broken bones, and it was later found that these children had vitamin D deficiency which caused brittle bone syndrome.

False accusations are not uncommon. There are many different ways they are made. Firstly, when one partner is looking for ways to 'punish' the other or an attempted act of revenge from a partner or spouse. Secondly, when a belligerent child uses false accusations as a means of manipulating parents. Such children seek to use social services as a tool of intimidation (most children act honourably towards their parents). Thirdly, when a concerned person suspects that a child is being abused.

The local authority might get involved with your family if they are concerned about child abuse. Firstly, if the reports of abuse are not substantiated, they may choose not to do anything about it, there will be 'no action taken'. Secondly, they may decide that the child is not at risk of significant harm but instead a child in need, and that the family needs support to protect the well-being of the child. Thirdly, they may involve the police to carry out further investigations to establish the facts of the case, and decide accordingly. Whether you are accused rightly or wrongly, it is crucial for you to:

- get legal advice
- speak to the social worker to find out what their intentions are.
- check what is on the file to make sure that it has been recorded accurately
- ensure that your lawyer is present before making any statements to the authorities.
- record all interactions you have with child services and or the police.
- keep all pieces of evidence, such as emails, text messages, telephone records that can assist in proving that the allegations made against you are false.
- gather relevant evidence to support your case. This may include statements by family members, friends, co-workers or neighbours.
- co-operate fully and follow the advice of your lawyer.

THE 'SOCIAL WORKER – FAMILIES' PARTNERSHIP

Social workers recognize the primary importance of human relationships. Sarah Gillinson, in the article '*Why relationships* are key to *good social work*' published in the Guardian, writes:

> "*Positive interactions between social workers and families are essential, but too often policies and practices act as a barrier. It's no wonder service users have a mixed experience – social workers manage a tricky balance. They do their best to support families to grow safer, more nurturing environments for their children, while at the same time assessing risk with a view to removing a child if they can't reduce it. It's hard to build relationships when your job is to take a family to court unless things change. This is especially hard in a system that encourages box ticking rather than relationship building, and that often demands a focus on a family's weaknesses rather than strengths.*
>
> *Frontline practitioners deal with large caseloads, under pressure to assess and monitor risk and comply with many rules and regulations. They are not incentivised or supported to build the mutual understanding upon which good relationships are based – relationships that can make all the difference for an individual or family, and reduce risk to a child. Without this kind of human interaction there are no relationships. Without relationships, there is no trust. And without trust there is only so much a social worker can do.*'[299]

A study from the Harvard Centre on the Developing Child found that the essential factor in the success of services provided by care professionals depend on the quality of their relationship with the families in question. When practitioners listen, build trust and connect with families to find ways to explore solutions together, then they can obtain the best possible outcomes for children.[300]

Notwithstanding, society has a legitimate interest in childrearing and a moral obligation to intervene whenever parents who fail to meet their responsibilities put their children at risk.

CHALLENGES OF SOCIAL WORKERS

The Department for Education 2019 report *'Experimental statistics: Children and family social work workforce in England, year ending September 30, 2018'*, revealed that 4,490 (full-time equivalent) social workers had left their job in the year ending September 30, 2018, compared with 3,880 in the previous year.[301]

Being a social worker can be satisfying because you are helping individuals make a difference in their lives and to boost the capacity for social functioning. You solve problems and promote social change for the greater good of society. While it is satisfying, studies have found that social workers have high workloads and a lack of resources to help service users, thus contributing to stress and poor working conditions.

A survey of 1600 social workers by Bath Spa University with the British Association of Social Workers (BASW) and the Social Workers Union (SWU) into the working conditions of social workers found 52% of UK social workers intend to leave the profession within 15 months. A total of 55% of those working in children's services intend to leave social work.[302]

The Health and Care Professions Council (HCPC) should ensure that social workers operate effectively and their professional deficiencies supported and improved rather than always finding blame or failings in individual frontline workers. This *'blame culture'* narrative further devalues the profession. While regulators have to ensure proper social work practice; understanding why failures occur is of paramount importance. Some people may see social workers as unsympathetic to their actions, but they mean the best. Some see them as dividing families, yet they safeguard the vulnerable. The press and media may vilify them but without their support, many would be lost. We may not always agree with their course of action, but they are still available – working under extreme pressures to meet our needs. They may make mistakes, ignore cultural realities and make subjective decisions, but they are human too. When things go wrong, let us take into consideration their noble profession and give them the benefit of the doubt – to err is human, to forgive divine.

"I believe the best service to the child is the service closest to the child,
and children who are victims of neglect, abuse,
or abandonment must not also be victims of bureaucracy.
They deserve our devoted attention, not our divided attention."

[Kenny Guinn, Politician and Former Governor of Nevada]

CONCLUSION

Research has shown that our attachment history–the quality of attachment we had with our own parents–is strongly related to our parenting behaviours, and in turn, to the type of attachment, our children will have to us.

The following questions should be considered by new parents:

1. What did you admire about the manner you were parented?
2. What would you not like to see repeated with your children?
3. How has your relationship with your parents progressed since childhood?

Dr Siegel and co-author Mary Hartzell, in the book, *Parenting from the Inside Out: How a Deeper Self-Understanding Can Help You Raise Children Who Thrive'*, present evidence-based research in the field of child development which shows that the principal factor is not the thing we experience in our childhood, rather it is how we understand the effects of those experiences in our lives. Dr Siegel suggests that parenting allows us to reflect on our own early experiences as we create a loving attachment with our children. A difficult childhood does not necessarily mean that you are bound to re-create negative interactions with your children. But it requires self-understanding, an inside-out approach to parenting, to break the negative patterns of family interactions from being transmitted down through the generations.[303]

The duty of parents is to choose behaviours that will support children's emotional well-being rather than repeating old patterns.

The Practice of Forgiveness[304]

Dr. Tyler VanderWeele, co-director of the Initiative on Health, Religion, and Spirituality at the Harvard T.H. Chan School of Public Health recommends the REACH method as an effective way to practice forgiveness. R-E-A-C-H stands for Recall, Emphasize, Altruistic gift, Commit, and Hold.

1. **Recall.** The first step is to recall the wrongdoing in an objective way. The goal is not to think of the person in a negative light nor to wallow in self-pity, but to come to a clear understanding of the wrong that was done.

2. **Empathise.** Next, try to understand the other person's point of view regarding why he or she hurt you, but without minimizing or downplaying the wrong that was done.

3. **Altruistic gift.** This step is about addressing your own shortcomings. Recall a time when you treated someone harshly and were forgiven. How did it make you feel? Recognizing this helps you realize that forgiveness is an altruistic gift that you can give to others.

4. **Commit.** Commit yourself to forgive.

5. **Hold.** Finally, hold on to your forgiveness. This step is tough because memories of the event will often recur. "Forgiveness is not erasure - rather, it's about changing your reaction to those memories," says Dr Tyler VanderWeele.

"It's not an easy journey, to get to a place where you forgive people. But it is such a powerful place, because it sets you free."

[Tyler Perry, Actor, Writer and Producer]

CHAPTER 15

─── ❧ ───

CONCLUSION – THE RULES OF LIFE

> *And you, beloved, are the light of the world. A city built on a hilltop cannot be hidden. Similarly, it would be silly to light a lamp and then hide it under a bowl. When someone lights a lamp, she puts it on a table or a desk or a chair, and the light illumines the entire house. You are like that illuminating light. Let your light shine everywhere you go, that you may illumine creation, so men and women everywhere may see your good actions, may see creation at its fullest, may see your devotion to Me, and may turn and praise your Father in heaven because of it.*
>
> [MATTHEW 5:14-16 THE VOICE]

MOVING THE GOAL POST

I n his book '*Recapture the Wonder*', Dr Ravi Zacharias, writes:

"*In the 1950s kids lost their innocence. They were liberated from their parents by well-paying jobs, cars, and lyrics in music that gave rise to a new term – the generation gap.*

In the 1960s, kids lost their authority. It was a decade of protest – church, state, and parents were all called into question and found wanting. Their authority was rejected, yet nothing ever replaced it.

In the 1970s, kids lost their love. It was the decade of me-ism dominated by hyphenated words beginning with self – self-image, self-esteem, self-assertion. It made for a lonely world. Kids learned everything there was to know about sex and forgot everything there was to know about love, and no one had the nerve to tell them there was a difference.

In the 1980s, kids lost their hope. Stripped of innocence, authority and love and plagued by the horror of a nuclear nightmare, large and growing numbers of this generation stopped believing in the future.

In the 1990s kids lost their power to reason. Less and less were they taught the very basics of language, truth, and logic and they grew up with the irrationality of a postmodern world.

In the new millennium, kids woke up and found out that somewhere in the midst of all this change, they had lost their imagination. Violence and perversion entertained them till none could talk of killing innocents since none was innocent anymore."[305]

MEDITATIONS OF EMPEROR MARCUS AURELIUS

Marcus Aurelius (AD 121-180) – Roman Emperor and Stoic philosopher, authored a series of challenging personal writings and reflections as he struggled to understand himself and how to live with maximum sanity and inner peace. These thoughts and writings form a collection of twelve books known as the *Meditations*. Translator Gregory Hays, notes in the introduction:[306]

> *"Ancient philosophy certainly had its academic side. But philosophy also had a more practical dimension. It was not merely a subject to write or argue about, but one that was expected to provide a "design for living" – a set of rules to live one's life by"*

In Book II of Meditations, Aurelius writes:

> *"When you wake up in the morning, tell yourself: The people I deal with today will be meddling, ungrateful, arrogant, dishonest, jealous, and surly. They are like this because they can't tell good from evil. But I have seen the beauty of good, and the ugliness of evil, and have recognised that the wrongdoer has a nature related to my own — not of the same blood or birth, but of the same mind, and possessing a share of the divine. And so none of them can hurt me. No one can implicate me in ugliness. Nor can I feel angry at my relative, or hate him. We were born to work together like feet, hands, and eyes, like the two rows of teeth, upper and lower. To obstruct each other is unnatural. To feel anger at someone, to turn your back on him: these are obstructions."*[307]

In Book V, Aurelius emphasises the virtue of work. He writes:

> *"At dawn, when you have trouble getting out of bed, tell yourself: 'I have to go to work – as a human being. What do I have to complain of, if I'm*

going to do what I was born for – the things I was brought into the world to do? Or is this what I was created for? To huddle under the blankets and stay warm?"

In the Emperor's philosophy, everything has a purpose. Man has a major duty to clear his mind of garbage and distraction and focus on the most important task that needs to be done. In other Meditations, he says:

- "If you are distressed by anything external, the pain is not due to the thing itself, but to your estimate of it; and this you have the power to revoke at any moment."

- "Whenever you are about to find fault with someone, ask yourself the following question: What fault of mine most nearly resembles the one I am about to criticize?"

- "Begin each day by telling yourself: Today I shall be meeting with interference, ingratitude, insolence, disloyalty, ill-will, and selfishness – all of them due to the offenders' ignorance of what is good or evil."

- "Everything we hear is an opinion, not a fact. Everything we see is a perspective, not the truth."

- "The happiness of your life depends upon the quality of your thoughts: therefore, guard accordingly, and take care that you entertain no notions unsuitable to virtue and reasonable nature."

- "Never esteem anything as of advantage to you that will make you break your word or lose your self-respect."

- "Don't go on discussing what a good person should be. Just be one."

- "If someone can prove me wrong and show me my mistake in any thought or action, I shall gladly change. I seek the truth, which never harmed anyone: the harm is to persist in one's own self-deception and ignorance."
- "The happiness of those who want to be popular depends on others; the happiness of those who seek pleasure fluctuates with moods outside their control; but the happiness of the wise grows out of their own free acts."

"Many of life's failures are people who did not realise how close they were to success when they gave up."

[Thomas Edison, Inventor and Businessman]

PRINCIPLES OF SUCCESSFUL LIVING

"I say this because I know what I am planning for you," says the Lord.
"I have good plans for you, not plans to hurt you.
I will give you hope and a good future."

[Jeremiah 29:11 New Century Version]

Solomon's Strategy for Success[308]

Mike Mazzalongo, the author of BibleTalk.tv article *'Solomon's Strategy for Success'*, draws inspiration from King Solomon, whom ancient texts record was determined to experiment with all of life's great enticements - diverse sensual and sexual pleasures; strong drink and its consequence; acquisition of knowledge; massive building projects and the exercise of political power. While experimenting with these, King Solomon was mindful to document his observations on how to achieve and maintain success throughout one's life. According to Mazzalongo, Solomon's seven strategies for success include:

1. You have Got to Give in Order to Get

"Do good wherever you go. After a while, the good you do will come back to you." [309]

A popular business principle states: "there is no return without investment and no reward without risk." Success requires the investment of time, effort, energy and self-discipline. Those who fail usually have excuses and blame, while those who succeed, do so because they were willing to forgo certain things in order to achieve their goals. As the old saying goes, *"the more you give, the more you get."*

2. Diversify

"Invest what you have in several different things. You don't know what bad things might happen on earth." [310]

Successful people recognise that sometimes (more often than not) bad things happen, and it is always wise to anticipate such events with a backup plan or second window of opportunity. Success sometimes occurs after several attempts and in areas we least imagine. Successful people advance as many of their talents as possible and maximise as many opportunities as time and energy permit.

3. Do not Worry About What You Cannot Change

"There are some things you can be sure of. If clouds are full of rain, they will pour water on the earth. If a tree falls – to the south or to the north – then it will stay where it falls."[311]

Solomon uses examples from nature to illustrate situations that we have no control or power to change once they occur. Our energy should be invested into viable causes and not worrying about past mistakes or those things that are impossible for us to control or change.

4. Do it Now

"But there are some things that you cannot be sure of. You must take a chance. If you wait for perfect weather, you will never plant your seeds. If you are afraid that every cloud will bring rain, you will never harvest your crops."[312]

Lost opportunities are usually the result of failure to take the first step towards our desired goal. Procrastinating robs time and energy. Putting off reasonable action plans for fear of failure is a recipe for a life of mediocrity. Without delay, successful people act on their dreams, goals, and vision.

5. You Never Know Until You Try

"You don't know where the wind blows. And you don't know how a baby grows in its mother's womb. In the same way, you don't know what God will do—and he makes everything happen. So begin planting early in the morning, and don't stop working until evening. You don't know what might make you rich. Maybe everything you do will be successful."[313]

There are things not seen (such as the wind), but they are nevertheless real. Success cannot be obtained or even noticed until a person attempts at something. Others may be blind to the likelihood of success because they do not value your vision or lack confidence in you. King Solomon encourages us to believe the evidence of the unseen, and to understand the power of faith.

6. Remember God's Judgment

"It is good to be alive. It is nice to see the light from the sun. You should enjoy every day of your life, no matter how long you live. But remember that you will die, and you will be dead much longer than you were alive. And after you are dead, you cannot do anything. So young people, enjoy yourselves while you are young. Be happy. Do whatever your heart leads you to do. Do whatever you want, but remember that God will judge you for everything you do."[314]

Humanity was never created for failures and unhappiness, but rather to be productive and enjoy the things that life offers, yet with responsibility and divine caution. The pleasure that success produces is neither the end of life nor its goal. Successful people know that success is a gift, and as such, are not self-absorbed by it nor do anything (even unethical) to maintain or keep it.

7. Success is Sweet, but Success is Short.

"Don't let your anger control you, and don't let your body lead you to sin. People do foolish things in the dawn of life while they are young."[315]

Solomon's advice to successful people is to enjoy while they have it because it is short-lived - a good suggestion for those who work hard to build families, businesses and careers but do not spend enough time to enjoy the fruit of their hard work. According to the King Solomon, there is nothing wrong with pursuing success, achieving goals and establishing dreams. After all, it was God who gave him the wisdom which he faithfully transmitted unto us. However, in doing this, we are cautioned to remember that to achieve final success, which is to live forever with God, we must follow His strategy for genuine success.

LUCIUS ANNAEUS SENECA (4 BC – 65 AD)

Lucius Annaeus Seneca, better known as Seneca the Younger (4 BC – 65 AD) was a Roman philosopher, writer and statesman, probably best known for being a tutor and advisor to Emperor Nero.[316]

On the brevity of life, Seneca, writes:

"It's not at all that we have too short a time to live, but that we squander a great deal of it. Life is long enough, and it's given in sufficient measure to do many great things if we spend it well. But when it's poured down the drain of luxury and neglect, when it's employed to no good end, we're finally driven to see that it had passed by before we even recognised it passing. And so it is – we don't receive a short life, we make it so."[317]

"There are no secrets to success. It is the result of preparation,
hard work, and learning from failure"

[Colin Powell, Retired US Army General and Statesman

THE BLESSINGS

Obey the LORD your God so that all these blessings will come and stay with you:

You will be blessed in the city and blessed in the country.

Your children will be blessed, as well as your crops; your herds will be blessed with calves and your flocks with lambs.

Your basket and your kitchen will be blessed.

You will be blessed when you come in and when you go out.

The LORD will help you defeat the enemies that come to fight you. They will attack you from one direction, but they will run from you in seven directions.

The LORD your God will bless you with full barns, and he will bless everything you do. He will bless the land he is giving you.

The LORD will make you his holy people, as he promised. But you must obey his commands and do what he wants you to do.

Then everyone on earth will see that you are the LORD's people, and they will be afraid of you.

The LORD will make you rich: You will have many children, your animals will have many young, and your land will give good crops. It is the land that the LORD promised your ancestors he would give to you.

The LORD will open up his heavenly storehouse so that the skies send rain on your land at the right time, and he will bless everything you do. You will lend to other nations, but you will not need to borrow from them.

The LORD will make you like the head and not like the tail; you will be on top and not on bottom. But you must obey the commands of the LORD your God that I am giving you today, being careful to keep them.[318]

ENDNOTES

1 Livingston, G. and Bialik, K. (2018). *7 Facts About U.S. Mothers*. Pew Research Centre. [Online]. Available at: https://www.pewresearch.org/fact-tank/2018/05/10/facts-about-u-s-mothers/ [Accessed 12 Apr. 2019].

2 Cervantes, W., Ullrich, R. and Matthew, H. (2007). *Developing Child*. National Scientific Council on the Developing Child. [Online]. Available at: https://developingchild.harvard.edu/wp-content/uploads/2015/05/Science_Early_Childhood_Development.pdf [Accessed 10 Apr. 2019].

3 National Academy of Sciences (2019). *National Academy of Sciences (NAS)*. [Online]. Available at: https:// nasonline.org/ [Accessed 12 Apr. 2019].

4 Steinberg, L. (2005). *The Ten Basic Principles of Good Parenting*. New York: Simon & Schuster Paperbacks.

5 Howe, N. and Strauss, W. (2000). *Millennials Rising: The Next Generation*. New York: Vintage Books.

6 Strauss, W. and Howe, N. (1992). *Generations: The History of America's Future, 1584 to 2069*. New York, NY: Quill.

7 Rouse, M. (2019). *What is Millennials (Generation Y)? - Definition from WhatIs.com*. WhatIs.com. [Online]. Available at: https://whatis.techtarget.com/definition/millennials-millennial-generation [Accessed 14 Oct. 2019].

8 Dimock, M. (2019). *Defining generations: Where Millennials end and Generation Z begins*. Pew Research Center. [Online]. Available at: https://www.pewresearch.org/fact-tank/2019/01/17/where-millennials-end-and-generation-z-begins/ [Accessed 14 Oct. 2019].

9 Ibid

10 Deloitte (2014). *The Deloitte Millennial Survey*. Deloitte. [Online]. Available at: https://www2.deloitte.com/content/dam/Deloitte/global/Documents/About-Deloitte/gx-dttl-2014-millennial-survey-report.pdf [Accessed 14 Oct. 2019].

11 Vogels, E. (2019). *Millennials stand out for their technology use, but older generations also embrace digital life*. Pew Research Center. [Online]. Available at: https://www.pewresearch.org/fact-tank/2019/09/09/us-generations-technology-use/ [Accessed 14 Oct. 2019].

12 Burke, R., Cooper, C. and Antoniou, A. (2015). The Multi-generational and Aging Workforce. Research Gate, p.122.

13 Livingston, G. and Bialik, K. (2018). *7 Facts About U.S. Mothers*. Pew Research Center. [Online]. Available at: https://www.pewresearch.org/fact-tank/2018/05/10/facts-about-u-s-mothers/ [Accessed 12 Apr. 2019].

14 Taylor, P. and Keeter, S. (2010). *Millenials – A Portrait of Generation Next: Confident. Connected. Open to Change*. Pew Research Center. [Online]. Available at: https://www.pewresearch.org/wp-content/uploads/sites/3/2010/10/millennials-confident-connected-open-to-change.pdf [Accessed 12 Apr. 2019].

15 Foot, D. and Stoffman, D. Boom (1998). Bust and Echo 2000: Profiting from the Demographic Shift in the New Millennium. Toronto: Macfarlane, Walter & Ross.

16 Matthew 10:8 New King James Version

17 Pells, R. and Romer, C. (2019). *Great Depression | Definition, History, Causes, Effects, & Facts*. Encyclopedia Britannica. [Online]. Available at: https://www.britannica.com/event/Great-Depression [Accessed 14 Oct. 2019].

18 Bryson, D. (2019). Family and Home, Impact of the Great Depression. [Online]. Available at: https://www.encyclopedia.com/economics/encyclopedias-almanacs-transcripts-and-maps/family-and-home-impact-great-depression [Accessed 14 Oct. 2019].

19 Watts, R. (2017). *A Boomer Parent's Apology to Millennials*. Forbes. com. [Online]. Available at: https://www.forbes.com/sites/nextavenue/2017/12/06/a-boomer-parents-apology-to-millennials/#5119098b24b6 [Accessed 12 Apr. 2019].

20 Bentley, G. and Mascie-Taylor, C. (2000). *Infertility in The Modern World*. Cambridge: Cambridge University Press, p.190.

21 Manby, C. (2018). *Do you have children? And if not, why not?*. The Independent. [Online]. Available at https://www.independent.co.uk/life-style/health-and-families/children-famillies-social-etiquette-childless-a8387831.html [Accessed 10 Mar. 2019].

22 Khazan, O. (2019). *How People Decide Whether to Have Children*. The Atlantic. [Online]. Available at: https://www.theatlantic.com/health/archive/2017/05/how-people-decide-whether-to-have-children/527520/ [Accessed 15 Mar. 2019].

23 Blackstone, A. (2014). *Doing Family without Having Kids*. Sociology Compass, 8(1), pp.52-62.

24 Sandler, L. (2013). *The Childfree Life: Having It All Without Having Children*. California: Time Magazine.

25 May, E. T. (1997). *Barren in the Promised Land*. Cambridge, MA: Harvard University Press.

26 Houseknecht, S. (1978). Voluntary Childlessness – A social psychological Model. *Alternative Lifestyles*, 1(3), pp.379-402.

27 LV (2016). *Cost of Raising a Child*. Press [Online]. Available at: https://www.lv.com/about-us/press/cost-of-a-child-2016 [Accessed 2 Apr. 2019].

28 Aarssen, L. W. and Altman, S. T. (2014). *Fertility Preference Inversely Related to 'Legacy Drive' in Women, But Not in Men: Interpreting the Evolutionary Roots, and Future, of the 'Childfree' Culture*. The Open Behavioral Science Journal. 6. Pp.37-43. [Online]. Available at: https://www.researchgate.net/journal/18742300_The_Open_Behavioral_Science_Journal [Accessed 16 Mar. 2019].

29 Krapf, M., Ursprung, H. and Zimmermann, C. (2014): Parenthood and Productivity of Highly Skilled Labor: Evidence from the Groves of Academe. IZA Discussion Paper, No. 7904.

30 Barker, S. B. and Barker, R. T. (1988). The human-canine bond: Closer than family ties. *Journal of Mental Health Counselling*, 10, pp. 46-56.

31 Stokes, S., Planchon, L., Templer, D. and Keller, J. (2002). Death of a Companion Cat or Dog and Human Bereavement: Psychosocial Variables. *Society & Animals*, 10(1), pp.93-105.

32 Dolan, P. (2019). *Happy Ever After*. London: Allen Lane.

33 Office for National Statistics (2017). Statistical Bulletin: Childbearing for women born in different years, England and Wales: 2016. Ons.gov. uk. [Online]. Available at: https://www.ons.gov.uk/peoplepopulationand-community/birthsdeathsandmarriages/conceptionandfertilityrates/bul-letins/childbearingforwomenbornindifferentyearsenglandandwales/2016 [Accessed 20 Sep. 2019].

34 Burton, N. (2017). *For Better for Worse*, [S.l.]: Acheron Press.

35 Benata, D (2008). *Never to Have Been: The Harm of Coming into Existence:* Oxford University Press.

36 Claire, M. (2019). *Meet the Anti-natalists, People Who Believe Having Kids Is Wrong*. [Online]. Available at: https://www.marieclaire.com/culture/a14751412/antinatalism/ [Accessed 15 Mar. 2019].

37 Cherry, K. (2019). *How to Deal With Tokophobia: Fear of Childbirth*. Verywell Mind. [Online]. Available at: https://www.verywellmind.com/tokophobia-overview-4684507 [Accessed 16 Oct. 2019].

38 Hofberg, K. and Brockington, I. (2000). Tokophobia: An unreasoning dread of childbirth. A series of 26 cases. *British Journal of Psychiatry*, 176(1), pp.83-85.

39 Hofberg, K. (2003). Fear of pregnancy and childbirth. *Postgraduate Medical Journal*, 79(935), pp.506-507.

40 Ganapathy, T. (2015). Tokophobia among First Time Expectant Fa-

thers. *International Journal of Psychiatric Nursing*, 1(1), p.99.

41 1 Corinthians 7:32 New Living Translation.

42 Baumrind, D. (1991). The Influence of Parenting Style on Adolescent Competence and Substance Use. *The Journal of Early Adolescence*, 11(1), pp.56-95.

43 Markham, L. (2015). *Peaceful Parent, Happy Kids*. New York: Perigee Book.

44 Ginott, H., Ginott, A. and Goddard, H. (2004). *Between parent and child*. New York: Random House.

45 Bernstein, D. (2013). *Essentials of Psychology*. Boston, MA: Cengage Learning. p.368

46 Bernstein, D. (2013). *Essentials of Psychology*. Boston, MA: Cengage Learning.

47 National Academy of Sciences, 2016. *Parenting Matters: Supporting Parents of Children Ages 0-8*. Washington, DC: The National Academy of Sciences.

48 Ibid., p. 219.

49 Encyclopedia Britannica. (2019). *Sir Edward Burnett Tylor | British anthropologist*. [online] Available at: https://www.britannica.com/biography/Edward-Burnett-Tylor [Accessed 28 Aug. 2019].

50 Bornstein, M. (2012). Cultural Approaches to Parenting. *Parenting*, 12(2-3), p. 213

51 Ibid., p. 213.

52 Kwak, K. (2003). Adolescents and their parents: A review of intergenerational family relations for immigrant and non-immigrant families. Human Development, 46(2-3), 15-136.

53 Harwood R. L., Schoelmerich, A., Schulze, P. A., and Gonzalez, Z. (1999). Cultural differences in maternal beliefs and behaviors: a study of middle-class Anglo and Puerto Rican mother-infant pairs in four everyday

situations. *Child Development,* 70(4), pp.1005-16.

54 Mcclelland Institute. (2019). Cultural Differences in Parenting Practices: What Asian American Families Can Teach Us [Online]. Available at: https://mcclellandinstitute.arizona.edu/files/ResearchLink2_1.pdf [Accessed 9 Aug. 2019].

55 Marcia Carteret, M. (2013). *Culturally-Based Differences in Child Rearing Practices | Dimensions of Culture. Dimensions of culture.* [Online]. Available at: https://www.dimensionsofculture.com/2013/09/how-individualism-and-collectivism-manifest-in-child-rearing-practices/ [Accessed 24 Jul. 2019].

56 Bernstein, D. (2013). *Essentials of Psychology.* Boston, MA: Cengage Learning. p.368.

57 Chua, A. (2012). *Battle hymn of the Tiger Mother.* London: Bloomsbury.

58 Paiva, N.D. (2008). South Asian parents' constructions of praising their children. Clinical Child Psychology and Psychiatry, 13(2), 191-201.

59 Nesteruk, O. and Marks, L. (2011). Parenting in Immigration: Experiences of Mothers and Fathers from Eastern Europe Raising Children in the United States. *Journal of Comparative Family Studies,* 42(6), pp.809-825.

60 Cheney, A., Nieri, T., Davis, E., Prologo, J., Valencia, E., Anderson, A., Widaman, K., Reaves, C. and Sullivan, G. (2019). The Sociocultural Factors Underlying Latina Mothers' Infant Feeding Practices. Global Qualitative Nursing Research, 6(1-11).

61 Small, M. (2001). *Kids: How Biology and Culture Shape the Way We Raise Our Children.* New York: Doubleday.

62 Power, T. (2013). Parenting Dimensions and Styles: A Brief History and Recommendations for Future Research. *Childhood Obesity,* 9(s1), pp.S-14-S-21.

63 Nesteruk, O. and Marks, L. (2011). Parenting in Immigration: Experiences of Mothers and Fathers from Eastern Europe Raising Children in the United States. *Journal of Comparative Family Studies,* 42(6), pp.809-825.

64 UNICEF (2007). *Child poverty in perspective: An overview of child well-being in rich countries.* UNICEF. [Online]. Available at: https://www.unicef.org/infobycountry/files/ChildPovertyReport.pdf [Accessed 17 Mar. 2019].

65 ONS (2018). *Overview of the UK population.* Office for National Statistics. [online] Available at: https://www.ons.gov.uk/peoplepopulationandcommunity/populationandmigration/populationestimates/articles/overviewoftheukpopulation/november2018 [Accessed 5 Apr. 2019].

66 Guy, C. (2013). *Fractured Families: Why stability matters | The Centre for Social Justice.* [Online]. The Centre for Social Justice. Available at: https://www.centreforsocialjustice.org.uk/library/fractured-families-stability-matters [Accessed 30 Aug. 2019].

67 The Centre for Social Justice (2017). Centre for Social Justice Polling on Public Attitudes to Family in Policy: Summer 2017. Center for Social Justice. [Online]. Available at: https://www.centreforsocialjustice.org.uk/core/wp-content/uploads/2017/09/Family_Polling_Data.pdf [Accessed 7 Nov. 2019].

68 Strong, M. (2012). *Church for the Fatherless.* Downers Grove, Ill.: IVP Books, p.10.

69 U.S. Department of Justice (1988). What can the federal government do to decrease crime and revitalize communities? : January 5-7, 1988 panel papers. The National Institute of Justice and the Executive Office for Weed & Seed. [Online]. Available at: https://www.ncjrs.gov/pdffiles/172210.pdf. [Accessed 6 Jun 2019].

70 Oliker, D. (2011). *The Importance of Fathers.* [online] Available at: https://www.psychologytoday.com/us/blog/the-long-reach-childhood/201106/the-importance-fathers. [Accessed 19 Mar. 2019].

71 Horn, W. (1997). You've Come A Long Way, Daddy. Hoover Institution. [Online]. Available at: https://www.hoover.org/research/youve-come-long-way-daddy [Accessed 20 Mar. 2019].

72 Kamarck, E., and Galston, W., (1990). Putting Children First: A Progressive Family Policy for The 1990s. Washington, DC: *Progressive Policy Institute,* p.4.

73 Horn, W. (1997). *You've Come A Long Way, Daddy.* Hoover Institution. [Online]. Available at: https://www.hoover.org/research/youve-come-long-way-daddy [Accessed 20 Mar. 2019].

74 U.S. National Commission on Children (1991). *Beyond Rhetoric: A New American Agenda for Children and Families: Summary: Final Report of the National Commission on Children,* DIANE Publishing (1995), p.18.

75 Horn, W. (1997). You've Come A Long Way, Daddy. [Online]. Hoover Institution. Available at: https://www.hoover.org/research/youve-come-long-way-daddy [Accessed 21 Oct. 2019].

76 Ibid.

77 Hetherington, E. and Kelly, J. (2002). *For better or for worse.* New York: W. W. Norton & Company.

78 Sarkadi, A., Kristiansson R. and Oberklaid, F. (2008). *Fathers' Involvement and Children's Developmental Outcomes: A Systematic Review of Longitudinal Studies.* Acta Paediatrica, 97(2), pp.153-158.

79 HuffingtonPost (2008). *HuffPost is now part of Oath.* [Online]. Available at: https://www.huffingtonpost.co.uk/2008/06/15/obamas-fathers-day-speech_n_107220.html? [Accessed 6 Jun. 2019].

80 Martin, G. (2019). *The Phrase finder.* [Online]. Available at: https://www.phrases.org.uk/meanings/a-woman-needs-a-man-like-a-fish-needs-a-bicycle.html. [Accessed on 6 Jun].

81 Cashion, B. (1982). Female-Headed Families: Effects on Children and Clinical Implications. *Journal of Marital and Family Therapy,* 8(2), pp.77-85.

82 Nielsen, L. (2014). Shared Physical Custody: Summary of 40 Studies on Outcomes for Children. *Journal of Divorce & Remarriage,* 55(8), pp.613-635.

83 Warshak, R. (2014). Social science and parenting plans for young children: A consensus report. *Psychology, Public Policy, and Law,* 20(1), pp.46-67.

84 Bergström, M., Fransson, E., Fabian, H., Hjern, A., Sarkadi, A. and Salari, R. (2017). Preschool children living in joint physical custody ar-

rangements show less psychological symptoms than those living mostly or only with one parent. *Acta Paediatrica,* 107(2), pp.294-300.

85 Bergström, M., Fransson, E., Modin, B., Berlin, M., Gustafsson, P. and Hjern, A. (2015). Fifty moves a year: is there an association between joint physical custody and psychosomatic problems in children?. *Journal of Epidemiology and Community Health,* 69(8), pp.769-774.

86 Barras, J. (2002). *Whatever happened to daddy's little girl?.* New York: Ballantine Pub. Group

87 Popenoe, D. (1996). *Life without Father.* New York: The Free Press, p. 163.

88 Haug, W., Compton, P., and Courbage, Y. (2000). The Demographic Characteristics of National Minorities in Certain European States: *Population Studies.* 2(31), Council of Europe Directorate General III, Social Cohesion, Strasbourg.

89 House, P. (2003). *Want your church to grow? Then bring in the men.* Baptist Press. [Online]. Available at: http://www.baptistpress.com/bpnews.asp?ID=15630 [Accessed 3 Apr. 2019].

90 Gungor, M. (2019). Mark Gungor on Family. [Online]. Available at: https://markgungor.com/products/mark-gungor-on-family-cd?_pos=1&_sid=7c3f1335b&_ss=r [Accessed 3 Apr. 2019].

91 Woodard, K. (2006), *Father Knows Best,* Western Standard.

92 National Fatherhood Initiative, a. (2017). *Fatherless Children Statistics and Other Data on Fatherhood* | NFI. Fatherhood.org. [Online]. Available at: https://www.fatherhood.org/fatherhood-data-statistics [Accessed 17 Mar. 2019].

93 The Fatherless Generation. (2018). *Statistics.* [Online]. Available at: https://thefatherlessgeneration.wordpress.com/statistics/ [Accessed 20 Mar. 2019].

94 Wilson, K. (2000). *Where's Daddy?: The Mythologies Behind Custody Access Support.* Richmond: Harbinger Press.

95 Ephesians 6: 4 New International Version.

96 Miller, D. (2014). Train Up a Child: What Does Proverbs 22:6 Actually Mean? SBC Voices. [Online]. Available at: https://sbcvoices.com/train-up-a-child-what-does-proverbs-226-actually-mean/ [Accessed 4 Apr. 2019].

97 Gibran, K. (1923). *The Prophet*, New York: Alfred A. Knopf , p. 17.

98 Krapfl, J. (2016). Behaviorism and Society. *The Behavior Analyst*, 39(1), pp.123-129.

99 Malone, J. (2014). Did John B. Watson Really "Found" Behaviorism?. *The Behavior Analyst*, 37(1), pp.1-12.

100 Watson, J. B. (1930). *Behaviorism*, (Rev. ed.) Chicago: University of Chicago Press. p. 82

101 MacLeod, S. Nature vs. Nurture in Psychology (2018). Simply Psychology [Online]. Available at: https://www.simplypsychology.org/naturevsnurture.html [Accessed 4 Apr. 2019].

102 Ephesians 6:4 Expanded Bible

103 Seay, A., Freysteinson, W. and McFarlane, J. (2014). Positive Parenting. *Nursing Forum*, 49(3), pp.207.

104 Rodrigo, M. (2010). Promoting Positive Parenting in Europe: New challenges for the European Society for Developmental Psychology. *European Journal of Developmental Psychology*, 7(3), 282.

105 Miller, L. (2015). *The Spiritual Child: The New Science on Parenting for Health and Lifelong Thriving*. St. Martin's Press. p.26.

106 Miller, L. (2015). *The Spiritual Child: The New Science on Parenting for Health and Lifelong Thriving*. St. Martin's Press.

107 Ibid, p.3

108 Mileant, A. (2001). *The Upbringing of Children*. Missionary Leaflet 55E. Fatheralexander.org. [Online]. Available at: https://www.fatheralexander.org/booklets/english/child.htm [Accessed 24 Mar. 2019].

109 Chen, Y. and VanderWeele, T. (2018). Associations of Religious Upbringing with Subsequent Health and Well-Being from Adolescence to Young Adulthood: An Outcome-Wide Analysis. *American Journal of Epidemiology*, 187(11), pp.2355-2364.

110 Equipping the Next Generation (2011). *Christian Research Journal*, [Online]. 32(4). Available at: https://www.equip.org/article/equipping-the-next-generation/ [Accessed 22 Mar. 2019].

111 Department for Education and Skill (1989) *The Elton Report* (1989) DES. [Online]. Available at: http://www.educationengland.org.uk/documents/elton/elton1989.html [Accessed 22 Mar. 2019].

112 Shin, L. (2013). *The 5 Most Important Money Lessons To Teach Your Kids*. Forbes.com. [Online]. Available at: https://www.forbes.com/sites/laurashin/2013/10/15/the-5-most-important-money-lessons-to-teach-your-kids/#3f97f7768269 [Accessed 22 Mar. 2019].

113 Kim, J. and Chatterjee, S. (2013). Childhood Financial Socialization and Young Adults' Financial Management. *Journal of Financial Counselling and Planning*, 24, (1) 61-79.

114 Hebrews 6:12 New International Version.

115 Proverbs 21:20 The Living Bible.

116 2 Thessalonians 3:10 New King James Version.

117 Luke 16:10 New Living Translation.

118 Luke 12:15 New Life Version

119 Proverbs 22:7 Expanded Bible.

120 Proverbs 22:1 Amplified Bible.

121 Proverbs 22:15 International Standard Version.

122 Proverbs 29:15 New International Version.

123 Mileant, A. (2001). *The Upbringing of Children*. Missionary Leaflet 55E. [Online]. Fatheralexander.org. Available at: https://www.fatheralexander. org/booklets/english/child.htm [Accessed 24 Mar. 2019].

124 Ibid.

125 Guidance for Effective Discipline. (1998). Pediatrics, 101(4), pp.723-728

126 1 Kings 1:6 New Living Translation.

127 1 Kings 1:6 Contemporary English Version.

128 1 Kings 1:6 New English Translation.

129 1 Samuel 2:12 Amplified Bible.

130 1 Samuel 2:22-25 Easy-to-Read Version.

131 Cloud, H. and Townsend, J. (1992). *Boundaries: When To Say Yes, When To Say No To Take Control Of Your Life*. Grand Rapids: Zondervan.

132 Ballenger, M. (2017). The Biblical difference between Discipline, Punishment, and Consequences. ApplyGodsWord.com. [Online]. Available at: https://applygodsword.com/the-biblical-difference-between-discipline-punishment-and-consequences/ [Accessed 30 Aug. 2019].

133 Ingram, C. (2006). *Punishment Versus Discipline - Focus on the Family*. [Online]. Focus on the Family. Available at: https://www.focusonthe-family.com/parenting/punishment-versus-discipline/ [Accessed 19 Apr. 2019].

134 Keener, C. (2003). *The IVP Bible background commentary*. Downers Grove, Ill: InterVarsity Press, p.552.

135 Flander, G. (2016). *International Day of Families: Four pillars of parenting | Poliklinika za zaštitu djece i mladih grada Zagreba*. Poliklinika za zaštitu djece i mladih grada Zagreba. [Online]. Available at: https://www.poliklinika-djeca. hr/english/featured/directors-note/international-day-of-families-four-pillars-of-parenting/ [Accessed 19 Apr. 2019].

136 Curtis, P. (2008). Schools 'replacing parents' as moral guide. The Guardian. [Online]. Available at: https://www.theguardian.com/education/2008/mar/10/schools.children [Accessed 19 Apr. 2019].

137 Ackerly, R., 2013. Should Schools Teach Values or is that the Parents' Responsibility?. *Genius In Children*, [Online]. Available at: http://geniusinchildren.org/2013/09/17/should-schools-teach-values-or-is-that-the-parents-responsibility/ [Accessed 19 April 2019].

138 Barry, E. (2012). *Fed-up teachers: 'Raise your own kids'*. NewsComAu. [Online]. Available at: https://www.news.com.au/national/raise-your-own-kids-teachers/news-story/aa04c1614752272bc39ae5ab6bda6ec8 [Accessed 19 Apr. 2019].

139 Greengrass, M. (2003). Giving to others linked to longer life. *Monitor on Psychology*, 34(2), p.17.

140 Henry, D. (2015). Generosity, *Christian Reflection: A Series in Faith And Ethics*, The Institute for Faith and Learning, p. 11.

141 Weissbourd, R. (2019). Turning the Tide II: How Parents and High Schools Can Cultivate Ethical Character and Reduce Distress in The College Admissions Process — Making Caring Common. Making Caring Common. [Online]. Available at: https://mcc.gse.harvard.edu/reports/turning-the-tide-2-parents-high-schools-college-admissions [Accessed 8 Oct. 2019].

142 Altman, D. (2003). *Living kindness*. Oregon City, OR: Moon Lake Media.

143 Ottoni-Wilhelm, M., Estell, D. and Perdue, N. (2014). Role-modelling and conversations about giving in the socialization of adolescent charitable giving and volunteering. *Journal of Adolescence*, 37(1), pp.53-66.

144 Weisman, C. (2008). *Raising Charitable Children*. St Louis, Mo.: F.E. Robbins & Sons. p.1

145 2 Corinthians 8:2-3 Good News Translation.

146 Luke 17:33 New International Version.

147 Smith, C. and Davidson, H. (2014). *The paradox of generosity*. Oxford: Oxford University Press.

148 Firestone, L. (2014). *The Benefits of Generosity*. Huffpost.com. [Online]. Available at: https://www.huffpost.com/entry/the-benefits-of-generosity/ [Accessed 31 Oct. 2019].

149 Making History Now (2019). *Christian Generosity: Some Ground Rules from the Bible and the Early Church*. [Online]. Available at: https://makinghistorynow.wordpress.com/2019/01/29/ground-rules-for-generosity-scripture/ [Accessed 26 Mar. 2019].

150 Weissbourd, R., Anderson, T., Cashin, A. and McIntyre, J. (2018). *The Talk: How Adults Can Promote Young People's Healthy Relationships and Prevent Misogyny and Sexual Harassment*. Making Caring Common. [Online]. Available at: https://mcc.gse.harvard.edu/reports/the-talk [Accessed 27 Mar. 2019].

151 Eudaimonia Report, Central YMCA.

152 Xia, M., Fosco, G., Lippold, M. and Feinberg, M. (2018). A Developmental Perspective on Young Adult Romantic Relationships: Examining Family and Individual Factors in Adolescence. *Journal of Youth and Adolescence*, 47(7), pp.1499-1516.

153 Hall, A. (2018). *Only one-third of British employees happy with work-life balance, study shows*. The Independent. [Online]. Available at: https://www.independent.co.uk/news/health/uk-employees-work-life-balance-happy-third-pressure-sleep-loss-impacts-a8387546.html [Accessed 5 Apr. 2019].

154 World Health Organization (1999). Healthy Living: What is a Healthy Lifestyle?. Copenhagen: WHO Regional Office for Europe. [Online]. Available at: http://www.who.int/iris/handle/10665/108180 [Accessed 28 Mar. 2019]

155 Sotos-Prieto, M., Bhupathiraju, S., Mattei, J., Fung, T., Li, Y., Pan, A., Willett, W., Rimm, E. and Hu, F. (2017). Association of Changes in Diet Quality with Total and Cause-Specific Mortality. *New England Journal of Medicine*, 377(2), pp.143-153.

156 Reames, R. (2011). *Parents Set The Example: Kids And Adults Should Exercise Together.* Huffpost.com. [Online]. Available at: https://www.huffpost.com/entry/parents-set-the-example.

157 NHS (2018). *Effects of smoking on the body.* Smokefree. [Online]. Available at: https://www.nhs.uk/smokefree/why-quit/smoking-health-problems [Accessed 6 Apr. 2019].

158 Jha, P., Ramasundarahettige, C., Landsman, V., Rostron, B., Thun, M., Anderson, R., McAfee, T. and Peto, R. (2013). 21st-Century Hazards of Smoking and Benefits of Cessation in the United States. *New England Journal of Medicine,* 368(4), pp.341-350.

158 World Health Organisation (2018). *Tobacco.* [Online]. Available at: https://www.who.int/news-room/fact-sheets/detail/tobacco [Accessed 6 Apr. 2019].

159 Tynan, M., Polansky, J., Titus, K., Atayeva, R. and Glantz, S. (2017). *Tobacco Use in Top-Grossing Movies — United States, 2010–2016.* [Online]. Available at: https://www.cdc.gov/mmwr/volumes/66/wr/mm6626a1.htm?s_cid=mm6626a1_w#suggestedcitation [Accessed 30 Mar. 2019].

160 World Health Organisation (2018). *Tobacco.* [Online]. Available at: https://www.who.int/news-room/fact-sheets/detail/tobacco [Accessed 6 Apr. 2019].

161 CDC (2019). Substance Use during Pregnancy. CDC. [Online]. Available at: https://www.cdc.gov/reproductivehealth/maternalinfanthealth/substance-abuse/substance-abuse-during-pregnancy.htm [Accessed 23 Oct. 2019].

162 Reproductive Facts (2014). *Smoking and Infertility.* Reproductive facts. [Online]. Available at: https://www.reproductivefacts.org/news-and-publications/patient-fact-sheets-and-booklets/documents/fact-sheets-and-info-booklets/smoking-and-infertility/ [Accessed 23 Oct. 2019].

163 Nyaboe, R. (2016). *World No Tobacco Day.* [Online]. HEALTH GUIDE 911. Available at: https://www.healthguide911.com/2016/05/world-no-tobacco-day.html [Accessed 30 Mar. 2019].

164 Nice.org.uk. (2010). *Smoking: stopping in pregnancy and after childbirth.* [online] Available at: https://www.nice.org.uk/guidance/ph26/resources/ smoking-stopping-in-pregnancy-and-after-childbirth-pdf-1996240366789 [Accessed 9 Nov. 2019].

165 1 Corinthians 6: 12 Amplified Bible

166 1 Corinthians 6:20 New International Version.

167 1 Corinthians 10:31 New King James Version.

168 Cherukupalli, R. and Perucic, A. (2018). Affordability of cigarettes products in the WHO Report on the Global Tobacco Epidemic, 2017. *Tobacco Induced Diseases,* 16(1).

169 GOV.UK. (n.d.). *Cost of smoking to the NHS in England: 2015.* [Online]. Available at: https://www.gov.uk/government/publications/cost-of-smoking-to-the-nhs-in-england-2015/cost-of-smoking-to-the-nhs-in-england-2015 [Accessed 30 Mar. 2019].

170 NHS (2018). *Risks: Alcohol Misuse.* [Online]. Available at: https:// www.nhs.uk/conditions/alcohol-misuse/risks/ [Accessed 30 Mar. 2019].

171 Philippians 2:3-4 The Passion Translation.

172 CDC (2019). Substance Use during Pregnancy | CDC. [Online]. Available at: https://www.cdc.gov/reproductivehealth/maternalinfanthealth/substance-abuse/substance-abuse-during-pregnancy.htm [Accessed 23 Oct. 2019].

173 Nice.org.uk. (2008). *Updated NICE guideline published on care and support that women should receive during pregnancy.* [online] Available at: https://www. nice.org.uk/guidance/cg62/documents/updated-nice-guideline-published-on-care-and-support-that-women-should-receive-during-pregnancy [Accessed 9 Nov. 2019].

174 D'mello, B. (2015). *What Does It Take To Become An Extraordinary Archer?.* Science ABC. [Online]. Available at: https://www.scienceabc.com/ sports/draw-back-bow-science-archery.html [Accessed 9 Apr. 2019].

175 Kindlon, D. (2003). *Tough Times, Strong Children: Lessons from the Past for Your Child's Future.* New York: Miramax Books/Hyperion.

176 Patz, A. (n.d.). *Failure Is an Option.* Parents.com. [Online]. Available at: https://www.parents.com/kids/development/behavioral/failure-is-an-option/ [Accessed 1 Apr. 2019].

177 Every child matters. (2003). [London]: Stationery Office.

178 Proverbs 4: 25 Amplified Bible Classic Edition.

179 Hebrews 6:12 New International Version.

180 Ephesians 4:16 New Living Translation.

181 1 John 5:14-15 New International Version.

182 Deuteronomy 6:6-7 The Living Bible.

183 Proverbs 27:17 Amplified Bible.

184 Ephesians 6:10 Contemporary English Version.

185 North Carolina State University. (2012). Parenting more important than schools to academic achievement, study finds. *Science-Daily.* [Online]. Available at: https://www.sciencedaily.com/releases/2012/10/121010112540.htm [Accessed 19 Apr. 2019].

186 2 Corinthians 6:2 New Living Translation.

187 Cronenwett, S., (1982). "Response to Symposium on Sex and Children," in *Character Policy,* edited by E. A. Wynne, Lanham, Md.: University Press of America, p. 101.

188 Sellgren, K. (2017). *Sex education compulsory in schools.* BBC News. [Online]. Available at: https://www.bbc.co.uk/news/education-39116783 [Accessed 27 Sep. 2019].

189 UNESCO (2018). *International Technical Guidance on Sexuality Education.* 2nd Rev. ed. Paris: UNESCO, p.16.

190 Haffner, D. and Ott, K. (2011). *A time to speak: Faith Communities and Sexuality Education,* Westport, CT: Religious Institute, 2, pp.25-26.

191 Ibid pp.9-10.

192 Ibid p.10.

193 Scottish Government (2017). *Equally Safe: Delivery Plan*. Scottish Government. [Online]. Available at: https://www.gov.scot/publications/equally-safe-delivery-plan-scotlands-strategy-prevent-violence-against-women/ [Accessed 7 Nov. 2019].

194 Hookham, M. and Manning, S. (2019). *Children as young as SIX are to be given self-touching lessons*. Mail Online. [Online]. Available at: https://www.dailymail.co.uk/news/article-7490415/Children-young-SIX-given-compulsory-self-touching-lessons.html [Accessed 28 Sep. 2019].

195 Ibid.

196 Ibid.

197 CPS (2019). *Rape and Sexual Offences - Chapter 2: Sexual Offences Act 2003 - Principal Offences, and Sexual Offences Act 1956 - Most commonly charged offences | The Crown Prosecution Service*. [Online]. Available at: https://www.cps.gov.uk/legal-guidance/rape-and-sexual-offences-chapter-2-sexual-offences-act-2003-principal-offences-and [Accessed 28 Sep. 2019].

198 Unwin, J. (1934). *Sex and Culture*. Oxford University Press.

199 En.wikipedia.org. (n.d.). *J. D. Unwin*. [Online]. Available at: https://en.wikipedia.org/wiki/J._D._Unwin#cite_note-2 [Accessed 27 Sep. 2019].

200 Chamie, J. (2016). *320 Million Children in Single-Parent Families — Global Issues*. Globalissues.org. [Online]. Available at: http://www.globalissues.org/news/2016/10/15/22568 [Accessed 1 Apr. 2019].

201 U.S Census Bureau (2017). Fathers in the United States. Census.gov. [Online]. Available at: https://www.census.gov/schools/resources/news/fathers.html [Accessed 21 Oct. 2019].

202 IMDB (2006). *The Pursuit of Happyness*. [Online]. Available at https://www.imdb.com/title/tt0454921/ [Accessed on 21 Oct].

203 OECD (2011). *Doing Better for Families*, OECD, Paris.

204 Office for National Statistics (2017) *Families and Households*: 2017. ONS, Table 1.

205 U.S. National Commission on Children (1991). Beyond Rhetoric: A New American Agenda for Children and Families: Summary: Final Report of the National Commission on Children, DIANE Publishing (1995), p.18.

206 Waldfogel, J., Craigie, T. and Brooks-Gunn, J. (2010). Fragile Families and Child Wellbeing. *The Future of Children*, 20(2), p.87.

207 Leach, P. (2014). *The vengeful mothers who tear fathers from their children's lives*. Mail Online. [Online] Available at: https://www.dailymail.co.uk/femail/article-2678528/The-vengeful-mothers-tear-fathers-childrens-lives-Britains-parenting-guru-one-unspoken-scandals-age.html [Accessed 30 Sep. 2019].

208 Lanstrom, E. (1983). *Christian Parent Burnout*. St. Louis, Mo.: Concordia.

209 Association for Psychological Science (2019). Parental burnout can lead to harmful outcomes for parent and child. *Science Daily*. [Online]. Available at: http://www.sciencedaily.com/releases/2019/08/190828080538.htm [Accessed Oct. 24 Oct. 2019]

210 Hubert, S. and Aujoulat, I. (2018). Parental Burnout: When Exhausted Mothers Open Up. *Frontiers in Psychology*, 9.

211 Roskam, I., Raes, M. and Mikolajczak, M. (2017). Exhausted Parents: Development and Preliminary Validation of the Parental Burnout Inventory. *Frontiers in Psychology*.

212 Leach, P. (2014). *The vengeful mothers who tear fathers from their children's lives*. Mail Online. [Online]. Available at: https://www.dailymail.co.uk/femail/article-2678528/The-vengeful-mothers-tear-fathers-childrens-lives-Britains-parenting-guru-one-unspoken-scandals-age.html [Accessed 2 Sep. 2019].

213 European Commission (n.d.). The United Nations Convention on the Rights of the Child (CRC). European Commission. [Online]. Available at: https://ec.europa.eu/anti-trafficking/legislation-and-case-law-international-legislation-united-nations/united-nations-convention-rights_en [Accessed 2 Sep. 2019].

214 Pruett, M., Hoganbruen, K. and Jackson, T. (2000). The Best Interest of the Child. *Journal of Divorce & Remarriage*, 33(1-2), pp.47-63.

215 UK Home Office (2009). Section 55: *Best Interest of the Child*. Borders, Citizenship and Immigration Act 2009.

216 1 Kings 3:24–27 New King James Version.

217 Pedro-Carroll, J. (2011). *Divorce and separation | How Parents Can Help Children Cope with Separation/Divorce | Encyclopaedia on Early Childhood Development.* Encyclopaedia on Early Childhood Development. [Online]. Available at: http://www.child-encyclopedia.com/divorce-and-separation/according-experts/how-parents-can-help-children-cope-separationdivorce [Accessed 1 Apr. 2019].

218 Early Intervention Foundation (2019). *About Early Intervention.* EIF. [Online]. Available at: https://www.eif.org.uk/why-it-matters. [Accessed 1 Apr. 2019].

219 Moorhead, J. (2014). *It's wrong to use children as a weapon in divorce or separation.* The Guardian. [Online]. Available at: https://www.theguardian.com/lifeandstyle/2014/jun/21/wrong-to-use-children-as-weapon-divorce-separation [Accessed 1 Sep. 2019].

220 Moroni, G. (2017). *Rowing parents might be more harmful to child development than divorce, study suggests.* University of York. [Online]. Available at: https://www.york.ac.uk/news-and-events/news/2017/research/rowing-harmful/ [Accessed 1 Oct. 2019].

221 Mooney, A., Oliver, C. and Smith, M. (2009). *Impact of family breakdown on children's well-being.* [Annesley]: Dept. for Children, Schools and Families (University of London), pp.7-8.

222 Turkat, I. (1995). Divorce related malicious mother syndrome. *Journal of Family Violence,* 10(3), pp.253-264.

223 Kruk, E. (2015). *Recent Advances in Understanding Parental Alienation.* Psychology Today. [Online]. Available at: https://www.psychologytoday. com/gb/blog/co-parenting-after-divorce/201507/recent-advances-in-understanding-parental-alienation [Accessed 7 Oct. 2019].

224 Finnigan, L. (2017). Divorced parents who pit children against former partners 'guilty of abuse'. *The Telegraph.* [Online]. Available at: https://www.telegraph.co.uk/news/2017/02/12/divorced-parents-pit-children-against-former-partners-guilty/ [Accessed 7 Apr. 2019].

225 Jones, R. (2019). *Families Need Fathers - Home.* Fnf.org.uk. [Online]. Available at: https://fnf.org.uk/ [Accessed 7 Apr. 2019].

226 TED Talk (2016). [video] Directed by J. Harman. http://ted.com/ tedx: YouTube.

227 Kruk, E., (2018). Alienation as a Form of Emotional Child Abuse: Current State of Knowledge and Future Directions for Research. *Family Science Review,* 22 (4), pp.146-148.

228 NSPCC. (n.d.). *Separation, divorce and contact.* [Online]. Available at: https://www.nspcc.org.uk/preventing-abuse/keeping-children-safe/separation-divorce-and-contact/ [Accessed 1 Apr. 2019].

229 Leach, P. (2014). *Family Breakdown:* Helping Children Hang on to Both Their Parents. London: Unbound.

230 Leach, P. (2018). *Putting the children first when you divorce.* Robinson.

231 Fincham, F. and Hall, J. (2005). Parenting and the marital relationship. In T. Luster & L. Okagaki (Eds.), *Parenting: An ecological perspective (pp. 206-207).* Hillsdale, NJ: Erlbaum. 2005, pp.206-207.

232 Cummings, E. and Davies, P. (2011). *Marital Conflict and Children.* New York: The Guilford Press.

233 Hughes, R. (2005). *The Effects of Divorce on Children.* Urbana, IL: University of Illinois Extension.

234 Pedro-Carroll, J. (2011). *Divorce and separation | How Parents Can Help Children Cope With Separation/Divorce | Encyclopaedia on Early Childhood*

Development. Encyclopaedia on Early Childhood Development. [Online]. Available at: http://www.child-encyclopedia.com/divorce-and-separation/according-experts/how-parents-can-help-children-cope-separation-divorce [Accessed 1 Apr. 2019].

235 Pedro-Carroll, J. (2011). *Divorce and separation | How Parents Can Help Children Cope with Separation/Divorce | Encyclopedia on Early Childhood Development.* Encyclopedia on Early Childhood Development. [Online]. Available at: http://www.child-encyclopedia.com/divorce-and-separation/according-experts/how-parents-can-help-children-cope-separationdivorce [Accessed 7 Apr. 2019].

236 APA (n.d.). [Online]. Available at: https://www.apa.org/helpcenter/stepfamily [Accessed 8 Apr. 2019].

237 Pasley, K., Dollahite, D., and Ihinger-Tallman, M. (2000). *What we know about the Role of the Step-parent.* Step-families Quarterly [Online]. Available at: stepfamiles.info [Accessed 8 Apr. 2019].

238 Code, D. (2009). *To raise happy kids, put your marriage first.* New York: Crossroad Pub. Co.

239 The State of the World's (2017). New York: UNICEF.

240 Gibbs, S. (2018). *Apple's Tim Cook: 'I don't want my nephew on a social network'.* The Guardian. [Online]. Available at: https://www.theguardian.com/technology/2018/jan/19/tim-cook-i-dont-want-my-nephew-on-a-social-network [Accessed 8 Apr. 2019].

241 Twenge, J. M., Martin, G. N., and Campbell, W. K. (2018). *Decreases in psychological well-being among American adolescents after 2012 and links to screen time during the rise of smartphone technology.* Emotion, 18(6), 765-780.

242 Chou, H. and Edge, N. (2012). *"They Are Happier and Having Better Lives than I Am": The Impact of Using Facebook on Perceptions of Others' Lives.* Cyberpsychology, Behavior, and Social Networking, 15(2), pp.117-121.

243 Primack, B., Shensa, A., Sidani, J., Whaite, E., Lin, L., Rosen, D., Colditz, J., Radovic, A. and Miller, E. (2017). *Social Media Use and Perceived Social Isolation among Young Adults in the U.S.* American Journal of Preventive Medicine, 53(1), pp.1-8.

244 Psychology Today (2019). *Dopamine*. PsychologyToday. [Online]. Available at: https://www.psychologytoday.com/gb/basics/dopamine [Accessed 17 Oct. 2019].

245 Ciaccia, C. (2017). *Facebook, cocaine, opioids: How addictive is the social network?*. Fox News. [Online]. Available at: https://www.foxnews.com/tech/facebook-cocaine-opioids-how-addictive-is-the-social-network [Accessed 17 Oct. 2019].

246 Haynes, T. (2018). Dopamine, Smartphones & You: A battle for your time - Science in the News. Science in the News. [Online]. Available at: http://sitn.hms.harvard.edu/flash/2018/dopamine-smartphones-battle-time/ [Accessed 17 Oct. 2019].

247 Sini, R. (2017). *'You are being programmed' - ex-Facebook VP*. BBC News. [Online]. Available at: https://www.bbc.co.uk/news/blogs-trending-42322746 [Accessed 17 Oct. 2019].

248 Wakefiled, J. (2018). *Facebook 'no place' for young children*. BBC News. [Online]. Available at: https://www.bbc.co.uk/news/technology-42872603 [Accessed 1 Oct. 2019].

249 Deloitte (2019). *Deloitte Global Millennial Survey 2019*. Deloitte. [Online]. Available at: https://www2.deloitte.com/global/en/pages/about-deloitte/articles/millennialsurvey.html [Accessed 14 Oct. 2019].

250 London School of Economics (2018). *Preparing for a Digital Future*. London School of Economics and Political Science. [Online]. Available at: http://www.lse.ac.uk/media-and-communications/research/research-projects/preparing-for-a-digital-future [Accessed 1 Apr. 2019].

251 Radesky, J., Kistin, C., Zuckerman, B., Nitzberg, K., Gross, J., Kaplan-Sanoff, M., Augustyn, M. and Silverstein, M. (2014). *Patterns of Mobile Device Use by Caregivers and Children during Meals in Fast Food Restaurants*. Pediatrics, 133(4), pp.e843-e849.

252 Hutton, J., Dudley, J., Horowitz-Kraus, T., DeWitt, T. and Holland, S. (2019). Associations Between Screen-Based Media Use and Brain White Matter Integrity in Preschool-Aged Children. *JAMA Pediatrics*, p.e193869.

253 American Academy of Pediatrics (2018). *Children and Media Tips from the American Academy of Pediatrics*. AAP. [Online]. Available at: https://www.aap.org/en-us/about-the-aap/aap-press-room/news-features-and-safety-tips/Pages/Children-and-Media-Tips.aspx [Accessed 1 Apr. 2019].

254 Moorehead, B. (1995). *Words Aptly Spoken*. Goodreads. Kirkland, WA: Overlake Christian.

255 Furedi, F. (2010). Celebrity Culture. *Society*, 47(6), pp.493-497.

256 Uhls, Y. and Greenfield, P. (2019). *The Rise of Fame: An Historical Content Analysis*. Cyberpsychology.eu. [Online]. Available at: https://cyberpsychology.eu/article/view/4243/3289 [Accessed 1 Apr. 2019].

257 Rosenblum, E. (2013). *Fixated on Fame? You're Not Alone. A Look at the Growing Obsession with Being a Star*. Teen Vogue. [Online]. Available at: https://www.teenvogue.com/story/celebrity-fame-obsession [Accessed 1 Apr. 2019].

258 Mayo Clinic (2019). Body Dysmorphic disorder. Mayo Clinic. [Online]. Available at: https://www.mayoclinic.org/diseases-conditions/body-dysmorphic-disorder/symptoms-causes/syc-20353938 [Accessed 1 Apr. 2019].

259 YMCA England & Wales (2018). *Young people face great expectations to look perfect*. YMCA England & Wales. [Online]. Available at: https://www.ymca.org.uk/latest-news/young-people-face-great-expectations-to-look-perfect [Accessed 1 Apr. 2019].

260 Abraham, A. and Zuckerman, D. (2011). Adolescents, Celebrity Worship, and Cosmetic Surgery. *Journal of Adolescent Health*, 49(5), pp.453-454.

261 Surgery (2017). *Statistics*. Surgery. [Online]. Available at: https://www.surgery.org/media/statistics [Accessed 1 Apr. 2019].

262 Taylor, J. (2010). *Parenting: Know Your Children's Enemy*. Psychology Today. [Online]. Available at: https://www.psychologytoday.com/us/blog/the-power-prime/201001/parenting-know-your-childrens-enemy [Accessed 1 Apr. 2019].

263 Ingleson, K. (2017). *What is Erotomania?* Medical News Today. [Online]. Available at: https://www.medicalnewstoday.com/articles/319145. php [Accessed on 1 Apr. 2019].

264 Derenne, J. and Beresin, E. (2014). *Body Image, Media, and Eating Disorders.* Academic Psychiatry, 30(3), 257-261.

265 AAP (2016). *American Academy of Pediatrics Announces New Recommendations for Children's Media Use.* AAP [Online]. Available at: https://www.aap.org/en-us/about-the-aap/aap-press-room/Pages/American-Academy-of-Pediatrics-Announces-New-Recommendations-for-Childrens-Media-Use.aspx [Accessed 1 Apr. 2019].

266 Strasburger, V. and Hogan, M. (2013). *Children, Adolescents, and the Media.* Pediatrics, 132(5), pp.958-961.

267 Bar-On, M. E, Broughton, D. D., Buttross, S., Corrigan, S., Gedissman, A., Rosario González De Rivas, M., Rich, M., Shifrin, D. L., Brody, M., Wilcox, B. L., Hogan, M., Holroyd, H. J., Reid, L., Norman, S. S., Strasburger, V., StoneChildren, J., (2001). Adolescents and Television. *Pediatrics*, 107(2), pp.423-426.

268 Radesky, J. and Christaki, D. (2016). Media and Young Minds. *Pediatrics*, 138(5), p.e20162591.

269 AACAP (2016). *Gangs and Children.* No. 98 [Online]. Available at: https://www.aacap.org/aacap/families_and_youth/Facts_for_Families/FFF-Guide/Children-and-Gangs-098.aspx [Accessed 1 Apr. 2019].

270 Family Lives (n.d.). Gangs. Family Lives. [Online]. Available at: https://www.familylives.org.uk/advice/teenagers/behaviour/gangs/ [Accessed 12 Apr. 2019].

271 UK Home Office. (2014). *Advice to Parents and Carers on Gangs.*

272 Bort, J., Pflock, A. and Renner, D. (2005). *Mommy Guilt: Learn to Worry Less, Focus on What Matters Most, and Raise Happier Kids,* New York: American Management Association.

273 Pew Research Center's Social and Demographic Trends Project. (2015). *Raising Kids and Running a Household: How Working Parents Share The Load.* [Online]. Available at: https://www.pewsocialtrends. org/2015/11/04/raising-kids-and-running-a-household-how-working-parents-share-the-load/ [Accessed 1 Apr. 2019].

274 Dube, R. (2017). *Father's Day survey: 63 percent of working dads envy stay-at-home dads.* TODAY.com. [Online]. Available at: https://www.today.com/parents/today-com-father-s-day-survey-reveals-dads-deepest-thoughts-t112695 [Accessed 1 Apr. 2019].

275 Grille, R. (n.d.). *Parent Guilt: A Silent Epidemic - The Natural Child Project.* Naturalchild.org. [Online]. Available at: https://www.naturalchild. org/articles/robin_grille/parent_guilt.html [Accessed 1 Apr. 2019].

276 Pfeffer, J. (2018). *Dying For a Paycheck.* New York: Harper Business.

277 Smith, A. (2011). *Are You a Guilty Parent?.* Psychology Today. [Online]. Available at: https://www.psychologytoday.com/gb/blog/healthy-connections/201109/are-you-guilty-parent [Accessed 9 Oct. 2019].

278 Oxford University Press (2019). Oxford Reference. Oxford University Press. [Online]. Available at: https://www.oxfordreference.com/ [Accessed 9 Oct. 2019].

279 Bettelheim, B. (1988). *A good Enough Parent.* New York: Vintage Books.

280 Luke Chapter 15:11-31 The Passion Translation

281 Keller, T. (2009). *The prodigal God.* London: Hodder.

282 Psalm 51:5 New International Version.

283 Galatians 6:7 The Passion Translation.

284 Proverbs 19:18 New Century Version.

285 Kruk, E. (2018). Parental Alienation as a Form of Emotional Child Abuse: Current State of Knowledge and Future Directions for Research. *Family Science Review,* 22 (4), p.145.

286 Kruk, E. (2018). Parental Alienation as a Form of Emotional Child Abuse: The Current State of Knowledge and Directions for Future Research. *Family Science Review*, 22 (4), 141-164.

287 Von Boch-Galhau, W. (2018). "Parental Alienation (Syndrome) - A serious form of psychological child abuse," *Mental Health and Family Medicine*, 13, 725-739.

288 Harman, J., Kruk, E. and Hines, D. (2018). "Parental Alienating Behaviors: An Unacknowledged Form of Family Violence," *Psychological Bulletin*, 144 (12), p.1275-1299.

289 Kruk, E. (2018). Parental Alienation as a Form of Emotional Child Abuse: The Current State of Knowledge and Directions for Future Research. *Family Science Review*, 22 (4), p.152.

290 Mark 10:14-16 The Living Bible.

291 Luke 11:4 The Passion Translation.

292 Wilcox, P. (2012). Is Parent Abuse a Form of Domestic Violence?. *Social Policy and Society*, 11(02), p. 277.

293 Cottrell, B. (2001). Parent abuse: The abuse of parents by their teenage children. Ottawa: Family Violence Prevention Unit. p. 3

294 1 Corinthians 10:6 The Passion Translation.

295 Romans 15:4 Easy-to-Read Version.

296 2 Samuel 15 – 18 New King James Version.

297 Family Lives (n.d.). *Teen violence help and advice for parents.* Family Lives. [Online]. Available at: https://www.familylives.org.uk/advice/teenagers/behaviour/teen-violence-at-home/ [Accessed 12 Apr. 2019].

298 Herman, L. (2013). *The Bill Of Rights For Parents Of Adult Children.* Forbes.com. [Online]. Available at: https://www.forbes.com/sites/nextavenue/2013/10/23/the-bill-of-rights-for-parents-of-adult-hildren/#154e93f520ab [Accessed 4 Sep. 2019].

299 Gillinson, S. (2017). *Why relationships are key to good social work.* The Guardian. [Online]. Available at: https://www.theguardian.com/social-care-network/2017/mar/21/why-relationships-are-key-to-good-social-work [Accessed 7 Oct. 2019].

300 Shonkoff, J. and Fisher, P. (2013). *Rethinking evidence-based practice and two-generation programs to create the future of early childhood policy.* Development and Psychopathology, 25(4pt2), pp.1635-1653.

301 GOV.UK. (2019). *Children's social work workforce 2018.* [Online]. Available at: https://www.gov.uk/government/statistics/childrens-social-work-workforce-2018 [Accessed 7 Oct. 2019].

302 Ravalier, J. (2018). *UK Social Workers: Working Conditions and Wellbeing.* BASW. [Online]. Available at: https://www.basw.co.uk/resources/uk-social-workers-working-conditions-and-wellbeing-0 [Accessed 28 Oct. 2019].

303 Siegel, D. and Hartzell, M. (2013). *Parenting from the inside out.* New York: Tarcher Perigee

304 VanderWeele, T. (2019). *The power of forgiveness.* Harvard Health. [Online]. Available at: https://www.health.harvard.edu/mind-and-mood/the-power-of-forgiveness [Accessed 8 Oct. 2019].

305 Zacharias, R. (2005). *Recapture the wonder.* Nashville, TN: Thomas Nelson.

306 Aurelius, M. (2002). *Meditations.* (Translated by Gregory Hays). New York: Modern Library.

307 Stevenson, D. (2009). *The Internet Classics Archive | The Meditations by Marcus Aurelius.* Classics.mit.edu. [Online]. Available at: http://classics.mit.edu/Antoninus/meditations.html [Accessed 4 Sep. 2019].

308 Mazzalongo, M. (2015). *Solomon's Strategy for Success.* BibleTalk.tv. [Online]. Available at: https://bibletalk.tv/solomons-strategy-for-success [Accessed 17 Apr. 2019].

309 Ecclesiastes 11:1 Easy-to-Read Version.

310 Ecclesiastes 11:2 Easy-to-Read Version.

311 Ecclesiastes 11:3 Easy-to-Read Version.

312 Ecclesiastes 11:4 Easy-to-Read Version.

313 Ecclesiastes 11:5-6 Easy-to-Read Version.

314 Ecclesiastes 11:5-6 Easy-to-Read Version.

315 Ecclesiastes Chapter 11:10 Easy-to-Read Version.

316 Philosophers (2012). *Seneca the Younger.* Philosophers.co.uk. [Online]. Available at: http://www.philosophers.co.uk/seneca-the-younger.html [Accessed 4 Sep. 2019].

317 Holiday, R. and Hanselman, S. (2016). *The Daily Stoic: 366 Meditations on Wisdom, Perseverance, and the Art of Living: Featuring new translations of Seneca, Epictetus, and Marcus Aurelius.* London: Profile Books. pp.1.3–4a

318 Deuteronomy 28:2-13 New Century Version

INDEX

A

B

D

E

F

G

H

I

J

K

L

M

N

R

S

T